Writing in Limbo

ALSO BY SIMON GIKANDI

Reading the African Novel

Reading Chinua Achebe: Language and Ideology in Fiction

Writing in Limbo

MODERNISM AND CARIBBEAN LITERATURE

Simon Gikandi

CORNELL UNIVERSITY PRESS

ITHACA AND LONDON

Open access edition funded by the National Endowment for the Humanities/ Andrew W. Mellon Foundation Humanities Open Book Program.

First published 1992 by Cornell University Press.

Library of Congress Cataloging-in-Publication Data

Gikandi, Simon.
    Writing in limbo : modernism and Caribbean literature / Simon Gikandi.
        p. cm.
    Includes bibliographical references and index.
    ISBN-13: 978-0-8014-2575-2 (cloth) — ISBN-13: 978-1-5017-1990-5 (pbk.)
    1. Caribbean fiction (English)—History and criticism. 2. Modernism (Literature)—Caribbean Area. 3. Carpentier, Alejo, 1904– Siglo de las luces.
I. Title.
823—dc21   91-23284

For Jamie McDonald

Contents

Acknowledgments   ix

Introduction: Modernism and the Origins of Caribbean
   Literature   1

1 Caribbean Modernist Discourse: Writing, Exile, and
   Tradition   33

2 From Exile to Nationalism: The Early Novels of George
   Lamming   66

3 Beyond the *Kala-pani*: The Trinidad Novels of Samuel
   Selvon   107

4 The Deformation of Modernism: The Allegory of History in
   Carpentier's *El siglo de las luces*   139

5 Modernism and the Masks of History: The Novels of Paule
   Marshall   168

6 Writing after Colonialism: *Crick Crack, Monkey* and *Beka
   Lamb*   197

7 Narration at the Postcolonial Moment: History and
   Representation in *Abeng*   231

   Conclusion   252

   Index   257

Acknowledgments

This book began as a study of the influence of modernism on George Lamming's theory and practice of fiction and ended up as an examination of what Edouard Glissant once called the Caribbean irruption into modernity. In trying to reconsider the meaning of modernity as seen from the "margins" of the modern world system, and in struggling to connect modernism, as a theoretical category, to colonialism and nationalism—the two ideas that have determined the production of modern Caribbean literature—I have incurred several personal and professional debts. I wish to thank the American Council of Learned Societies, whose generous grant enabled me to complete my research for this book in both the Caribbean and England. I completed the book as an Andrew Mellon Faculty Fellow at Harvard University, and I thank the fellowship and its director for providing funding at a time when I needed relief from teaching duties. I thank the two anonymous readers for Cornell University Press: their enthusiasm for my work was as validating as their criticisms were constructive; among other things, they reminded me about the importance of historicizing cultural production.

I discovered Caribbean literature and its centrality in the cultures of the African diaspora as an undergraduate at the University of Nairobi,

and I owe thanks to Micere Mugo for introducing me to Lamming and
Brathwaite and to Wanjiku Mwotia with whom I studied Césaire; I
read Carpentier in a class taught by Kavetsa Adagala and I would like
to thank her and Wambui Githiora, the other student in the course, for
a memorable year.

At the University of Massachusetts at Boston, it was my luck to have
a group of students who, despite working under very difficult circumstances, shared my fascination with African and Caribbean literature,
history, and culture. I take this opportunity to thank some of these
students for their interest and support: Stephanie Major, Liliana
Green, Marty Stanford, Lionel Rogers, and Patrick Sylvain; Sheila
Mabry, for having taught me how to read Michelle Cliff; and Juan-
damarie Carey-Brown, who has provided friendship and invaluable
research assistance. I have also been fortunate to have the friendship
and professional support of Jim Miller, Bob Fox, and Julie Winch, and I
am grateful for that. Finally, I thank Jamie McDonald for being a
patient witness to this book, for her boundless enthusiasm for its
subject and her sustenance during its production.

A section of Chapter 6 first appeared as "Narration in the Post-
Colonial Moment: *Crick Crack, Monkey*," in *Ariel: A Review of Interna-
tional English Literature* 20, 4 (1989), 18–30. The same article has been
reproduced in *Past the Last Post: Theorizing Post-Colonialism and Post-
Modernism*, ed. Ian Adam and Helen Tiffin (Calgary: University of
Alberta Press, 1991). The article is reprinted here with permission.
Selections from Edward Kamau Brathwaite, *The Arrivants* (Oxford
University Press, 1973), are used by permission of Oxford University
Press.

S. G.

Writing in Limbo

Introduction: Modernism and the Origins of Caribbean Literature

Even if every date that permits us to separate any two periods is arbitrary, none is more suitable, in order to mark the beginning of the modern era, than the year 1492, the year Columbus crosses the Atlantic Ocean.

—Tzvetan Todorov, *The Conquest of America*

My mother said I'd be alone
and when I cried (she said)
I'd be Columbus of my ships
and sail the gardens round
the tears that fell into my hand.

—Edward Kamau Brathwaite, "Limbo"

Caribbean literature and culture are haunted by the presence of the "discoverer" and the historical moment he inaugurates. For if Columbus's "discovery" of the Americas and his initial encounter with the peoples of the New World have paradigmatic value in the European episteme because they usher in a brave new world, a world of modernity and modernist forms, as Tzvetan Todorov assumes in my first epigraph, these events also trigger a contrary effect on the people who are "discovered" and conquered. And while Eurocentric scholars have been eager to claim the conquest of the Americas as a radical and exemplary event that opens up the Old World's reconceptualization of its cultural traditions and temporality, and the constitution of the colonial other, Caribbean writers and scholars exhibit extreme anxiety and ambivalence toward the beginnings of modernity and modern-

1

ism.[1] This book is about this historical anxiety and ambivalence and the cultural and narrative forms Caribbean writers have developed both to represent and to resist the European narrative of history inaugurated by Columbus and the modern moment.

European admirers of modernity—most notably Todorov—may perceive Columbus as the quintessential figure of a modernity that breaks through the limits of tradition, leading us into what Bartolomé de Las Casas called "that time so new and like no other"; but for many Caribbean writers, the "discovery" was tantamount to what George Lamming would call "an unwelcome invasion of the American spine," a disastrous prelude to slavery and colonialism.[2] Indeed, given the consequences of the European "modernization" of the New World, it appears almost impossible for Caribbean writers to accept Todorov's claim that "we are all the direct descendants of Columbus," and that it is with him that "our genealogy begins."[3] For the victims of slavery, colonialism, and indentured labor, it would be even more difficult to be comfortable in Jürgen Habermas's Hegelian conceptualization of the year 1500 as an "epochal threshold."[4] On the contrary, Caribbean writers, like their counterparts in the colonial and postcolonial worlds of Africa and Asia, are skeptical about any liberational claims for modernism and modernity because, as Simon During has noted in his excellent discussion of the relationship between modernity, colonization, and writing, the concept of the modern often derives its force from its Eurocentrism and its capacity to propel European expansion—"the West is modern, the modern is the West. By this logic, other societies can enter history, grasp the future, only at the price of their destruction."[5]

Since entry into the European terrain of the modern has often demanded that the colonized peoples be denied their subjectivity, language, and history, it would be tempting to argue that Caribbean writers have sought new modes of expression and representation by rejecting modernity and by seeking or revalorizing ancestral sources from Africa and India. Indeed, some Caribbean writers and critics

1. For the "modernist implications" of the conquest of America, see Tzvetan Todorov, *The Conquest of America*, trans. Richard Howard (New York: Harper, 1984), pp. 1–5.
2. Here I have adopted Lamming's notion that Caribbean music has invaded the English spine. See *The Pleasures of Exile* (London: Allison and Busby, 1984), p. 77. Las Casas is quoted by Todorov, p. 5.
3. Todorov, p. 5.
4. Jürgen Habermas, *The Philosophical Discourse of Modernity: Twelve Lectures*, trans. Frederick G. Lawrence (Cambridge: MIT Press, 1990), p. 5.
5. Simon During, "Waiting for the Post: Modernity, Colonization, and Writing," *Ariel: A Review of International English Literature* 20 (October 1989), 31.

Introduction

have explicitly rejected modernism, especially the "high" bourgeois variety that developed in Europe after the First World War, as a dangerous fallacy that represses the historicity of art and its function as a form of social critique. For example, Michael Thelwell, the eminent Jamaican novelist and critic, has argued that modernism has had a corrupting influence on twentieth-century Caribbean fiction; it functions as "the excuse and justification for a general retreat from [a] wide-ranging engagement with social and moral questions."[6]

And yet there is a sense in which Caribbean writers cannot escape from modernism and its problematic issues, especially the questions of language, history, and the colonial subject which it raises. Generations of Caribbean writers and intellectuals have had to bear the burden of modern European history and its ideologies as that history was initiated by the "discovery" and then transformed, shaped, and even distorted by subsequent events and institutions such as the plantation system and the colonial condition. In this context, it was perhaps inevitable that the mother of the poetic speaker in Brathwaite's poem (which I use as my second epigraph) would sooner or later invoke the name of Columbus in her attempts to show her son ways of navigating a Caribbean world that Europe had tried to refashion in its own image. For whatever ideological positions Caribbean writers such as Brathwaite, Lamming, and others have taken on the meaning of the "discovery," they are all forced to redefine themselves in relation to this moment. They realize that the time inaugurated by the European colonization of the Americas sets up a modern tradition of representation which still haunts the Caribbean.

Thus the history initiated by the conquest and invention of America has become what George Lamming once called "a sad and hopeful epic"; it destroys aboriginal cultural forms, but it also enables the Caribbean discourse of resistance and cultural transformation in which old African cultures become "modernized" by African slaves as they struggle to survive in a hostile terrain invaded by "human heroes and victims of an imagination shot through with gold."[7] My basic premise, then, is that Caribbean writers cannot adopt the history and culture of European modernism, especially as defined by the colonizing structures, but neither can they escape from it because it has overdetermined Caribbean cultures in many ways. Moreover, for peoples of

6. Michael Thelwell, "Modernist Fallacies and the Responsibility of the Black Writer," in *Duties, Pleasures, and Conflicts: Essays in Struggle* (Amherst: University of Massachusetts Press, 1987), p. 221.
7. Lamming, *The Pleasures of Exile*, p. 17.

3

African and Asian descent, the central categories of European modernity—history, national language, subjectivity—have value only when they are fertilized by figures of the "other" imagination which colonialism has sought to repress. In this sense, Caribbean modernism is highly revisionary. As Wilson Harris, possibly the most self-conscious Caribbean modernist, has argued, *modern* "implies an ongoing and unceasing re-visionary and innovative strategy that has its roots in the deepest layers of that past that still address us."[8]

This book is primarily concerned with this revisionary strategy in West Indian literature, a strategy necessitated by Caribbean writers' attempts to rescue their cultures from what Michel de Certeau, writing on the conquest of the New World, has called the discourse of European power which uses the New World "as if it were a blank, 'savage' page on which Western desire will be written."[9] Because the Africa diaspora was constituted, as Paul Gilroy says, in "a milieu of dispossession," modernity and modernism in the Caribbean pose a set of questions different from that raised in an Anglo-American context.[10] Does the Caribbean writer, driven by what Edouard Glissant calls "the daring adventure of modernity," reject tradition and literary continuity in order to "give meaning to the reality of [the] environment"?[11] If this is the case, what is the status of borrowed European (and hence colonial) literary conventions and of African traditions brought to the Caribbean by slaves and sustained by the peasantry? If Caribbean literature is both haunted and sustained by modernism and modernity, as I argue in this introduction, what exactly are the ideology and form of Caribbean modernism and how do they appropriate or reject the hegemonic European idea of the modern as an affect of Western reason and history?

The Irruption into Modernity

In order to contextualize Caribbean modernism and its cultural politics, we need to conceive it as opposed to, though not necessarily

8. Stephen Slemon, "Interview with Wilson Harris," *Ariel: A Review of International English Literature* 19 (July 1988), 48.

9. Michel de Certeau, *The Writing of History*, trans. Tom Conley (New York: Columbia University Press, 1988), p. xxv.

10. Paul Gilroy, *There Ain't No Black in the Union Jack: The Cultural Politics of Race and Nation* (London: Hutchinson, 1987), p. 219.

11. Edouard Glissant, *Caribbean Discourse: Selected Essays*, trans. J. Michael Dash (Charlottesville: University Press of Virginia, 1989), p. 146.

independent of, European notions of modernism. For there is a sense in which much hostility toward modernist Caribbean texts arises from the tendency to limit definitions of modernism to the twentieth century and to the high modernist aesthetic articulated by Anglo-American writers such as Ezra Pound, T. S. Eliot, and James Joyce. It is this rather limited conceptualization of modernism which has compelled Thelwell to argue, wrongly in my view, that modernist forms lead to the writer's abandonment of "history and cultural reality."[12] Thelwell's definition of modernism is further limited by his negation of the historical conditions that make Caribbean and Afro-American literature possible: in arguing that modernism is diffused "into the cultures of the African world, Black America, and the Caribbean . . . as a result of myth and institutions," he refuses to countenance the historical necessity of what one may call a Third World modernism distinct from the prototypical European form which, in Houston Baker's words, "is exclusively Western, preeminently bourgeois, and optically white."[13]

The long history of colonialism in the Caribbean, and the construction of its cultural landscape under European hegemony, have generated what Glissant aptly calls the region's irruption into modernity as a violent departure from the colonial tradition. Two themes, then, will help us conceptualize this irruption and the narrative and discursive techniques it generates: first, I argue that Caribbean modernism has evolved out of an anxiety toward the colonizing structure in general and its history, language and ideology in particular; second, I examine how this modernism, which is closely related to the process of creolization, develops as a narrative strategy and counter-discourse away from outmoded and conventional modes of representation associated with colonial domination and colonizing cultural structures.

Nowhere is the essential modernity of Caribbean literature as apparent as in the writers' anxiety toward their history; as John Hearne noted in his introduction to the 1976 Caribbean Arts Festival (Carifesta) anthology, "History is the angel with whom all we Caribbean Jacobs have to wrestle, sooner or later, if we hope for a blessing."[14] While European modernists would posit history as a nightmare from which the aesthetic imperative was going to rescue the artist, Caribbean literature has often been haunted by the projection of the Carib-

---

12. Thelwell, p. 221.
13. Thelwell, p. 236; Houston A. Baker, Jr., *Modernism and the Harlem Renaissance* (Chicago: University of Chicago Press, 1987), p. 6.
14. John Hearne, "Introduction," *Carifesta Forum: An Anthology of 20 Caribbean Voices*, ed. John Hearne (Kingston: Institute of Jamaica, 1976), p. vii.

bean colonial subject as either an ahistorical figure of European desire or simply a victim of the history of conquest and enslavement. Caribbean writers simultaneously represent colonial history as a nightmare and affirm the power of historicity in the slave community. This double gesture is not difficult to explain. The African slaves in the New World were denied their history as a precondition for enslavement; to claim subjectivity, they had to struggle for their essential historicity. In the plantation economy, as the Jamaican sociologist Orlando Patterson has observed, slaves were represented as socially dead, without cultural authority, excommunicated from their history, and isolated from their genealogy. The slave, says Patterson, was formally "isolated from his social relations with those who lived" and was "culturally isolated from the social heritage of his ancestors":

> He had a past, to be sure. But a past is not a heritage. Everything has a history, including sticks and stones. Slaves differed from other human beings in that they were not allowed freely to integrate the experience of their ancestors into their lives, to inform their understanding of social reality with the inherited meanings of their natural forebears, or to anchor the living present in any conscious community of memory. That they reached back for the past, as they reached out for the related living, there can be no doubt. Unlike other persons, doing so meant struggling with and penetrating the iron curtain of the master, his community, his laws, his policemen or patrollers, and his heritage.[15]

In spite of the repression of their history during the "middle passage," slaves sustained their culture by memories of the past, of severed kinship with Africa, and by the desire for an epistemology that preceded slavery. However, the point that needs to be foregrounded in Patterson's theory of slavery as social death, and indeed of Caribbean culture as a whole, is the extent to which slaves were denied a consciousness of their historicity. Slaves were not free to claim a historical consciousness independent of the slave master, nor were they allowed to anchor their lives around value systems imported from Africa; as a result, historicity (as distinct from history) was something to be struggled for against the machinery of the plantation and the colonial state. Since colonial modernity denied the Caribbean an "other" history—a version of events distinct from the conventional European narrative in which the islands exist solely as a project of the

15. Orlando Patterson, *Slavery and Social Death: A Comparative Study* (Cambridge: Harvard University Press, 1982), p. 5.

6

conqueror's expansionism—West Indian writing would come to function as a forced entry (into history) through the iron curtain of colonial culture. This forced entry, however, would not be merely an attempt to reclaim a repressed past through the imaginary act; it would also function as an attempt to invent an emancipatory Caribbean narrative of history. As Roberto Marquez has observed, the reconstitution of the Caribbean past, which also demands a critical examination of the past, establishes "the prehistory of the present—active, unreconciled, unpropitiated, contradictory, continuing or permanent presence—and the proper ground for establishing the entelechy, cultural and national, of a Caribbean ethos."[16]

A Caribbean narrative of history is further necessitated by the colonized writers' need to contest the meaning and method of colonial historiography, especially its totalizing gestures. Glissant has observed that in the historiography of colonial modernism—in which history is a "highly functional fantasy of the West"—the process of historicization involves both a strategic dislocation of the colonized and the ideological imposition of "a single History, and therefore of power."[17] Furthermore, colonial history, whose system of signs is an integral part of the narrative of domination and control, attempts, in the words of J. Michael Dash, to "fix reality in terms of a rigid, hierarchical discourse":

> In order to keep the unintelligible realm of historical diversity at bay, History as system attempts to systematize the world through ethnocultural hierarchy and chronological progression. Consequently, a predictable narrative is established, with a beginning, middle, and end. History then becomes, because of this almost theological trinitarian structure, providential fable or salvational myth. . . . History ultimately emerges as a fantasy peculiar to the Western imagination in its pursuit of a discourse that legitimizes its power and condemns other cultures to the periphery.[18]

In their quest for a decolonized Caribbean discourse, however, many West Indian writers consider what Dash calls a trinitarian structure to be the Achilles' heel of colonial historiography: in assuming that there is only one history, Western history, colonial discourse is

16. Roberto Marquez, "Nationalism, Nation, and Ideology: Trends in the Emergence of a Caribbean Literature," in *The Modern Caribbean*, ed. Franklin W. Knight and Colin A. Palmer (Chapel Hill: University of North Carolina Press, 1989), p. 324.
17. Glissant, p. 93.
18. J. Michael Dash, "Introduction," in Glissant, *Caribbean Discourse*, p. xxix.

blind to the fragmentation and diversity that will return to haunt it. Indeed, the very historical moments in which European history appears triumphant because it has achieved, through the conquest of the other, the Hegelian dream of modernity as the manifestation of the Absolute Spirit, contain within them the strains that rupture the totality of the colonizing structure. These strains attract Caribbean writers and intellectuals because they seem to provide an opportunity for subverting colonial discourse at its foundations. Thus Lamming is attracted to Caribbean history in the late sixteenth and early seventeenth centuries because "it's a period which contains all the stresses that go with an emerging nationalism."[19] However, in considering this period in which the European powers seemed to have consolidated their control over the islands, the Caribbean novelist—writing in the period of decolonization—is not seduced by the imperial ideas that dominated the sixteenth and seventeenth centuries, but by their corollary—nationalism and national identity. Similarly, while the history of Martinique has been written in the colonial text as the continuity of French history—the temporary abolition of slavery (1794), emancipation (1848), and departmentalization (1946) are all presented as consequences of central events in French history—Glissant seeks to expose the "real discontinuity beneath the apparent continuity of our history."[20] In both cases, the central paradigms of colonial historicity—systematization, chronology, and closure—are heavily contested.

Some Caribbean writers have, of course, suggested that to escape the prisonhouse of colonial history, the writer must expunge history from the imaginary text altogether. The most important proponent of this view, which is akin to the high modernist desire to transcend history as a precondition for liberating the self from its alienating structures, is Derek Walcott, the St. Lucia poet. In "The Muse of History," Walcott argues that the great poets of the New World reject history because it is "fiction, subject to a fitful muse, memory"; history chains writers to the past and thus forecloses the language of liberation; a literature that "serves" historical truth "yellows into polemic or evaporates in pathos."[21] For Walcott, "the truly tough aesthetic of the New World neither explains nor forgives history. It refuses to recognize it as a creative or culpable force. This shame and awe of history possess poets of the Third World who think of language as enslave-

---

19. Quoted in George Kent, "Caribbean Novelist," *Black World* 22 (March 1973), 14.
20. Glissant, p. 91.
21. Derek Walcott, "The Muse of History," in Hearne, *Carifesta Forum*, p. 112.

ment and who, in a rage for identity, respect only incoherence or nostalgia."[22]

Does Walcott, then, see the poetic act as truly liberating only if it secures the writing self a niche in what Linda Hutcheon calls, in another context, "the hermetic ahistoric formalism and aestheticism" of high modernism?[23] Or is Glissant closer to the truth when he suggests that what Walcott rejects is not the validity of historicity but the valorization of inherited categories of history and an "affirmation of the urgency of a revaluation of the conventions of analytical thought?"[24] Clearly, some of Walcott's best poetry (the "Schooner's Flight," for example) is generated by the tension between language and the "burden of history" which the poet consigns to others in his poetic theory. In the circumstances, the poet seems to become enmeshed in history the more he tries to escape from it.

Glissant's suggestion that what is at issue in Walcott's devalorization of history is the desire to deconstruct the analytic conventions of that history is pertinent to the Caribbean's quest for its own modes of representation because, as we will see in several chapters in this book, the march of European modernist history in the New World is often posited as the triumph of reason and the systematization of time and space. In the circumstances, Walcott's refusal to recognize history as a creative force is really a negation of a European model of history anchored on notions of progress and temporal closure. In contrast, a decolonized discourse seeks forms of representing a history of displacement and reversal and valorizes strategies of inscribing and evoking what Maximilien Laroche, the Haitian writer, has called "the otherness of identity" found in the "theater of our contradictions."[25] My other intention in this study is to argue that Caribbean modernism has developed to articulate the identities constituted by such historical contradictions.

In arguing for a Caribbean modernism that contests colonial history,

22. Walcott, "The Muse of History," p. 112.

23. The phrase is used by Linda Hutcheon in *A Poetics of Postmodernism: History, Theory, Fiction* (New York: Routledge, 1988), p. 88. As I try to show in subsequent chapters, the kind of problematization of history which Hutcheon attributes to postmodernism—in reaction against the "modernist period"—has been one of the defining attributes of what I refer to as Caribbean modernism.

24. Glissant, p. 65.

25. See Maximilien Laroche's contribution to the discussion in *Process of Unity in Caribbean Society*, ed. Ileana Rodriguez and Marc Zimmerman (Minneapolis: Institute for the Study of Ideologies, 1983), p. 111; and Patrick Bellegarde-Smith, *In the Shadow of Powers: Dantès Bellegarde in Haitian Social Thought* (Atlantic Highlands, N.J.: Humanities Press, 1985), pp. 181–82.

I am well aware that this modernity and its forms may still be imprisoned in the very European paradigms it seeks to negate. The risk of formulating a theory of Caribbean modernism which is haunted by the shadows of the colonizing structures is, of course, enormous: we cannot tell when a counter-discourse finally breaks away from the discourse it critiques, nor does my placement of Caribbean narratives in the gap between a colonial and a decolonized narrative, between Europe and Africa, provide much certainty or ideological consolation. But this risk is worth taking for two reasons: First, any turn to Africa or India for an ideological rescue plan does not seem to mitigate the anxieties of European history discussed above. At best, as Edward Brathwaite's trilogy, *The Arrivants*, has shown so well, Africa is only a prelude to the adventure of Caribbean modernity. The Caribbean writer returns to Africa not in search of a cure for alienation and displacement, nor to overcome the psychological gap denoted by the middle passage, but to evolve a genealogy of his or her origins; this genealogy leads to the development of a radical consciousness of history, but it also actualizes the trauma of imperialism which has overrun the ancestors.

My contention, then, is that Caribbean writing is not so much motivated by the desire to recover an "original" model—the unhistoried African body that predates slavery and colonialism—as by the need to inscribe Caribbean selves and voices within an economy of representation whose institutional and symbolic structures have been established since the "discovery." If we accept Glissant's basic argument that the essential modernity of New World writers is the desire to write a new history of the region, Africa does not proffer an ideal history to counter the disorder of colonialism, except at the expense of mystification. The slave trade, says Glissant, is the journey "that has fixed in us the unceasing tug of Africa against which we must paradoxically struggle today in order to take root in our rightful land. The motherland is also for us the inaccessible land."[26]

Glissant's double gesture—he affirms the necessity of Africa in the Caribbean consciousness even as he asserts its remoteness—points to the second reason why I risk adopting modernism as a conceptual category: even when it is haunted by its imposed metropolitan identity and its desired ancestral image, the Caribbean imagination is sustained by the tug of both Europe and Africa. This tug, which can be as

26. Glissant, pp. 160–61.

enriching and ennobling as it can be depreciative and enslaving, has often functioned as the enabling condition of Caribbean social thought and cultural production at crucial historical junctures. For example, in nineteenth-century Haiti, as Patrick Bellegarde-Smith notes in an excellent examination of Haitian social thought, the newly independent ruling class could not countenance the value of the African-derived language and culture of the peasantry; indeed, this class could not countenance the possibility of a Haitian national culture independent of France. The men who had fought and defeated French enslavement held a firm belief that the Americas constituted a new social practice that, nevertheless, perpetuated the old European spirit. Bellegarde-Smith notes that in both Haiti and the Hispanic islands that became independent at the end of the nineteenth century, the predominant social theory was that the Americas would improve upon Europe, with which they shared a "common culture"; at the time of independence, "there was seemingly no alternative to modernization seen as westernization."[27]

It was in reaction to this assumed continuity between Europe and the Caribbean that a later generation of Caribbean writers such as Jean Price Mars and Aimé Césaire sought to revalorize Africa in the Caribbean imagination. As Césaire told Charles Rowell, "If Senghor and I spoke of Negritude, it was because we were in a century of exacerbated Eurocentrism, a fantastic ethnocentrism, that enjoyed a guiltless conscience."[28] In any case, irrespective of where they sought their identity, Caribbean writers could not escape the anxieties generated by their historical conditions—they were colonial subjects and they had to write for or against colonial modernism. Whether they were Eurocentric or Afrocentric, these writers lived in a colonial condition that was, by its very definition, an extreme state of anxiety.

But before I trace these anxieties, especially as they are manifested in language and subjectivity, I want to emphasize my basic contention

27. Bellegarde-Smith, p. 181. The strategic position of modernism and literary production in the New World has been discussed by Roberto Gonzalez Echevarria in numerous essays. His observation that "Latin America as a concept and as a political reality was created at the outset of modernity, that is to say, at the historical juncture that also brought into being the question of cultural existence, both as a question and as a conceptual need" applies equally to the Caribbean basin. See *The Voice of the Masters: Writing and Authority in Modern Latin American Literature* (Austin: University of Texas Press, 1985), p. 11. Gonzalez Echevarria discusses the conjunction of modernity and historicity in "Literature of the Hispanic Caribbean," *Latin American Literary Review* 8 (Spring–Summer, 1980), 4–5.

28. Charles Rowell, "It Is through Poetry That One Copes with Solitude: An Interview with Aimé Césaire," *Callaloo* 12 (Winter 1989), 55.

that the colonial anxiety does not necessarily disable the colonized writer; rather, it enables a narrative of liberation in the colonizer's language. The colonized writer who suffers a crisis of identity because he or she cannot feel at home in imposed colonial spaces is inevitably driven to subvert the given form and language. Also, as Houston A. Baker has observed in his seminal study of Afro-American modernism, this kind of anxiety can indeed open up radical discursive possibilities:

> Modernist "anxiety" in Afro-American culture does not stem from a fear of replicating outmoded forms or of giving way to bourgeoisie formalisms. Instead, the anxiety of modernist influence is produced, in the first instance, by the black spokesperson's necessary task of employing audible extant forms in ways that move clearly *up*, masterfully and resoundingly away from slavery.[29]

For Caribbean peoples, however, "re-sounding" away from slavery and colonization demanded a certain reconceptualization of the colonial language and its ideological terrain. The result was a creole culture that according to Patrick Taylor "enabled peoples disrupted by the slave trade to recreate themselves, to distance themselves from those who tried to control their minds."[30] Modern Caribbean writers are framed by this creole culture on one side and the colonial episteme on the other side.

Modernism: Creolization and Maroonage

In what space, wonders Glissant in a crucial moment in *Caribbean Discourse*, is a poetics of Antillean writing going to be articulated? Since the European metropolitan space is too compromised (it carries all the baggage of enslavement and colonization) and the African terrain is inaccessible, Glissant, like many of his contemporaries, has sought to position his art and discourse in a "twilight" consciousness between the ancestral sources and the colonizing structures. Because it is not fixed in any epistemic position, or rather does not have to see the appropriation of one paradigmatic value (for example the Euro-

---

29. Baker, p. 101.
30. Patrick Taylor, *The Narrative of Liberation: Perspectives on Afro-Caribbean Literature, Popular Culture, and Politics* (Ithaca: Cornell University Press, 1989), pp. 228–29.

pean language) as the negation of another value (such as African folklore or religion), the twilight consciousness offers limitless ideological possibilities; from a linguistic perspective, the twilight zone is not indebted to old social and cultural models, conventions, or idioms. Most important, as Dash observes in relation to Glissant's poetics, the writer who operates in the space between cultural traditions draws inventive energies from "creative schizophrenia": speaking an androgynous idiom, this writer does not have to choose between self and community, between a private discourse and a national language, or even between the subjective experience and historical traditions.[31] On the contrary, this kind of writer is able to move from one value to the other and to break the binary oppositions that sustain such values as mutually exclusive entities. As Wilson Harris notes, the twilight situation, which "half-remembers, half-forgets," enables "the language of consciousness" to "rediscover and reinform itself in the face of accretions of accent and privileges, the burden of 'sacred' usage or one-sidedness."[32]

In the circumstances, the Caribbean writer cannot be the slave of a canonical tradition that burdens us with its "sacred" claims; on the other hand, unlike their European counterparts, Caribbean writers have no need to retreat from their social environment or cultural traditions. The capacity to reject epistemological fixations turns the language of Caribbean literature into what Walcott calls an instrument of deliverance from servitude; existing in the twilight zone of colonial culture, blacks in the New World were forced to forge "a language that went beyond mimicry, a dialectic which had the force of revelation as it invented names for things, one which finally settled on its own mode of inflection, and which began to create an oral culture of chants, jokes, folksongs and fables."[33] Moreover, enslaved blacks could lay claim to the New World through a creative use of the social spaces in which they were imprisoned, thereby reverting their terrible irruption into the plantation system into a fundamental value to which all other values in the slave community could refer. In other words, the slaves' journey from the Old World to the New World would open up the African imagination to other temporal and spatial possibilities, while

31. Dash, "Introduction," p. xxvi.
32. Wilson Harris, *Tradition, the Writer, and Society: Critical Essays* (London: New Beacon Publications, 1973), p. 64. See also Derek Walcott's literary manifesto, "What the Twilight Said: An Overture," in *Dream on Monkey Mountain and Other Plays* (New York: Farrar, 1970), pp. 3–40.
33. Walcott, "What the Twilight Said," p. 17.

at the same time demanding a new idiom and form. The "modernization" of African cultures in the Caribbean (what has come to be known as creolization) is the process by which exiled Africans set out to develop modernist ways of seeing, knowing, and representing their dislocated culture—aware, no doubt, of its aboriginal sources, but motivated by the need to account for new social and historical forms.

The most dramatic metaphor for this process of cultural transformation is the limbo dance. Edward Brathwaite, who sees the limbo dance as a metacode for New World writing in general, speculates that the dance evolved on the slave ships in the middle passage as a therapy for the cramped conditions in the holds: it was a creative way of using limited dancing space.[34] For Wilson Harris, the limbo dance is an appropriate metaphor for the middle passage, which serves as a gateway between Africa and the Caribbean and as a form of cultural dislocation, a figure of the doubleness that infuses Caribbean writing. Thus, although the middle passage represents the temporal moment when the slaves are dislocated from Africa, it is also a challenge to them to reassemble their cultural fragments, fuse their multiple ethnic identities, and appropriate imprisoned social spaces; the "dislocation of interior space serves as a corrective to a uniform cloak or documentary stasis of imperialism."[35] Indeed, in most Caribbean writing, dislocation and its imaginary correctives go hand in hand; however, they are both functions of the stasis of imperialism which they seek to subvert.

Being in "limbo" does have its anxieties, but what makes this cultural space attractive to Caribbean writers is its generation of ironic forms that undermine the authority of imperialist discourse and its dominant figures. Readers of Edward Brathwaite's poem "Limbo" can fail to recognize its ironic undercurrent only at their own peril. For one thing, the authority of the mother who throws her son ashore and asks him to navigate his ship in tears like Columbus in reverse is called into question by her state of mind—she is described as the "cracked mother," mad in the sense that she is unaware of the absurdity of the Columbian model she holds up for her son.[36] After all, if Columbus was such a good navigator, why did he end up in the wrong place?

34. See Edward Brathwaite, "Limbo," in *The Arrivants: A New World Trilogy* (London: Oxford University Press, 1973), pp. 179–205. Brathwaite provides an important historical notation on the limbo dance in his glossary to this collection of poems (p. 274).

35. Wilson Harris, *Explorations: A Selection of Tales and Articles 1966–1981*, ed. Hena Maes-Jelinek (Geding Sovej, Denmark: Dangaroo Press, 1981), p. 28.

36. Brathwaite, "Limbo," p. 170. All further references to the poem are included in the text.

Surely the European model is one that needs to be questioned and made ironic at every juncture.

The ironic nature of the poem becomes even more apparent when we recognize the contradictory terms Brathwaite uses to re-present the inaugural moments of Caribbean modernity. On the sea of his tears the boy sees three nuns who later turn out to be emblems of Columbus's ships—"Santa Marias with black silk sails" (p. 180)—and slowly he realizes that to replay the journey of the discovery, that is, to adopt European forms to represent Caribbean conditions, he must at the same time negate his selfhood and become an agent of domination and repression. And yet, what choice does the subject have? His predicament is made worse by the realization that an ideal history of the Caribbean is ultimately inaccessible except as fantasy: "We wanted land as it should be," says the poetic speaker, "hard and firm; the trees deep-rooted / the orchards well spaced / churches quiet and heavy as stone" (p. 183). The reality, however, is a reversal of such expectations, for the islands have lost their balance, "suddenly fallen and drowned" (p. 184).

Thus a modernist anxiety generates irony in this poem: the poetic speaker, now reduced to a function of the colonizing structure, does not even know how to navigate his own world: "how will new maps be drafted? / Who will suggest a new tentative frontier? / How will the sky dawn now?" (p. 184). Such questions about maps and boundaries are symptoms of the "inner dichotomy" (what Marshall Berman, in a general history of modernism, calls the "inner sense of living in two worlds simultaneously") through which the categories of colonial modernism and modernity emerge.[37] The most obvious manifestation of this dichotomy is the fact that the poetic speaker seeks to map a Caribbean landscape but he speaks a European language already loaded with Eurocentric figures.

Another source of anxiety for Caribbean writers is the uneasy convergence of modernism and colonialism, especially in those cases where colonized writers have aligned themselves with the European literary avant-garde. For it was not uncommon, especially in the colonial period, for colonized writers to use forms and figures borrowed

37. Marshall Berman, *All That Is Solid Melts into Air: The Experience of Modernity* (New York: Penguin, 1988), p. 17; Berman's ideas on modernism, modernity, and modernization are discussed by Perry Anderson in "Modernity and Revolution" in *Marxism and the Interpretation of Culture*, ed. Cary Nelson and Lawrence Grossberg (Urbana: University of Illinois Press, 1988), pp. 317–34.

from European modernism as a point of entry into certain aspects of Western culture, or to "naturalize" European languages to Caribbean cultures. This process of naturalizing the dominant language has its parallels in doctrines of modernization in the region. For example, in his *Discourse on Colonialism*, Aimé Césaire is agitated by any notion that he is an "enemy of Europe" or the mere thought that he ever urged colonized peoples to return to "the ante-European past." On the contrary, the colonized peoples are the vanguard of the modernizing project; "it is the African who is asking for ports and roads, and colonialist Europe which is niggardly on this score . . . it is the colonized man who wants to move forward, and the colonizer who holds things back."[38]

Inevitably, there is a more important linguistic twist to this claim: Césaire works within the French language, but as he tells René Depestre in a 1967 interview, he has always striven to create a new language, a language "capable of communicating the African heritage." The old French language—which not only has supported an injust colonial praxis but has also become "burdensome, overused"—can be renewed by "an Antillean French, a black French that, while still being French, had a black character."[39] In other words, the French language could be "creolized" and thus forced to account for a different, Caribbean-centered experience. For many Caribbean writers and intellectuals, creolization has come to represent a unique kind of Caribbean modernism, one that resists the colonizing structures through the diversion of the colonial language and still manages to reconcile the values of European literacy with the long-repressed traditions of African orality.[40]

The notion of creolization as an essential component of Caribbean modernism has both a political and theoretical function. On one hand, the political function of creolization can be found in the writings and activities of the founders of Cuba and Haiti, the first Caribbean countries to become independent, who sought to harmonize the racial and caste differences brought about by the plantation system by promoting creolization as a process of refashioning the Old World into a new national culture. In the context of the Ten Years' War of Cuban independence (1868–78), for example, José Martí would posit cultural syncretism as the fundamental code for explaining Caribbean culture; the

38. Aimé Césaire, *Discourse on Colonialism*, trans. Joan Pinkham (New York: Monthly Review Press, 1972), p. 25.
39. Césaire, *Discourse*, pp. 66, 67.
40. See Glissant, pp. 122–28.

intermingling of cultural forms was a harnessing of "the elements composing the islands."[41] Earlier, in a newly independent Haiti, Toussaint L'Ouverture seems to have foreseen linguistic creolization as a gesture toward what Roberto Marquez calls "the control of the international language" in the service of the state:

> And this is because the new state has destroyed the economic substratum on which the prior state had depended; it has restructured the plantation relationship, and it has severed much of its continuity with the past. The revolution meant a beginning and a new basis, as well as an end to the old bases. It was a beginning in which all elements, relations and norms in the realm of culture, aesthetics and linguistics would be recreated and resynthesized in function of the state's emergent political economy.[42]

On the other hand, creolization—in its theoretical and more contemporary strand—is appropriated as a figure of modernism because it opposes the synchronic vision of colonial historiography with the diachronic narrative of a cross-cultural imagination.[43] The colonial vision is presented as essentially synchronic because it insists on the fixation of the identity of the dominated; the narrative of creolization, on the other hand, insists on the transmutation and transformation of the colonial subject—and its culture—toward a realm of freedom. According to Edward Brathwaite, who has written more on creolization than any other Caribbean historian, the matrix of creolism signalizes both the adaptation of ancestral forms to the Caribbean environment and the quest for alternatives to European cultural traditions. Creolism thus suggests "subtle and multiform orientations from or *towards* ancestral origins": "In this way, Caribbean culture can be seen in terms of a dialectic of development taking place within a seamless guise or continuum of space and time; a model which allows for blood flow, fluctuations, the half-look, the look both/several ways; which allows for and contains the ambiguous, and rounds the sharp edges off the dichotomy."[44]

Brathwaite's recognition that creolization must allow for fluctua-

41. Quoted in Marquez, "Nationalism, Nation, and Ideology," p. 298.
42. Roberto Marquez, contribution to the discussion in Rodriquez and Zimmerman, *Process of Unity in Caribbean Society*, p. 75.
43. I'm using *diachrony* here—in the sense popularized by Edward W. Said—as the process by which narrative destabilizes a hegemonic system of meanings and hence functions as an agent of change and transformation. See Said, *Orientalism* (New York: Vintage, 1979), p. 240.
44. Edward Brathwaite, "Caribbean Man in Time and Space," in Hearne, *Carifesta Forum*, p. 204.

tions has important consequences for my discussion. His eclectic description of creolism allows him to counter the orthodoxy of state doctrines of creolization which sometimes create the illusion that the relationship of all the parts that make the whole is egalitarian. He also recognizes that the kind of syncretism which some Caribbean writers seem to find in creolization portends a will to cultural synthesis which sometimes obscures the racial, ethnic, and caste tensions that often militate against the formation of a unified national or Pan-Caribbean culture. For Brathwaite, then, the central problem of Caribbean culture is not how to account for its totality but rather how to express "the extraordinary complexity of what we call creolization," how "to study the fragments/whole."[45] In other words, modern Caribbean writing will not be predicated on a theory of a unified organic self, or the non-problematic relationship among this self, its world, and language. For if we were to succumb to a sensual and essential theory of language and writing in which literature valorizes the "possibility of the integration of feeling/knowledge, rather than the split between the abstract and the emotional," as Barbara Christian has recently argued, then we would be sustaining one of the greatest illusions of colonialist discourse, its repression of differences, its futile struggle to represent the colonized as a junior and inferior partner in a Pax Britannica or other colonial mythology.[46] It is important to note that although it sustains a social and economic structure that draws from even the dubious wells of biological divisions, the colonial enterprise has cultivated a colonialist discourse (defined most aptly by Peter Hulme as "an ensemble of linguistically-based practices unified by their common deployment in their management of colonial relationships"[47]) as a key instrument of its cultural hegemony.

An integrated discourse of self is surely the ultimate or possibly utopian desire of Caribbean writing, but it can only be reached after the negotiation of a historically engendered split between the self and its world, between this self and the language it uses. The despair of Caribbean modernist literature—and also the condition that makes it possible—is expressed by the Haitian poet Léon Laleau in his 1931 "Trahison" (Betrayal):

45. Brathwaite, "Caribbean Man," p. 199.
46. Barbara Christian, "The Race for Theory," *Cultural Critique* 6 (Spring 1987), 55–56.
47. Peter Hulme, *Colonial Encounters: Europe and the Native Caribbean 1492–1797* (London and New York: Methuen, 1986), p. 2.

This haunted heart that doesn't fit
My language or the clothes I wear
Chafes within the grip of
Borrowed feelings, European ways.[48]

Laleau's dilemma—how to negotiate the chasm between a colonial language and an African-derived culture—has been echoed by many other Caribbean writers; in its most dramatic form, the problem of self-representation in an alienating language is exemplified by the suicide of the Haitian poet Edmond Laforest, who tied a Larousse dictionary around his neck before he drowned himself to protest the hegemony of the colonial library.[49]

Although the political desire to unify the fragments that mark the Caribbean landscape is urgent and necessary, the modern drama of creolization is marked by linguistic conflicts and cultural indentureship. So long as creolization is overdetermined by colonialism and neocolonialism, it still carries the Manichaeanism of the colonial situation and the violence it engenders. The relationship between the literate (European) and the oral (Caribbean) cultures, between the colonizer and the colonized, is, as Césaire succinctly notes, devoid of human contact; this relationship is "nothing but the relationship of domination and submission which turns the colonising man into a warder or a whip, and the indigenous man into an instrument of production."[50] Since the colonial language is an instrument of domination and submission, how is it going to be adapted to the narrative and discourse of liberation? Interestingly, the linguistic crisis the Caribbean writer faces at this juncture is similar to that which confronted European high modernist poets at about the same time Laleau, Laforest, and Césaire began to write: how can literary language face the pressures of its objective conditions and yet liberate itself from them?[51] My basic premise, then, is that the history of Caribbean literature can be written as the evolution of a discourse striving to establish its identity within the parameters defined by the European language and

48. Léon Laleau, "Betrayal," in *The Negritude Poets*, ed. Conroy Kennedy (New York: Thunder's Mouth Press, 1975), p. 15.
49. The episode is reported by Henry L. Gates, Jr., "Writing 'Race' and the Difference It Makes," *Critical Inquiry* 12 (Autumn 1985), 13.
50. Césaire, *Discourse*, p. 27.
51. For the pressures that generated the language of European high modernism, see Alan Wilde, *Horizons of Assent: Modernism, Postmodernism, and the Ironic Imagination* (Baltimore: Johns Hopkins University Press, 1981), p. 99; and Theodor Adorno, *Aesthetic Theory*, trans. C. Lenhardt, ed. Gretel Adorno and Rolf Tiedemann (London: Routledge, 1984), p. 49.

culture which it strives to disperse. My argument here is that Caribbean writers, in response to their historical marginalization, have evolved a discourse of alterity which is predicated on a deliberate act of self-displacement from the hegemonic culture and its central tenets. The Maroon is the most visible symbol of this gesture of cultural *dédoublement*.

According to Richard Price, runaway African slaves managed to maintain their autonomy from the dominant culture by both mastering European modes of resistance and improvising American ones; in Maroon societies, ideological commitment to "things African" was formulated through "nascent but already powerful plantation-forged Afro-American cultures."[52] Many Caribbean writers have hence adopted maroonage as a metaphor for cultural production in foreign lands and, specifically, for writing in a colonial situation. Cultural maroonage, argues Depestre, is a subversive strategy adopted by slaves "to restructure their disembodied components of their historical identity in the unfamiliar world," to find "the new truth of their lives," or to "rework their shredded African traditions."[53] Like the slaves fleeing into the hills to establish autonomy, the modern Caribbean writer seeks to rework European forms and genres to rename the experience of the "other" American.

But Depestre's claim, in another context, that maroonage is a form of "escape from western culture," needs to be qualified in one important respect: this escape has never been complete.[54] Indeed, as Richard Price observes of the original Maroons, the survival of autonomous African communities in the New World always depended on a paradoxical relationship with the plantation structure; while Maroons were, "from one perspective, the antithesis of all that slavery stood for, they were at the same time everywhere an embarrassing visible

52. "Introduction: Maroons and Their Communities," in *Maroon Societies: Rebel Communities in the Americas*, ed. Richard Price (New York: Anchor, 1973), p. 28. See also Franklin W. Knight, *The Caribbean: Genesis of a Fragmented Nationalism* (New York: Oxford University Press, 1978), pp. 69–73; and Mavis C. Campbell, *The Maroons of Jamaica 1655–1796* (Trenton, N.J.: Africa World Press, 1990). The most comprehensive examination of the theme of resistance in Caribbean literature is Selwyn Cudjoe's *Resistance and Caribbean Literature* (Athens: Ohio University Press, 1980).

53. René Depestre, "Hello and Goodbye to Negritude," in *Africa in Latin America: Essays on History, Culture, and Socialization*, ed. Manuel Moreno Fraginals, trans. Leonor Blum (New York: Holmes and Meier, 1984), pp. 258–59.

54. René Depestre, "Problems of Identity for the Black in the Caribbean," in Hearne, *Carifesta Forum*, p. 62.

part of these systems."[55] Maroonage as Houston Baker has argued, evinces a discourse that adopts skills and knowledge borrowed from the "master culture" to represent "a community of national interests set in direct opposition to the general economic, political, and theological tenets of a racist land."[56]

Nowhere is maroonage as a gesture of discursive Caribbean modernism as evident as in Césaire's *Cahier*, a text in which linguistic resistance is underwritten by a parasitic relationship to the language community the poet opposes. Simply put, the *Cahier*, one of the most radical gestures in Caribbean literature, is also indebted to, possibly haunted by, the European modernist models it adopts to strike at the foundations of Eurocentrism. As A. James Arnold has noted in his comprehensive study of negritude and modernism, to attack the world view that engendered slavery and colonialism, Césaire was "constrained by his education to forge weapons out of the adversary's own arsenal."[57] Arnold proceeds to formulate Césaire's agonized relationship to the European tradition in terms that explain the modernist bent in Caribbean writing: "As a black Martinican, Césaire stood inside and outside the culture of France and of Europe. His struggle was to prove especially painful and its outcome especially problematic because in attacking modern Europe he was at the same time attacking a part of himself."[58] As Caliban, Césaire would use the ecumenical language of high modernism to amplify his call for "decolonization within the bounds of the dominant cultures," but he was painfully imprisoned in the French language.[59]

Now, to the extent that it seeks to disperse the already written discourse of colonialism, the maroonage gesture Caribbean writers associate with Caliban is commensurate with that act of dispersal which, according to Michel Foucault, realizes a new discursive formation by opening different possibilities of "reanimating already existing themes, of rousing opposed strategies, of giving way to irreconcilable interests, of making it possible, with a particular set of concepts, to

55. Richard Price, "Introduction: Maroons and Their Communities," in *Maroon Societies*, p. 21.
56. Baker, p. 77.
57. A. James Arnold, *Modernism and Negritude: The Poetry and Poetics of Aimé Césaire* (Cambridge: Harvard University Press, 1981), p. 70.
58. Arnold, p. 70.
59. Césaire, *Discourse*, pp. 67, 68.

play different games."[60] Within this formulation, a new Caribbean discourse is generated by the colonized writer's guerrilla attack on the dominant culture through what Césaire would call a "surrealistic" onslaught. Reflecting on his linguistic strategies in the *Cahier*, Césaire notes that the power of his poem, especially its ability to break through the silence imposed on the Caribbean peoples by the colonizer through the colonial language, is largely due to his use of poetic maneuvers to deconstruct the "already written" aspects of colonial discourse, and to his use of surrealistic techniques as weapons "to explode the French language" and ignite a process of disalienation.[61]

Patrick Taylor's conclusion that Césaire's poem is bound and possibly disabled by "its own starting point"—the poet's assimilationist tendencies and his implicit acceptance of "the white myth"—is quite valid, but this hindrance should not draw attention away from the linguistic radicalism embedded in the structure of the *Cahier*.[62] Whatever its limitations, what makes Césaire's poem so remarkable in the discourse of decolonization is its initial conceptualization as a fragment that, nevertheless, exists as the preliminary toward a whole: the poet falls back on the "discourse of deracination" borrowed from European modernism to explode the colonizer's claim of an integrated Caribbean culture (i.e., one integrated to the empire). The instruments of displacement are valorized; psychological and cultural dysfunction is foregrounded as an object that blocks consciousness and the self's access to its true nature; the dispersal of the dominant figures of colonial discourse, and the celebration of the negative, realize the poetic act.[63]

We can better appreciate the power and value Césaire bestows on displacement if we recall that the poet's point of entry into the *Cahier* (his entry into the French language as it were) is itself an absence, a twilight zone—"At the end of the wee hours." This absence, however, is the incentive to new meanings: in the "inert town" of the poet's

---

60. Michel Foucault, *The Archeology of Knowledge and the Discourse on Language*, trans. A. M. Sheridan Smith (New York: Pantheon, 1982), pp. 36–37.

61. Césaire says he was ready to accept surrealism because it was "a weapon that exploded the French language. It shook up absolutely everything. This was very important because the traditional forms—burdensome, overused forms were crushing me." See *Discourse*, p. 67.

62. Taylor, p. 181.

63. Ronnie Scharfman, "Repetition and Absence: The Discourse of Deracination in Aimé Césaire's 'Nocturne d'une nostalgie,'" *The French Review* 56 (March 1983), 572. See also Serge Gavronsky, "Aimé Césaire and the Language of Politics," *French Review* 56 (December 1982), 273–80; and Joan Dayan, "The Figure of Negation: Some Thoughts of a Landscape by Césaire," *The French Review* 56 (February 1983), 411–21.

birth, the speaker is confronted by a throng "detoured from its true cry," suggesting that the poetic utterance cannot be constructed on perceptual figures (p. 35). In the tradition of his European modernist counterparts, as discussed by Alan Wilde, Césaire falls back on language not "as a means of discovering or evoking some final and ultimate 'Truth,' but as a way of releasing the self and thereby making the phenomenal world . . . the scene of purposeful action."[64] The poetic voice is painful and fragmented, however, and the speaker is forced to enunciate in the ill-defined zone of deracination. Because Césaire can only create meanings by writing about silence, absence, death, and denial, his discourse effectively exists in a space of double inscription: it traces the same lines along which the colonizer has structured the black subject, but this gesture is a form of subversion— it has assumed opposite and reversed ideological value.

What is important for us to note, however, is that Césaire's notion of displacement is not the Derridian sojourn in the wilderness of uncertainty. While Derrida argues that displacement does not "overturn" the authority of the old truth, and does not, as a result, take place as an event ("It does not occupy a simple place. It does not take place *in* writing"[65]), Césaire posits the dislocation of old meanings as the prelude to the creation of new ones in writing. Linguistic displacement is imperative to the poetics of decolonization because, by tracing the historical and discursive origins of the subject's dislocation, the poet transcends his or her limitations through writing. What Joan Dayan calls Césaire's language of copia is evidence of his ability (or desire) to turn displacement into a performative event that will enable him to "find a voice amid the remnants of an idiom springing from historical realities and ways of cognizance alien to his own."[66] In the twilight zone of colonialism, the displaced subject returns and embraces "its land without a stale, / these paths without memory, these winds without memory, these / winds without a tablet," but instead of becoming overwhelmed by his alienation on the site of colonialism, he uses his absences to launch his "Full voice, ample voice" as "our wealth, our spear" (p. 49). And thus in New World modernism, the mastery of form goes hand in hand with its deformation; out of silence

---

64. Wilde, p. 99.
65. Jacques Derrida, *Dissemination*, trans. Barbara Johnson (Chicago: University of Chicago Press, 1981), p. 193.
66. Dayan, p. 415.

arises, like the phoenix, a new voice. This modern voice proposes a different reading of what Wilson Harris calls "the office of language."[67]

Reading Caribbean Modernism

But the greatest challenge facing any critic of Caribbean literature is one of epistemology and historical periodization. For if Caribbean modernism implies an unceasing process of revisionism, as Wilson Harris has constantly insisted, it also presents us with innumerable difficulties of definition and perspective.[68] As a Caribbean modernist who wants to appropriate the revolutionary linguistic strain in the literary avant-garde while renouncing the imperialism that under-writes the "discovery," Harris adopts a geographic metaphor to help him situate his aesthetic. Modernity, he argues, is an escarpment dividing the moment of conquest and loss for "the ancient American civilizations" from the temporal movements through which Europe renews and empowers itself: "This escarpment seen from another angle possesses the features of a watershed, main or subsidiary, de-pending again on how one looks at it."[69] The position of the writer on this escarpment is possibly the most urgent issue in the quest for a Caribbean hermeneutics.

Thus if George Lamming seems intent on transforming the original error of "discovery" into an American gnosis, it is because he realizes, as do many of his contemporaries, that what is at stake in the repre-sentation of the islands is not the discovery of an original model or presence, but the projection of new desires and ideologies. The value of Columbus's adventure, notes Lamming, lies in its ironic results, which show that the original purpose of a journey "may sometimes have nothing to do with the results that attend upon it."[70] In simple hermeneutical terms, modernity in the Caribbean has always man-ifested itself in contradictory and often antagonistic tendencies, which need to be stressed because they explain many of the shifts in Carib-

---

67. Quoted in Sandra E. Drake, *Wilson Harris and the Modern Tradition* (Westport, Conn.: Greenwood, 1986), p. 10. My reflections on a particular kind of Caribbean modernism are indebted to Drake's discussion of the ways in which "non-Western paradigms also constitute part of the Modernist tradition" (p. xii).

68. See Harris's interview with Slemon, p. 48.

69. Wilson Harris, *Tradition, the Writer, and Society* (London: New Beacon Books, 1973), pp. 30–31.

70. Lamming, *The Pleasures of Exile*, p. 36.

bean discourse in the twentieth century. Clearly, any periodization of Caribbean literature will always remain suspect and possibly undesirable; a "schematic history," censures J. Michael Dash, may gain in "shapeliness but lose a sense of the diversity and contradictions of the events it attempts to explain."[71] Dash proceeds to provide an alternative recuperation of Caribbean literary history—one transcending "the hierarchical, the fixed, the linear"—which I have adopted as my model in selecting texts and periods of study: "In tracing [the writer's] concern with the expressiveness and redeeming force of language, we may well see the Caribbean writer as a modern Quixote, relying on his imagination in order to confer meaning on an elusive and complex reality."[72]

Each of the chapters in this book focuses on what I consider to be significant points in the imaginary journey of Caribbean writers as they struggle to explicate or confer meanings on the complex realities of the region. In Chapter 1, for example, my emphasis is on themes of displacement and exile in C. L. R. James's *Beyond a Boundary* and George Lamming's *The Pleasures of Exile.* I am well aware of a certain uneasiness among many Caribbean writers and intellectuals as to any foregrounding of fragmentation and exile in Caribbean discourse, but my assumption here is that any meaningful account of Caribbean literature cannot ignore the angst that has generated some of the most powerful texts on the colonial situation. It is not by accident that such narratives (notable examples include Edgar Mittelholzer's *A Morning at the Office* and V. S. Naipaul's *A House for Mr. Biswas*) are concerned with the insecure position of the colonial subject in an emerging social order and his or her attempt to develop a meaningful relationship with the alienating historical context of colonialism and of the dominant European culture. As Selwyn Cudjoe has observed in his study of Naipaul's works, the colonial subject writes to externalize the past in order to examine it. "Once having externalized the past, he can bear the pain caused by such an examination."[73] Thus even a narrative on the failure of the colonial subject to find a site of identity in the colonized landscape still affords us insight into the dialectic that defines this subject—"his alienation, the immanent nature of his social

71. J. Michael Dash, "The World and the Word: French Caribbean Writing in the Twentieth Century," *Callaloo* 11 (Winter 1988), 113.
72. Dash, "The World and the Word," p. 115.
73. Selwyn R. Cudjoe, *V. S. Naipaul: A Materialist Reading* (Amherst: University of Massachusetts Press, 1988), p. 61.

existence, the particularity of his social being, and the historical dimension of his existence."[74]

Rather than denying the historicity of the Caribbean experience, a concern with displacement and exile becomes the first major attempt by Caribbean writers to engage the colonial condition on their own terms. Furthermore, as a historical condition and literary code, exile is not a subjective quest by the Caribbean avant-garde to escape their fixed and fetishized places in the colonial culture. On the contrary, as Jean D'Costa and Barbara Lalla observe in *Voices in Exile* (an exemplary study of some of the earliest texts of Caribbean expression), "The experience of exile is central to Jamaican history and to the making of language in a Jamaica which spelled banishment for most of its people."[75] The centrality of exile is further underscored by Lamming, who insists that "to be colonial is to be a man in a certain relation; and this relation is an example of exile."[76]

Furthermore, there is a vital epistemological consequence to the condition of exile: it forces an earlier generation of Caribbean writers (especially in the 1940s and 1950s) to an irreversible cognizance of their cultural schizophrenia; in turn, this awareness of division comes with what Walcott has aptly called "a gradual sense of a loss of innocence about history."[77] This loss of innocence is the central paradigm in James's *Beyond a Boundary*. As I argue in the next chapter, in his seminal discourse on cricket—as both metaphor and metonym for the colonial situation, its culture and its institutions—James was able not only to reverse entrenched notions about play, class, color, and nationalism, but also to mediate the two modes of desire (the bourgeois and the popular) which defined the colonial relationship. Moreover, as Sylvia Wynter has succinctly noted, the pattern of *Beyond a Boundary*, "working out the logic of its own motifs, uncovers 'large areas of human existence,' as James points out, that his 'history, economics, politics' had left unaccounted for. Here it reveals that a separation, a gap appeared between the mode of popular desire, i.e., what the masses wanted to live by and what the 'ruling elements' wanted them to live by."[78] This gap of desire has important formal and discursive implica-

74. Cudjoe, *V. S. Naipaul*, p. 73.
75. "Introduction," *Voices in Exile: Jamaican Texts of the 18th and 19th Century*, ed. Jean D'Costa and Barbara Lalla (Tuscaloosa: University of Alabama Press, 1989), p. 1.
76. *The Pleasures of Exile*, p. 156.
77. Charles H. Rowell, "An Interview with Derek Walcott," *Callaloo* 11 (Winter 1988), 81.
78. Sylvia Wynter, "In Quest of Matthew Bondman: Some Cultural Notes on the Jamesian Journey," in *C. L. R. James: His Life and Work*, ed. Paul Buhle (London: Allison and Busby, 1986), p. 131.

tions, which I discuss in my analysis of the discourse of decolonization in the works of James and Lamming.

In Chapter 2, I discuss narrative strategies in Lamming's early fiction as one way of examining some of the most important issues confronting Caribbean culture in the age of decolonization, more specifically, the problem of language and representation. Beginning with the important nationalist uprisings of the 1930s (*In the Castle of My Skin*), moving us through the immigration of many West Indians to the metropolis in the 1950s (*The Emigrants*), and culminating with the apotheosis of decolonization as the affirmation of national culture (*Season of Adventure*), Lamming's early novels represent the drama of liberation and its problematic issues while tracing the cycles of contemporary Caribbean history. Lamming is, by his own confession, a very thematic writer, and the central themes of his novels have been discussed definitively in some excellent critical studies. Given the existence of substantial critical literature on Lamming and the politics and poetics of the colonial situation, my concern in this chapter is to shift emphasis from the overt rhetoric of Lamming's novels to more specific questions about language—as it relates to representation and identity—and the value and function of the act of narration itself. I will try to show that Lamming's novels are remarkable for their self-conscious subversion of traditional conventions of realism and their rejection of coherence in narrative language.

This subversive strain might be explained by Lamming's historical proximity to high modernism, but it is more probably a result of his acute understanding of the problems of language in a colonial situation. In the colonial encounter, Lamming once told George Kent,

> Caliban received not just words, but language as symbolic interpretation, as instrument of exploring consciousness. Once he had accepted language as such, the future of his development, however independent it was, would always be in some way inextricably tied up with that pioneering aspect of Prospero. Caliban at some stage would have to find a way of breaking that contact, which got sealed *by language*, in order to structure some alternative reality for himself.[79]

My close reading of *In the Castle of My Skin* shows how the colonized subjects' striving to use language as an instrument of consciousness always seems to reach a dead end, forcing them to restructure and

79. Kent, p. 88.

reinvent their language in order to have a handle on a colonial reality and history previously foreclosed from them. Moreover, narrative, and the act of narration, have immense powers to counter the colonial vision; against the stasis of imperialism, narrative introduces the disruptive power of temporality. My theoretical premise here is best articulated by Edward Said in *Orientalism*:

> Narrative asserts the power of men to be born, develop, and die, the tendency of institutions and actualities to change, the likelihood that modernity and contemporaneity will finally overtake "classical" civilizations; above all, it asserts that the domination of reality by vision is no more than a will to power, a will to truth and interpretation, and not an objective condition of history. Narrative, in short, introduces an opposing point of view, perspective, consciousness to the unitary web of vision; it violates the serene Apollonian fictions asserted by vision.[80]

The narrative deconstruction of the colonial vision which dominates Caribbean literature is often seen as a prelude to a unified national consciousness in each of the islands. A central concern in the Trinidad novels of Samuel Selvon, which I discuss in Chapter 3, is the need to imagine a national community in which the different cultures in the island can be harmonized into a modern nation, a community of language and shared consciousness. Selvon's ideological and narrative concerns revolve around the forms in which East Indians in Trinidad can overcome the mythologies surrounding their cultures, mythologies that have often come between them and the black population of the island. Narrative provides Selvon with an apparatus for imagining and realizing the dream of creolization through the evocation of a calypso aesthetic. Here the calypso functions as a metaphor of an emerging, or imagined, nationhood. As Albert Gomes once observed in regard to the period covered by Selvon in *A Brighter Sun*, "The calypso singer has begun to announce in his songs that our ethnic 'potpourrie' is a reality, and that its many pots have begun to pour one into the other. The welding of our polyglot community is taking place before our eyes in the 'tents' and the weddings of our culture are being celebrated right there."[81] The desire for the polyglot community—and the problems that block its realization—function as a central paradigm in Selvon's novels.

---

80. Said, ep. 240.
81. Quoted by F. Gordon Rohlehr, "The Folk in Caribbean Literature," in *Critical Perspectives on Sam Selvon*, ed. Susheila Nasta (Washington, D.C.: Three Continents Press, 1988), p. 36.

As products of the colonial situation, the writers examined here are all preoccupied with larger problems of history and historiography. But one problem that permeates the Caribbean experience and the discourse on decolonization is the repression and distortion of a Caribbean version of global events. Glissant tells the story of the Guadaloupean patriot Colonel Delgrès, who in 1802 blew up himself and three hundred of his compatriots rather than give in to the edict that reintroduced slavery in the French colonies in the region. But when this event was written into the March 1848 proclamation abolishing slavery, the French government "asserted that Guadaloupeans had *themselves demanded* the reimposition of slavery in 1802."[82] Consequently, in order to "repossess their historical spaces," argues Glissant, Caribbean countries have to find a detour around the ideological blockades put up by European history.

Although my selection of Alejo Carpentier's *El siglo de las luces* (*Explosion in a Cathedral*) as the focus of Chapter 4 may appear unusual in a study devoted primarily to Anglophone Caribbean novels, the text affords me an opportunity to discuss the ways Caribbean narratives penetrate and unsettle the discourse of history itself. Set during the period of the French Revolution and the Enlightenment, this novel shows how the "other" America functioned to call the philosophy of European history into question. As Roberto Gonzalez Echevarria has asserted, this novel "centers on that moment when the various versions of history are pitted against each other in an attempt to reach a master version."[83] However, the European drive for a master version of history is haunted and ultimately reverted by the black slaves who articulate their history using carnivalesque strategies that parody the Western desire for rationalization. In this regard, I concur with Gonzalez Echevarria's assertion that Carpentier's novel is important to the Caribbean literary tradition "because of the way in which it delves into the very core of the dilemma of what constitutes American history and how to narrate it."[84]

A similar preoccupation with the forms of black history in the New World is central to the narrative strategies Paule Marshall adopts in the novels I examine in Chapter 5. In *The Chosen Place, the Timeless People*, in

82. Glissant, p. 62.
83. Roberto Gonzalez Echevarria, "Socrates among the Weeds: Blacks and History in Carpentier's *Explosion in a Cathedral*," in *Voices from Under: Black Narrative in Latin America and the Caribbean*, ed. William Luis (Westport, Conn.: Greenwood, 1984), p. 37.
84. "Socrates among the Weeds," p. 37.

particular, the drive for modernization in the postcolonial period is often a mask of power adorning a new native ruling class, which has appropriated the ideological configurations of the colonizing structures to justify its class domination. Marshall's critique of a nationalist ideology that betrays its own aspirations and logic is already prefigured by Lamming, who, at the end of *In the Castle of My Skin*, details the rise to power of a native ruling class (symbolized by Slime, the school teacher). In aligning itself with the planters, this ruling class negates the original dream of nationalism and independence as the apotheosis of decolonization, thus exposing the modern state as what Jean Franco aptly calls "a kind of illusionist which needs the past only as a lament and whose miracle is the economic miracle of dependency."[85]

In this context, as Frantz Fanon notes in his famous critique of nationalism, "National consciousness, instead of being the all-embracing crystallization of the innermost hopes of the whole people, instead of being the immediate and most obvious result of the mobilization of the people, will be in any case only an empty shell, a crude and fragile travesty of what it might have been."[86] Many novels produced by Caribbean writers after independence are variations on Fanon's critique: from Lamming's later works (especially *Season of Adventure*) to more recent novels such as Earl Lovelace's *The Wine of Astonishment* and Michael Thelwell's *The Harder They Come*, the novel provides a framework for questioning previous assumptions about culture and identity, political independence, ethnicity, class, and gender. These are the kinds of "Third World" novels which, in Jean Franco's words, "offer a motley space in which different historical developments and different cultures overlap. What they enact is the unfinished and impossible project of the modernizing state."[87]

At the same time, many Caribbean writers believe that one reason national discourse has been found wanting in the postcolonial period is that it sustains its own forms of exclusion, especially in relation to questions of class, gender, and sexuality. A significant critique of nationalist discourse as a system of patriarchal power emerges in Caribbean literature as early as 1960 in Lamming's *Season of Adventure*,

---

85. Jean Franco, "The Nation as Imagined Community," in *The New Historicism*, ed. H. Aram Veeser (New York: Routledge, 1989), p. 206.

86. Frantz Fanon, *The Wretched of the Earth*, trans. Constance Farrington (New York: Grove Press, 1968), p. 148.

87. Franco, "The Nation," p. 205.

where the failure and collapse of an independent Caribbean nation are attributed to the exclusion of the poor and women from power. In the character of Fola, who represents the feminine principle in Caribbean culture, Lamming seeks regeneration in the power of women. Although she is an educated member of the Caribbean middle class, Fola is, like the peasantry in the island, also marginalized in relation to the patriarchal institutions of the postcolonial state. Shared exclusion gives her the license to identify with popular culture, however; by undergoing the vodun Ceremony of Souls she positions herself against "the civilised honour of the whole republic," an act of abnegation which brings her into an encounter "with her forgotten self."[88] As Sandra Pouchet Paquet concludes in her reading of the novel, Fola's quest for her unknown father "is ultimately the search for an alternative tradition that accommodates the African and peasant roots of the San Cristobal community, long obscured by colonial history."[89]

Lamming's introduction of the gender factor into the discourse on national identity sets the stage for contemporary Caribbean women writers such as Merle Hodge, Zee Edgell, and Michelle Cliff, whose works I examine in the last two chapters of this book. While I would hesitate to argue that the three women writers I discuss hold any magic keys to the postcolonial phenomenon in Caribbean literature, a "feminist" challenge to previous assumptions about modernism and nationalism is imperative for an understanding of the major debates taking place in the region today. For one thing, the problem of national identity and modernity in the Third World has too often been limited by its failure to confront its gender bias. As Franco observes in another context, the modern allegory of the nation is presented primarily as centering on the crisis of male identity; in the process women function as "the territory over which the quest for (male) national identity passed, or . . . the space of loss."[90] Thus in discussing her politics and poetics, Olive Senior, a leading Jamaican writer, observes that while ideological issues may not have changed significantly in Caribbean literature since independence, there has been a reconfiguration of the form in which such issues are explored: "The fact that Caribbean women writers have now come to the fore is opening up to us a

88. George Lamming, *Season of Adventure* (London: Allison and Busby, 1979), pp. 68 and 50.
89. Sandra Pouchet Paquet, *The Novels of George Lamming* (London: Heinemann, 1982), p. 70.
90. Jean Franco, *Plotting Women: Gender and Representation in Mexico* (London: Verso, 1989), p. 131.

completely new approach to the topic of the Caribbean mother—one of our great literary preoccupations—and of our relationship with that mother. It is also, I believe, personalizing the socio-political issues."[91]

And while I am aware that all generalizations are dangerous because they are often blind to the exception to the rule, Caribbean women writers seem more amenable to formal experimentation than their male counterparts. Michael Thelwell's *The Harder They Come* negotiates the same ideological terrain as Cliff's *Abeng* and Erna Brodber's *Jane and Louisa Will Soon Come Home*, but the three texts are motivated by different assumptions about literary form. Thelwell advocates "realism" and is contemptuous of modernist forms that emphasize fragmentation instead of coherence; he argues that the modernist novel "is quite useless for the projection of political and moral vision or statement. Its tone is parodic and its impulses contemptuous—both of the reader and of observable reality."[92] Cliff and Brodber, on the other hand, adopt fragmentation and parody as key elements of their narrative strategies; by breaking up and parodying the master code, they seek reconnection with their historical reality. In both cases, however, what is important for my study is the extent to which a new generation of Caribbean women writers is revising the project of their male precursors who had, in turn, revised and dispersed the colonial canon. My hope is that both male and female revisionings of colonial discourse and the re-presentation of previously excluded Caribbean selves will also force us to revise our notions of modernism and its relationship to colonialism and to so-called postcolonialism.

91. Charles H. Rowell, "An Interview with Olive Senior," *Callaloo* 11 (Summer 1988), 485.
92. Thelwell, p. 225.

1

Caribbean Modernist Discourse: Writing, Exile, and Tradition

> But if true exile is a condition of terminal loss, why has it been transformed so easily into a potent, even enriching, motif of modern culture?
> —Edward Said, "Reflections on Exile"

> Wat a joyful news, Miss Mattie
> I feel like me heart gwine burs
> Jamaica people colonizing
> Englan in reverse
> —Louise Bennett, "Colonization in Reverse"

The most important literary and cultural documents in the Caribbean tradition—Aimé Césaire's *Cahier*, Frantz Fanon's *Black Skin, White Masks*, C. L. R. James's *The Black Jacobins*, V. S. Naipaul's *A House for Mr. Biswas*, and George Lamming's *In the Castle of My Skin*—were produced in exile. Because of this simple fact, any attempt to map the directions in which contemporary Caribbean writing has developed, or to account for the emergence of a distinctly Caribbean literary tradition, must investigate the phenomenon of exile as a historical and existential condition. In other words, exile and the displacement it engenders constitute the ground zero of West Indian literature, its radical point of departure; exile generates nationalism and with it the desire for decolonized Caribbean spaces. It is not insignificant, Edouard Glissant wrote in 1981, that "the first cry of Caribbean Negritude was for *Return*." As he says, "The truth is that exile is within us from the outset, and is even more corrosive because we have not managed to drive it into the open with our precarious assurances nor have we succeeded all together in dislodging it. All Caribbean poetry is a witness to this."[1] Although it is doubtful that the writers of the texts mentioned above wrote simply to dislodge or dispel the condition of exile, many of them used exile (in intense cases of ironic reversal and dispersal) as an instrument for transcending the prison-house of colonialism. In both a psychological and an ideological sense, exile would be adopted as an imaginary zone distanced from the values and structures of colonialism; it would hence be posited as the point of departure for the anticolonial discourse that was to generate most of the novels I discuss in this book.

Now, I do not intend to claim any special status for the condition of exile in Caribbean writing or even to suggest that exile was the only route toward a literary tradition in the islands. Indeed, exile has become such a dominant term in the theorization of twentieth-century literature that, leaving the specific historical experiences of Caribbean writers aside, there is a sense in which most contemporary literature is a product of the sense of cultural orphanage which defines the modern condition.[2] Because exile was one of the most dominant tropes in the ideologies of high modernism—which tended to evoke cultural displacement as a form of artistic privilege—it was inevitable that those Caribbean writers who aligned themselves with the European avant-garde would adopt exile and its rhetoric as the gesture that, by individuating and universalizing artistic production, would also liberate the writer from his or her "compromised" literary traditions. Thus, for V. S. Naipaul, exile and and displacement—which he defines as "one's lack of representation in the world; one's lack of status"—secure the colonized writer's position as an individual who, uncorrupted by national interests, becomes a reasonable and objective commentator on colonial and postcolonial societies.[3] As Rob Nixon has observed, for Naipaul being an exile "is a term privileged by high modernism and associated with the emergence of the metropolis as a crucible for a more international, though still European or American-based, culture."[4]

1. Edouard Glissant, *Caribbean Discourse: Selected Essays*, trans. J. Michael Dash (Charlottesville: University Press of Virginia, 1989), pp. 153–54.

2. According to Edward Said, "We have become accustomed to thinking of the modern period itself as spiritually orphaned and alienated, the age of anxiety and estrangement." See "Reflections on Exile," *Granta* 13 (Autumn 1984), 159.

3. Quoted by Rob Nixon in "London Calling: V. S. Naipaul and the License of Exile," *South Atlantic Quarterly* 87 (Winter 1988), 9.

4. Nixon, p. 10.

This more recent, and possibly retrospective, view of exile and its connection to literary reputation has been examined in many excellent commentaries on Naipaul and is not my concern here.[5] Instead, my focus is on the rather paradoxical question posed by Said in the epigraph, a question that informs most Caribbean literature published before independence: how can exile and displacement be transformed into a powerful discourse of decolonization and the sources of a literature of national identity? In *The Pleasures of Exile*, which I discuss in greater detail later in this chapter, Lamming makes the important proposition that although the condition of exile is universal, it is configured differently in the West Indies because of its overdetermination by colonialism. According to Lamming, "When the exile is a man of colonial orientation, and his chosen residence is the country which colonised his own history, then there are certain complications."[6]

According to Lamming, among the many complications raised by the writer's state of exile and his or her affiliation with the metropolitan culture, two are particularly pertinent to the relationship between writing and displacement in Caribbean writing. First, the colonized imagination suffers from a certain anxiety in relation to the colonial language and its culture; the exiled writers might find themselves in much-improved circumstances once they have become established in the metropolitan centers, but their "whole sense of cultural expectations" has not greatly changed; exiled West Indian writers arrive and travel "with the memory, the habitual weight of a colonial relation" (p. 25). Second, and as a consequence of the first complication, colonized writers can only break away from the colonial mentality by returning imaginatively to the native land to "grapple with that colonial structure of awareness which has determined West Indian values"; they use the novel "as a way of investigating and projecting the inner experiences of the West Indian community" (pp. 36, 37). As I argue in my Introduction, the dialectic of loss and return which Lamming attributes to the exiled imagination is the structuring principle in Césaire's *Cahier*. But this dialectic acquires an even greater resonance in Lamming's *The Pleasures of Exile* and C. L. R. James's *Beyond a Boundary*, the two texts around which I anchor my discussion in this chapter: here exile explicitly generates nationalism and its corollary discursive and narrative strategies.

5. See, for example, Selwyn R. Cudjoe, *V. S. Naipaul: A Materialist Reading* (Amherst: University of Massachusetts Press, 1988), pp. 193–226.

6. George Lamming, *The Pleasures of Exile* (London: Allison and Busby, 1984), p. 24. All further references are included in the text.

But to understand how a condition of loss is reversed into a discourse on nationalism—which is defined by Said as "an assertion of belonging in and to a place, a people, a heritage"[7]—we must first return to the historical conditions that prompted an earlier generation of Caribbean writers to define colonialism as essentially a state of perpetual exile. Indeed, to understand why many Caribbean writers sought to invent a literary tradition to compensate for their state of unbelonging, we must begin with an examination of these writers' existential condition. We must begin by understanding why long before they sought their African roots, or even tried to adopt the African-derived popular cultures of the Caribbean into their poetics, West Indian writers had to settle scores with the colonial tradition that produced them.

Exile and the Generation of Caribbean Discourse

The existential situation of the black writer in the colonial Caribbean is best captured by James in an 1969 essay discussing the Beacon literary circle which, in the Trinidad of the 1930s, sought to establish cultural and literary autonomy in the West Indies. In reflecting on the colonial culture that had produced him, James draws attention to two rather contradictory propositions that are, nevertheless, crucial to an understanding of the decolonizing enterprise and its discourse. James begins by restating a point that is easily lost in the ideological rhetoric surrounding his life and work: "I want to make it clear that the origins of my work and my thoughts are to be found in Western European history and West European thought. . . . It is in the history and philosophy and literature of Western Europe that I have gained my understanding not only of Western Europe's civilisation, but of the importance of the underdeveloped countries."[8] James was to restate this point a few years before his death when he asserted that "we of the Caribbean have not got an African past. We are black in skin, but the African civilisation is not ours. The basis of our civilisation in the Caribbean is an adaptation of Western civilisation."[9] The author's insistence that his categories and conceptual system have been determined by Western culture is not simply an ideological aberration; he

7. Said, "Reflections on Exile," p. 162.
8. C. L. R. James, "Discovering Literature in Trinidad: the 1930s," in *Spheres of Existence: Selected Writings* (London: Allison and Busby, 1980), p. 237.

takes it a step further when he appropriates the colonial library as his literary point of departure:

> The atmosphere in which I came to maturity, and which has developed me along the lines that I have gone, is the atmosphere of the literature of Western Europe. In my youth we lived according to the tenets of Matthew Arnold; we spread sweetness and light, and we studied the best that there was in literature in order to transmit it to the people—as we thought, the poor, backward West Indian people.[10]

There is, however, an important contrary strain to this ostensible identification with the colonial tradition and its culture; while literacy and education shift the black elite away from the "backward West Indian people" toward the colonial master, they also expose the inherent state of cultural, social, and even racial dispossession which the two social classes share. The white members of the Beacon circle had opportunities to realize their talents in the colony, James notes in reference to Albert Gomes, but "we were black and the only way we could do anything along the lines we were interested in was by going abroad; that's how I grew up."[11] Indeed, James's growth—manifested in *Beyond a Boundary* as the transition from the English public school mentality to an embracement of nationalism—arises from a cognizance of the gap that defines his desires; he is educated to become a full-fledged member of the colonial club, but he is excluded from the same club because of his race and color. Thus, on one hand, a colonial education was promoted as the point of entry into the dominant political economy and culture; on the other hand, the colonial situation was inherently and immutably what Fanon would call a Manichaean world with compartmentalized social spaces unbridgeable by wealth, culture, or education.[12]

The colonial context would not allow for the kind of transcendental desires James sought through the "public school" code because the compartmentalized colonial context is, in Fanon's famous spatial metaphor, one that forecloses self-realization:

> This world divided into compartments, this world cut in two is inhabited by two different species. The originality of the colonial context is

9. See "An Audience with C. L. R. James," *Third World Book Review* 1 (1984), 6.
10. James, "Discovering Literature," p. 237.
11. James, "Discovering Literature," p. 238-39.
12. Frantz Fanon, *The Wretched of the Earth*, trans. Constance Farrington (New York: Grove Press, 1968), p. 41.

that economic reality, inequality, and the immense difference of ways of life never come to mask the human realities. When you examine at close quarters the colonial context, it is evident that what parcels out the world is to begin with the fact of belonging to or not belonging to a given race, a given species. In the colonies the economic substructure is also a superstructure. The cause is the consequence; you are rich because you are white, you are white because you are rich.[13]

Among the members of the Beacon circle, Albert Gomes might try to explain his difference from other Caribbean writers in terms of geographical location and individual choice—the others went away but he stayed at home—but James, who had come to examine the colonial situation differently and to know it better than he did in his youth, realized that sites of cultural production had nothing to do with education, social position, or even individual choice. For him, Gomes could stay because he was not born in the native side of the town and this gave him a kind of power which had nothing to do with talent or desire: "You stayed not only because your parents had money but because your skin was white; there was a chance for you, but for us there wasn't—except to be a civil servant and hand papers, take them from the men downstairs and hand them to the man upstairs."[14] Desires imprisoned by a fixed colonial relationship could only be released through displacement. Dispossessed in their own land, exiled Caribbean writers would reterritorialize themselves and hence reassert their identity through discourse and narration.

Moreover, because the colonized subject has also been entrapped in a colonial hermeneutics—previously, knowledge was only possible "under Western eyes"—self-understanding in the projected decolonized culture demands the appropriation of exile as a form of metacommentary on the colonial condition itself. Indeed, Fredric Jameson's critical discussion of the function of metacommentary in hermeneutics can help us understand the conceptual, but quite paradoxical, privilege accorded exile by colonized writers trying to take their place in a world from which they have hitherto been excluded. More specifically, Jameson isolates three functions of metacommentary which I find pertinent to my discussion: interpretation as a commentary on "the very conditions of the problem itself"; interpretation as an act of showing the interpreter's credentials and self-justification; and inter-

13. Fanon, *The Wretched*, pp. 39–40.
14. James, "Discovering Literature," p. 239.

pretation as an attempt by a society "to assimilate monuments of other times and places, whose original impulses were quite foreign to them and which required a kind of rewriting."[15] The first two functions are elaborated in Jan Carew's famous essay on exile and the Caribbean writer, while the final function is the key to understanding Lamming's theoretical reflections on exile.[16]

The importance of Carew's essay does not lie simply in his examination of the historical condition that makes the colonized subject an exile at home, but in the ways he reverses exile from a negative existential condition to a positive cultural hermeneutics: exile confers linguistic and ideological credentials on the Caribbean writer; displacement generates a discourse on nationalism and identity. At first glance, argues Carew, the condition of exile and loss militates against the development of a decolonized cultural tradition: the Caribbean writer is "a creature balanced between limbo and nothingness, exile abroad and homelessness at home, between the people on the one hand and the colonizer on the other."[17] Far from being rooted in a holistic tradition, the writer is imprisoned in a "mosaic of cultural fragments" which are witnesses to "successive waves of cultural alienation." The European fragment "is brought into sharper focus than the others," but it also masks its cultural incompleteness and violent history; worse still, this privileged European fragment is a source of mystification: "Hiding behind the screen of this European cultural fragment, the Caribbean writer oscillates in and out of sunlight and shadows, exile abroad and homelessness at home."[18]

If exile emasculates and mystifies, then how can Carew justify his claim that the Caribbean writer "by going abroad is in fact, searching for an end to exile"? What indeed are the credentials of the exiled writer? In Carew's view, exile accredits Caribbean writers by releasing them, in both a psychological and a temporal sense, from the spaces the colonizer has compartmentalized. In exile, the dispossessed writer has no allegiance to the colonized space and can hence traverse "a territory that his imagination encompasses without let or hindrance."[19] Writing in exile also enables the colonized writer to mediate the pro-

15. Fredric Jameson, "Metacommentary," in *The Ideologies of Theory: Essays 1971–1986*, vol. 1 (Minneapolis: University of Minnesota Press, 1988), p. 5.
16. Jan Carew, "The Caribbean Writer and Exile," in *Fulcrums of Change: Origins of Racism in the Americas and Other Essays* (Trenton, N.J.: Africa World Press, 1988), pp. 91–114.
17. Carew, p. 91.
18. Carew, p. 92.
19. Carew, p. 92.

hibitions of the colonial situation and to map the possibilities of decolonization. Because exile is the "second" encounter between the colonizer and the colonized, it summons forms of opposition whose goal is to reverse the colonial relationship itself; it is in exile that the colonized writer discovers what Fanon calls "the need of a complete calling into question of the colonial situation" as a prerequisite for a different state of habitation.[20] In this context, says Carew, exile is nothing short of a willed entry into history:

> The Caribbean writer and artist, if he must end his exile, is compelled by the exegesis of history to move back and forth from the heart of [Caribbean] cultural survivals into whatever regions of the twentieth century, the island, the continent or the cosmos, his imagination encompasses; and, in roaming across the ages of man in this bloodstained hemisphere, he must penetrate into the unfathomable silences where a part of the Amerindian past is entombed, he must gnaw at the bones of universal griefs, and the reservoir of compassion in his heart for the dispossessed must be limitless.[21]

Originally posited as a departure from the Caribbean, exile has been redefined as a self-willed entry into history and into previously enforced silences. Furthermore, "the journey by sea is an interlude between home and the Caribbean communities island abroad."[22]

Significantly, exile is also seen as Caliban's violent assimilation of Prospero's technology of language. In *The Pleasures of Exile*, where he seeks "to reflect and interpret the anxieties and aspirations of a Caribbean sensibility at home and abroad" ("Introduction to 1984 Edition"), Lamming conceives Caliban's appropriation of the master's international language as his point of entry into modernism. According to Lamming, Caliban's engagement with the colonial language represents his sense of exile and his ambivalent relationship to the colonial tradition. In seeking to establish the context in which the linguistic revolt of the colonized takes place, Lamming intends to use Shakespeare's *The Tempest* "as a way of presenting a certain state of feeling which is the heritage of the exiled and colonial writer from the British Caribbean" (p. 9). Because this canonical text was taught in the Caribbean to mask the real relationship between the colonial subject and the

20. Fanon, *The Wretched*, p. 37.
21. Carew, p. 108.
22. Carew, p. 113.

English literary tradition (the colonial text is disguised as a universal text even as it serves the interests of empire), Lamming is aware of the heretical intentions behind his rereading of Shakespeare. And yet, he says, "there are occasions when blasphemy must be seen as one privilege of the excluded Caliban" (p. 9).

By the same token, the emigration of the Caribbean writer to "the tempestuous island of Prospero's and his language" is not so much a journey of conquest in reverse as an attempt to expropriate the master's language to redefine and transform the colonized cultural space. According to Lamming, Caliban's new identity is not defined by his absolute rejection of his colonial education and its cultural traditions, but by his violent claims to an authority of language previously denied him—after all, Caliban is both colonized by language and excluded by language. Moreover, if Caliban is ultimately posited as the modernizer of the old colonial language, it is because his ambivalent position (as a descendant of both slaves and masters) gives him the freedom to transcend the Manichaean spaces that previously defined the relationship between the colonizer and the colonized:

> I am a direct descendant of Prospero worshipping in the same temple of endeavour, using his legacy of language—not to curse our meeting—but to push it further, reminding the descendants of both sides that what's done is done, and can only be seen as a soil from which other gifts, or the same gift endowed with different meanings, may grow toward a future which is colonised by our acts in this moment, but which must always remain open. [P. 15]

Here Lamming underscores two strains that are essential in the reconceptualization of Caribbean modernism: he moves Caliban's functions beyond the role of ressentiment and gestures toward the future; he also positions the Caribbean writer as a member of an avant-garde that rejects boundaries and closures, and seeks to enrich old texts with new meanings. In the task of endowing the European language with figures of the "other" imagination, the discourse on exile generates two important discursive strategies—displacement and repetition.

Clearly, if we perceive exile as something akin to the liminal phase in the ritual process, Caribbean writers write about, and within, an indeterminate space between the colonial economy of representation and the desired national culture; these writers operate in that ambiguous position defined by Victor Turner as lying "betwixt and between the

41

positions assigned and arrayed by law, custom, convention, and cere-monial."[23] In the circumstances, the strategy of displacement arises from the need to simultaneously deconstruct the colonial text and develop discourse as a form of cultural critique which will allow the writer to negate the Manichaean colonial relation and the compart-mentalized social space. As Mark Krupnick has observed in regard to cultural deconstruction, displacement allows the critic to reverse "a hierarchy or structure of domination" and to displace and dislodge the hegemonic discursive system.[24] Exile also insists on the trope of repe-tition not simply because colonized Caribbean writers see themselves as reproducing the journey through the middle passage in reverse, but also because repetition decenters old forms or exposes them as what Said would call "counterfeit imitation."[25] (Re)presented through fig-ures of the Caribbean imagination, the heritage shared by Caliban and Prospero acquires radically different meanings, accents, and reso-nances. To recuperate such meanings we must examine more closely the discursive strategies in two exemplary Caribbean texts on displace-ment and exile—James's *Beyond a Boundary* and Lamming's *The Plea-sures of Exile*.

History as Repetition and Play: *Beyond a Boundary*

In explaining how he came to write *Beyond a Boundary*, James estab-lishes the relationship between displacement and identity with a mem-orable flourish: "If the ideas originated in the West Indies it was only in England and in English life and history that I was able to track them down and test them. To establish his own identity, Caliban, after three centuries, must himself pioneer into regions Caesar never knew."[26] Taking West Indian colonial notions of the "mother country" to Eng-land, James tests the historical validity of such ideas by returning them to their metropolitan condition of possibility. But his encounter with England, rather than affirming the universality of the public school

---

23. Victor W. Turner, *The Ritual Process: Structure and Anti-Structure* (Chicago: Aldine, 1969), p. 95.

24. See Mark Krupnick's introduction in *Displacement: Derrida and After* (Bloomington: Indiana University Press, 1983), p. 1.

25. See Edward W. Said, *The World, the Text, and the Critic* (Cambridge: Harvard University Press, 1983), p. 124.

26. C. L. R. James, *Beyond a Boundary* (New York: Pantheon, 1983), Preface. All further references are in the text.

ethos that had shaped his character and identity, confronts the writer with the limits of his own knowledge about the colonial situation. In the course of his discourse and commentary on his colonial background, James comes to realize that the Arnoldian codes acquired through his public school education were not founded on the language, culture, and history of the Caribbean people; to establish his identity, he has to reincarnate what Fanon once called the "illuminating and sacred communication" of the nation.[27] At the end of his journey into the heart of the metropolis, the colonized writer also becomes cognizant of the gap that separates him from his native environment and cultural background.

As a result, the discourse on displacement is written in reverse, as it were: the moment of writing (the early 1960s) witnesses the triumph of Caribbean nationalism and the institution of the idea of the nation as the framework for a new West Indian culture. From this vantage point James looks back on the absences and ambivalences of nation and culture which defined his childhood and youth earlier in the century; the resulting discourse mediates the gap between previous displacement and a new identity as the colonial subject comes to terms with his social terrain. Above all, the colonized subject, by writing about the absence of a national culture and the loss of self in an adopted colonial identity that denigrates the popular sources of Caribbean culture, is able to evoke a genealogy of the negative. By underscoring his loss of self-knowledge and freedom—especially at that moment of identification with the hegemonic colonial culture—James suggests that he has finally developed a new consciousness of freedom; he can now see through the mask of "sweetness and light" and tap the previously unseen and unspoken aspects of his people's culture. Taking cricket as a synecdoche of colonial culture, James writes about how West Indians have adopted this symbol of the English upper class and reverted it into an expression of popular will, a mode of communicating an emerging national consciousness.

Moreover, James's manifest subject—the history of West Indian cricket—is also a ruse: as he asks in the preface to the book, "What do they know of cricket who only cricket know? To answer involves ideas as well as facts." Originally conceived as a symbol of the white middle class's control of the colonial space, the idea of cricket becomes radi-

27. Quoted in Patrick Taylor, The Narrative of Liberation: Perspectives on Afro-Caribbean Literature, Popular Culture, and Politics (Ithaca: Cornell University Press, 1989), p. 81.

cally dispersed in James's discourse: from its traditional conception as the expression of individual transcendence and a Puritan notion of self, cricket is radically reversed to represent the collective will for freedom and self-representation in Trinidad. Originally introduced as a symbol of English superiority and the continuity of English culture in the periphery of empire, cricket is appropriated and modernized to represent a new consciousness of freedom; it is redefined to contain "elements of universality that went beyond the bounds of the originating nation" (p. 164). And as I have already argued, the translation and transformation of borrowed or inherited categories are certainly among the most important issues in Caribbean modernist discourse.

Now, the reader of *Beyond a Boundary* will already sense modernist strategies of subversion and defamiliarization in the mixed generic conception at the heart of James's discursive strategy. Indeed, a reader encountering James's text for the first time can be forgiven for wondering how a history of cricket in the West Indies provides one of the central paradigms in my study—the notion that the Caribbean self must of necessity move from a position of silence and blankness to a cognizance of its own marginal status in the colonial economy of representation as a precondition for the recentering of the colonial subject in history. James must have pondered the same question when he wrote this book because he initiates his discourse with an epigraph that, rather than assuring the reader that he or she is in the familiar territory of the Caribbean *bildung*, goes out of its way to confuse the terms by which we read this text. In this succinct and carefully crafted epigraph, James is emphatic that his text is "neither cricket reminiscences nor autobiography"; rather, he offers us a document in which generic boundaries are collapsed and the distinction between facts and fiction, discourse and narrative, is rejected. The autobiographical form James adopts in the book is not a means toward writing a coherent history of self, but a structure for framing displacement in a temporal sequence "in relation to the events, the facts and the personalities which prompted them" (Preface).

Because James wants to be able to represent the dominant middle class perspective and at the same time to recover the popular culture the colonial bourgeoisie tried to repress, his discourse is informed by an urgent need to revise social meanings and to expose their ambivalences. For example, in the public school ethic, sport is supposed to solidify social and class bonds; but James has no doubt that "the clash of race, caste and class did not retard but stimulated West Indian cricket" (p. 72). This conclusion is valid, however, only because James is able to contradict, or to expose the contradictions inherent in, the dominant mode of discourse. The power of James's discourse can hence be attributed to his deliberate appeal to the dialectic of history and to what Richard Terdiman, in an influential discussion of theories of discourse, calls "an intricate and continuous interplay of stability and destabilization which produces the social world for all of its actors."[28] A crucial chiasmus develops as James tries to historicize cricket and to subvert its traditional representation in colonial discourse:

> I am . . . certain that in those years social and political passions denied normal outlets, expressed themselves so fiercely in cricket (and other games) precisely because they were games. Here began my personal calvary. The British tradition soaked deep into me was that when you entered the sporting arena you left behind you the sordid compromises of everyday existence. Yet for us to do that we would have had to divest ourselves of our skins. From the moment I had decided which club I would join the contrast between the ideal and the real fascinated me and tore at my insides. Nor could the local population see it otherwise. The class and racial rivalries were too intense. . . . Thus the cricket field was a stage on which selected individuals played representative roles which were charged with social significance. [P. 72]

Here the colonial strategy of containment generates reversals it could never countenance: the subject is taught that sport is an aesthetic activity divorced from the realities of race and class which define colonial society; but no sooner has he entered this ostensibly apolitical arena than he is confronted with the historical conflicts sports were supposed to resolve. The colonized subject becomes victimized by the politics he was supposed to transcend through play, but in the process he gains insight into the historical forces at work in his society. Against all expectations, it is through play that the subject recovers important categories such as race, class, culture, and even nation from the absolute silences of colonialism.

Furthermore, in order to articulate a native mode of what Terdiman calls perception and assertion, an important prerequisite for the essential displacement of the dominant perspective of the colonial world, James must constantly cast his struggle for repressed meanings as a struggle for territory, for spaces of representation.[29] As a matter of fact, James's point of departure is his quest for a "window to the world," a

28. Richard Terdiman, *Discourse/Counter-Discourse: The Theory and Practice of Symbolic Resistance in Nineteenth-Century France* (Ithaca: Cornell University Press, 1985), p. 13.
29. Terdiman, p. 13.

phrase he uses as a subtitle for the first part of the book. Here the author's concerns are phenomenological and perceptual: he has a deep concern for, even obsession with, acts of seeing and conceiving, a fascination with the social world as a large spectacle full of the images of men and women in motion, and an affinity for the dialectical relationship between persons and events. As a little boy, James perches on a window and watches the world, seeking a position from which things can be represented in their totality: "This watching from the window shaped one of my strongest early impressions of personality in society," he notes (p. 13).

In seeking a new mode of perception, the subject returns over and over again to the notion of selfhood, to the forms human beings take and the power and presence that propel them. This concern with forms of selfhood is an important way of countering the repression of the West Indian subject in the very activity (cricket) that was supposed to endow them with "character." In the process, the cricket field is represented as an arena in which contradictory meanings are produced. In fact, in James's discourse, the cricket field is both a metaphor and metonym, simultaneously a topos of identity and of displacement. As a metaphor, the cricket field functions as the inherited space of representation in which colonial peoples express their English identity: cricket is posited as the author's inheritance and "a good case could be made out for predestination, including the position of the house in front of the recreation ground and the window exactly behind the wicket" (p. 17). Cricket is a figure for James's previous identification with the colonial culture of his youth and the middle class desires it generated. But any mode of identification cricket may proffer is also exposed by the historical conflicts surrounding the game. As a metonym, then, cricket functions as a site in which original, colonial meanings, and the identities of colonial subjects, are displaced; it is a place where the sign and the signified no longer correspond.

In the cricket field, for example, Matthew Bondman proves to be a superb batsman, a "*genus Britannicus*"; but his performance in the field of play also foregrounds his "failure of character" in the public arena: "Matthew, so crude and vulgar in every aspect of his life, with a bat in his hand was all grace and style" (p. 14). There is a double irony in the gap that demarcates Bondman's two selves: on one hand, it appears that since the cricket field is the only place the lower classes can express themselves freely, play reveals the true self unencumbered by an imposed identity; on the other hand, it is possible that play abstracts the self from its real conditions of production. Like all ironies, the meanings to be adduced to the cricket field cut both ways. What is pertinent to my argument here is the extent to which such ironies open up a whole reconceptualization of the historical condition of the colonized. Bondman, as a player, has a different character from his "real" self precisely because he has turned the cricket field into what Sylvia Wynter calls "an alternative cosmology" and reconstituted play as a form of "underground culture."[30] In addition, notes Wynter, characters like Bondman find themselves in a world in which their powers and desires have been blocked and their radical historicity repressed; to release themselves from the "historicality of the productive forces," they have to demand the liberation of their will by being other than they are supposed to be.[31]

In semiotic terms, such ironic reversals are important instruments for evoking a protodialectical counter-discourse. In this kind of discourse, as Terdiman has shown, the author resists given meanings by asserting "alternative structures for conceiving the real," by inducing "some fissure or slippage in the apparent seamlessness and solidity of the dominant."[32] Representing the cricket field as a scene of *dédoublement*, James traces the ideological process by which the players become aware of their ironic relationship to the colonial dominant. The gap between the ideal of a common English tradition and the harsh realities of colonial oppression generates an alternative hermeneutics. Thus, in the cricket field, Bondman appears to be an incarnation of the perfect human being. On closer examination, however, Bondman is a slave; his batting strokes conceal, but also expose, his pitiful position as a man without status and representation in the colonial economy. Indeed, as James discovers soon enough, Bondman is adored as a player but devalued as a citizen; his performance in the field is celebrated, but he can't even get a decent job because of the color of his skin.

But as I have already suggested, James's awareness of the social displacement of his hero is the first lesson in what I have termed the negative genealogy of colonialism: "The contrast between Matthew's pitiable existence as an individual and the attitude people had toward

30. Sylvia Wynter, "In Quest of Matthew Bondman: Some Cultural Notes on the Jamesian Journey," in *C. L. R. James: His Life and Work*, ed. Paul Buhle (London: Allison and Busby, 1986), p. 137.
31. Wynter, p. 137.
32. Terdiman, p. 199.

him filled my growing mind and has occupied me to this day" (p. 14). In short, the disjuncture between the social field and the field of play forces James to develop a sense of his own historicity: the cricket field exposes the gap between self and other, assertions and realities, words and things. Henceforth, James's authority as an anticolonial writer will depend on his ability to find value in those gaps and disjunctions which the dominant discourse represses.

Although such ironies may have appeared to be minor slippages when they occurred, in discourse they are presented as part of a larger historical pattern which has acquired value retrospectively. In fact, James goes on to observe that at the moment of writing *Beyond a Boundary*, in the years when nationalism had validated the legitimacy of decolonization, the images of cricketers such as Matthew Bondman and Arthur Jones had "ceased to be merely isolated memories and fell into place as starting points of a connected pattern" (p. 17). Moved from a field of play (where they were valued solely as things) to the field of history (where they were connected to the destiny of the islands), these cricketers would mark the end of James's identification with colonial culture. The "unrecorded history" (p. 72) of such "minor" cricketers would become, in the discourse of decolonization, signs and reference points for the moment in which negative knowledge had forced James into an epistemological shift: "They were the end, the last stones put into place, of a pyramid whose base constantly widened, until it embraced those aspects of social relations, politics and art laid bare when the veil of the temple has been rent in twain as ours has been." These figures from the past, James asserts, echoing Hegel, are part of a frame of reference that "stretches east and west into the receding distance, back into the past and forward into the future" (p. 17).

Implicit in James's concern with patterns and frames of reference is a certain anxiety about what Wynter calls the "transformation of hierarchical categories into a continuum."[33] In many cases, he is drawn to questions of boundaries and borders because he is not always certain about the effectiveness or even decisiveness of moments of temporal transition: When does the colonial situation become transformed into the postcolonial condition? When do colonial subjects release themselves from the shadow of colonialism? For a book written in the liminal period of transition from the colonial culture to the postcolonial

33. Wynter, p. 141.

48

one, *Beyond a Boundary* is heavily overdetermined by temporal conjunctions where the reader might have expected disjunctions. In other words, James does not produce a discourse that promises or promotes a radical break in time (a break, for example, from the written moment to the moment of writing, from a colonial identity to a postcolonial one); rather, his accent is on a paradoxical temporal relationship between historical continuity and radical revisionism. His argument is that the present is rooted in the past and is a consequence of that past: "Hegel says somewhere that the old man repeats the prayers he repeated as a child, but now with the experience of a lifetime," he asserts (p. 17).

James evokes the Hegelian notion of repression as he tries to affirm a relationship between his "isolated" childhood memories and the "connected pattern" of history which he discovers at the moment of writing. Because the discourse of decolonization, which seeks to denigrate the authority and stability of colonial systems of meaning, is primarily a rewriting (with different modes and intentions) of what has previously been written about the colonial space, the temporal shift from the past to the present is also a form of repetition. Repetition is certainly central to James's struggle to develop a genealogy of knowledge and self in the colonial situation. Thus, at the end of a discourse whose central tropes are boundaries, how they are crossed and changed, the author can only assert the inevitable contiguity and continuity of the colonial ethic, saying—with a mixture of pride and frustration—that "we have travelled, but only the outlines of character are changed. I have changed little" (p. 246). There is, nevertheless, an interesting oxymoron in James's conclusion: he denies himself a radical transformation of self but, at the same time, he represents his life as a journey, evoking a metaphor that signifies shifts and movements in time and space. In essence, James's self has changed little, but its historical context has become transformed, if not ruptured. Indeed, the author posits his changeless "outline of character" as the only stable entity in the volatile history of colonialism and nationalism in the Caribbean.

At the same time, however, James is eager to remap the colonial spaces of his childhood as part of a scheme of willed entry into history. This remapping is a prelude to his questioning of previously unproblematic memories and also a way of transforming the colonial space into a realm in which self-realization is possible. As Patrick Taylor has observed in reference to Fanon, who had to transform his colonized spaces in similar ways, "Decolonization, as the entry into time and challenge to the colonizer's domination over history, transforms the lost space of the colony into the space, reconquered, of the new nation."[34] To live up to its promises, the new nation and its subjects must recover, rather than repress, their individual and collective memories; this process demands that the central codes of colonial culture be questioned rigorously. In this case, since the ideas that shaped James's character—the English public school ethic, the ideology of sport, and the English national spirit—were intended to reinforce the colonial order, the author has to develop a discursive strategy that reproduces and simultaneously subverts them. In the kinds of rewriting of the past we see in James—a rewriting that interrogates and even psychoanalyzes the boy who became a writer—such ideas are deprived of their ocular authority; represented as play rather than significant history, they are shown to produce not "good" character, but hopelessly displaced subjects. Although James tells us that he does not want to be liberated from his memories, such memories, recuperated through a decolonized prism, become an important medium of liberation—"once you have written down something your mind is ready to go further" (p. 65).

In an important study of nationalism and ideology in the emergence of Caribbean literature, Roberto Marquez has argued that one of the basic premises of the historical novel in the region is that a confrontation with history is also its reconstitution; a critical encounter with the past is "both the prehistory of the present . . . and the proper ground for establishing the entelechy, cultural and national, of a Caribbean ethos."[35] A similar principle underlies James's meditation on memory and history, especially in his use of repetition to conserve his field of discourse.[36] By replaying memories of his displaced childhood and youth, James is able to hold on to the weight of the past, to turn his accumulated experiences into a discourse on colonialism. In the circumstances, he would consider any liberation from memory (the sum of accumulated experiences) to be "a grievous loss, irreparable"—"I do not wish to be liberated from that past, and above all, I do not wish to be liberated from its future" (p. 65). Most of all, James insists on

34. Taylor, p. 82.
35. Roberto Marquez, "Nationalism, Nation, and Ideology: Trends in the Emergence of a Caribbean Literature," in *The Modern Caribbean*, ed. Franklin W. Knight and Colin A. Palmer (Chapel Hill: University of North Carolina Press, 1989), p. 324.
36. On the theory of repetition, see Said, *The World*, pp. 111–25.

temporal constancy to sustain an important dialectic in his writing—
the colonial past enables the postcolonial future:

> Most of this book had already been written when it so happened that I
> re-visited the West Indies after twenty-six years' absence and stayed
> there for over four years. Greedily I relived the past, every inch of it that
> I could find, I took part in the present (particularly a grand and glorious
> and victorious campaign to make a black man, Frank Worrell, captain of
> the West Indies team to Australia) and I speculated and planned and
> schemed for the future; among other plans, how to lay racialism flat and
> keep stamping on it whenever it raises its head, and at the same time not
> to lose a sense of proportion. [Pp. 65–66]

As we can see from this passage, James's discourse is motivated by the
need to confront the past and to retrieve useful knowledge from it; this
knowledge enables the author to maintain a sense of proportion as he
schemes for the future.

So if James's text surprises the reader by its constant return to the
primal scene of displacement and alienation, it is precisely because he
is propelled by what Said would call "a genealogy of knowledge and of
human presence" which, like desire, is defined by absence and lack.[37]
At this point, displacement is posited as redemptive because it can
now be rewritten as a pattern toward a totality: "A British intellectual
long before I was ten, already an alien in my own environment among
my own people, even my own family. Somehow from around me I had
selected and fastened on to the things that made a whole" (p. 28).
Amazingly, displacement even creates fluency in the writing subject.
For example, at the prestigious Queen's Royal College, James is asked
by one of the masters to write something for the school magazine:
"Such was my fanaticism that I could find nothing better to write about
than an account of an Oxford and Cambridge cricket match played
nearly a half century before, the match in which Codben for Cambridge dismissed three Oxford men in one over to win the match by
two runs" (p. 28). In this sentence alone, we can see the paradoxes
from which the text derives most of its power: James uses an ironic
tone that mocks his previous assimilation into English upper class
culture; at the same time, however, he reproduces with relish the
knowledge derived from that assimilation.

Moreover, the author's fluency about his displacement and his split

37. Said, *The World*, p. 117.

subjectivity indicates that his autobiography is not generated by a sense of inadequacy about the self. On the contrary, at the retrospective moment in which the discourse is generated, James sees his previous (mis)education as the source of his authority as a writer and psychoanalyst of colonialism: through his mastery of English culture and language he can persuade the reader that he now clearly understands the sources of his alienation, has mastered his displacement, and has trapped the colonial uncanny. At the moment of writing, he can mock the sacred text of his public school education, "the Gospel according to St. Matthew, Matthew being the son of Thomas, otherwise called Arnold of Rugby" (p. 29), and get away with it. Indeed, James confesses that most of the knowledge he has about his colonial childhood and youth is only realized "now as I write" (p. 32).

Implicit in the above statement is an important linkage between writing and self-knowledge: it is through writing that the subject realizes an alternative mode of knowledge, one opposed to the English public school code, "against all it formally stood for and all that I was supposed to do in it" (p. 32). Because writing and cricket realize a knowledge against the grain, as it were, James posits them as analogous in this book; as Hazel Carby has noted, "Literature and cricket are the two recurring motifs that figure the emergence of his political consciousness."[38] Furthermore, writing and cricket are represented as avenues out of the fixed site of colonial cultural production; through literature and cricket, the colonized subject views previous representations ironically and hence disperses them. Thus literature and cricket, two of the most obvious signifiers of English cultural hegemony in the West Indies, are "contaminated" by the colonized and turned into instruments of epistemological revenge.

Consider the example of cricket. As part of the social code in the colonizing structure, this game is supposed to bring out and sustain the snobbishness of English culture, its class divisions and racism; in colonial Trinidad, cricket clubs are segregated along class, racial, and color lines. Because it is so intimately tied to the public school code and the Arnoldian ideal of culture—"We lived according to the tenets of Matthew Arnold, spreading sweetness and light and the best that has been thought and said in the world" (p. 71)—cricket accentuates the author's displacement from the African-derived culture of his people. Ironically, because of his education and mastery of cricket history,

38. Hazel Carby, "Proletarian or Revolutionary Literature: C. L. R. James and the Politics of the Trinidadian Renaissance," *South Atlantic Quarterly* 87 (Winter 1988), 40.

young James finds, in his own displacement, certain social privileges, even when his dark skin serves as a reminder of the blockage engendered by colonial racism: "I moved easily in any society in which I found myself. So it was that I became one of those dark men whose 'surest sign of . . . having arrived is the fact that he keeps company with people lighter in complexion than himself' " (p. 59).

Now, as he relives the past, James knows that this privilege was also a form of limitation—it not only cut him off from "the popular side" but also delayed his political development "for years" (p. 59). Aligned with the elite in his youth, James fails to comprehend the ways the "popular side" has used the cricket field to subvert inherited colonial categories and laws. For even as the cricket field excludes and divides people in racial, color, and class terms, it is also the space in which the repressed returns to haunt the dominant. Here, especially in the record of the historical triumphs of the West Indies cricket teams over England and Australia, James finds the unconscious of history, the silent and unwritten side of experience which will eventually emerge as the true signifier of the West Indian spirit of resistance. Significantly, cricket becomes appropriated as an instrument of decolonization when the cricket players reconceive the playing field as a site of struggle rather than the place where the colonized reproduce the colonizer's world view. This revision of the ideology of the game is only possible, however, in a situation of crisis, a crisis that develops when the desires of the colonial elite collide with the nationalist stirrings of black people.

Indeed, the crisis in West Indian cricket has uncanny parallels to the political crisis that triggered Caribbean nationalism in the 1920s and 1930s. Both crises revolved around issues of representation and leadership: had the West Indian peoples mastered the colonial rules of conduct and political behavior well enough to be represented in the institutions of power, and could they provide their own leadership in the projected modernity of the colonial state? In the cricket field, black and East Indian players had become the backbone of the West Indies team, but the predominantly white cricket federation would not countenance the appointment of a black man to be captain of the West Indies because they believed that cricket would "fall into chaos and anarchy if a black man were appointed captain" (p. 76). In reality, James notes parenthetically, "by the grim irony of history we shall see that it was their rejection of black men which brought the anarchy and chaos and very nearly worse" (p. 76).

Denied a place at the settler's table—to use Fanon's expression—the colonized now understand the historicity of cricket: whereas before it was a mere game, cricket is now seen as a representation of all the contradictions and pressures that have so far defined the colonial relationship.[39] Furthermore, it will be in the place of play, where subjects are supposed to be dissociated from reality, that the repressed can truly express themselves. As depoliticized and unhistoried bodies, black people on the periphery of the colonial institutions will reenter history through play; after all, in the class and racial system of the British Caribbean, the cricket field is the only sphere "where competition was open" (p. 99). In a very significant way, then, James uses the politics of cricket not only to bring into his text the Hegelian struggle between the master and the slave, but also to gain access to the original and forgotten meaning of the Caribbean character and its will to nationhood.

To understand the affinity between cricket, character, and nation, we need to underscore James's subscription to a general Hegelian notion of the world-historical individual and his belief in the ability of certain typological characters to represent the collective spirit of an age or people. James's operating principle here is postulated quite strongly in his renowned study of Melville, where he argues that "the social and political ideas in a great work of imagination are embodied in human personalities, in the way they are presented, in the clash of passions, the struggle for happiness, the avoidance of misery." The representative character is a typological figure who contains "within a single self, at one and the same time, the whole history of the past, the most significant experiences of the world around him, and a clear vision of the future."[40] It seems, then, that for James and the Caribbean subject to liberate themselves from the colonial world view, they needed a heroic character who could register the retardation of colonialism, point to a utopian future beyond the confines of the established culture, activate the repressed consciousness of the West Indian people, and reverse the meaning and order of the colonial narrative of history.

The West Indian cricket fields would produce such a figure in the person of Laurie Constantine, the great batsman, whom James describes as "one man in his time" and whom he portrays both as the

39. Fanon, *The Wretched*, p. 39.
40. C. L. R. James, *Mariners, Renegades, and Castaways: The Story of Herman Melville and the World We Live In* (London: Allison and Busby, 1985), p. 122.

representative of repressed collective desires and also as the author's point of entry into a previously unknown national history. According to James, Constantine "belongs to that distinguished company of men who, through cricket, influenced the history of their time" (p. 105). Before Constantine's reputation as a cricketeer was established, it appears that the history of the West Indian people was "an absent cause." The Constantines were black people, and "off the cricket field the family prestige would not be worth very much. Constantine was of royal ancestry in cricket, but in ordinary life, though not a pauper, he was no prince. This contrast explains not all, but much" (p. 107). What does this social contrast explain and what does it repress? To answer this question, we must keep in mind that in his reconfiguration of the cricketeer as a cultural hero, James's immediate goal is to affirm his basic belief that play is a formalized realization of the best in the West Indian character. We must also remember that in endowing the player with a symbolic role, the author also points to the basic absence that all colonized peoples share irrespective of their accomplishments—the absence of political representation within a national framework.

The transformation of Constantine from a mere player to a national-ist figure parallels James's own emergence from the shadows of colo-nialism. As a public performer in the cricket field, Constantine is "a man conscious of his status" and of his subjectivity; he is indeed an actor in a drama in which reality has been suspended—his strokes are compared to the "single gesture of an actor in a long performance" (p. 109). Outside the field of play, however, the status of the hero is negligible: he cannot get a civil service job because of his color. This double existence (as a venerated player and an oppressed colonial subject) is crucial in James's analysis—he writes of a hero whose social existence mocks the heroic doctrines promoted by the public school codes; he writes of a national hero who fails to fulfill himself in the colony because he has no nation whose desires he can synthesize with his own. So Constantine's exclusion provides clear evidence, to both author and reader, that the West Indian character cannot be fulfilled in that colonial place of signification promoted by the public schools. The West Indian people look up to Constantine, expecting great things, but the hero has no national community to minister to, no cultural infrastructure. "A national hero must have a nation. The nation as it was could do nothing for the national hero except applaud," James concludes (p. 112).

It is this sense of "national" helplessness that forces Constantine, and later James, to question the doctrines that have so far governed their lives. For James, in particular, the denigration of Constantine as a human being expresses the limits of a history in which the national spirit is held hostage to the whims of the colonial other. To put it in terms of discursive strategies, in *Beyond a Boundary* James sustains the duality of Constantine as hero and victim for two reasons: first, the cricketeer's position mirrors the author's own sense of prohibitions and denials; second, the hero's tragic sense of betrayal debunks the cornerstone of colonial assimilationist policy. If the colonial system can treat the national hero so abjectly, can any of the "lesser" colonial subjects ever hope for fulfillment in the colonial situation? Constantine's response to this question would become evident both inside and outside the cricket field: by insisting on the essential historicity of the game—and its symbolic function in the colonial situation—Constantine would generate the West Indian renaissance "not only in cricket, but in politics and history and in writing" (p. 114). His example in cricket would be echoed in James's own writings: knowledge of the historical roots of displacement could be reversed into a positive genealogy of the colonized; by linking cricket to history and nationalism, Constantine initiated a new kind of discourse on the Caribbean.

Constantine is also central to discursive strategies in *Beyond a Boundary* because he helps to historicize James. Before he goes to England, James has been living in a world of texts, abstracted from his environment: "Intellectually I lived abroad, chiefly in England. What ultimately vitiated all this was that it involved me with the people around me only in the most abstract way" (p. 71). Even when he arrives in England at the invitation of Constantine (who has now become a major advocate of West Indian nationalism), James still cuts the figure of "the British intellectual . . . going to Britain" (p. 114), wary that Constantine's anti-imperialist views of the "mother country" are "unduly coloured by national and racial considerations" (p. 115). But heated discussions with Constantine force James to confront the "seductive generalizations" that have tied him to the mythology of England; he is exposed to "the politics of nationalism" (p. 117).

Colonialism in Reverse: *The Pleasures of Exile*

As I suggested at the beginning of this chapter, questions of nation and culture are generated in exile, where the mythology of empire—

especially the belief that the colonizer and the colonized share a common identity—is exposed by the harsh realities of race and nation. In the circumstances, the colonial contract has to be reread and rewritten, hence the need for a discourse that psychoanalyzes the character of the empire and its subjects. My basic assumption that exile generates self-knowledge in the colonial situation is supported by Lamming's early works, in which exile from home triggers a reconsideration of the relationship between the colonial character and the metropolitan center.

Of the many exiles and emigrants who inhabit Lamming's novels, none is as memorable as Trumper in *In the Castle of My Skin*. As I show in greater detail in the next chapter, Trumper struggles, as do many other colonial subjects, to get into history; but frustrated by the narrative and linguistic blocks the colonial system puts between him and his ancestral past, he rejects historical narrative altogether because "hist'ry ain't got no answers. You ain't a thing till you know it."[41] It is only when they know that they are just objects in the colonial narrative and political economy that Lamming's colonized subjects develop self-knowledge. What is remarkable about Trumper, however, is the extent to which his rejection of the historical narrative is triggered by his experiences in the United States: away from the Caribbean he is forced, by racism and the black nationalism that develops to counter it, to reconsider his previous identity with the colonizing structure and its history.

In *The Pleasures of Exile*, the reconsideration of the relationship between the margin and the center takes textual form; in many ways, the experience of exile is about reading and rereading the colonial narrative of history and the canonical text. In such texts, especially in the gaps his reading exposes, Lamming seeks his space of representation and identity. In reflecting on the meaning and ideological implications of rewriting the colonial experience, Lamming also questions certain doctrines of European modernity: the historical beginnings it is supposed to engender, the gift of language it is supposed to proffer, and indeed the assumption that in the modern world (the colonial world) a common identity is shared by the colonizer and the colonized. As a state of limbo, exile becomes Lamming's carnivalesque space of representation. According to Joyce Jonas, in this space where he is no longer

41. George Lamming, *In the Castle of My Skin* (New York: Schocken, 1983), p. 297.

bound by old laws concerning representation or interpretation, Lamming functions as a trickster:

> His task as a creative West Indian writer is to mount a perpetual assault on the *word* of assumed Eurocentric authority, to resist any and every world view that colonizes him and to assert, in place of the sacred "shrines" of Western cultural imperialism, an ongoing narrative activity that invites us to step outside the "given" into a limbo where imaginative new connections can be made, and where acts of reconstituting reality hold infinite possibilities.[42]

Although Jonas's remarks refer specifically to Lamming's fiction, she isolates three aspects that are central to my discussion of the discourse of exile in the Caribbean: to resist colonial authority, the writer devalorizes European cultural "shrines"; his or her discourse then invites us to step outside a world of given meanings and identities; finally, by establishing new semiotic and ideological connections between the colonizer and the colonized, the author sets out to reorder the narrative of history.

Colonization in reverse, as Louise Bennett reveals in the poem I use as my second epigraph, is an opportunity to rewrite the past backwards and as farce—Jamaicans going to England "Jus a pack dem bag an baggage / An tun history upside dung."[43] The irreverence with which Bennett rewrites colonialism in reverse is part of what Lamming, in *The Pleasures of Exile*, deems to be Caliban's "strange way of behaving sometimes" (p. 77). In an important examination of the decolonized episteme, Lamming borrows an example from the calypso, whose aesthetic subverts through historical and social irrelevance:

> Shortly after the sputnik went up, Lord Kitchner, the Trinidadian calypsonian, sang about it. An English communist was furious with me when I told him what the calypso was about. He was furious because the refrain of the song was:
>
> Columbus didn't need a dog.
>
> Kitch is no intellectual; he can see in his own way, and he communi-

---

42. Joyce E. Jonas, "Carnival Strategies in Lamming's *In the Castle of My Skin*," *Callaloo* 11 (Spring 1988), 359.

43. Louise Bennett, "Colonization in Reverse," in *The Penguin Book of Caribbean Verse in English*, ed. Paula Burnet (Harmondsworth: Penguin, 1986), p. 32.

cates with song. I am sure he has read little or no history, but note the instinctive return to the theme of Christopher Columbus. Kitch himself is a kind of Columbus in reverse; for his music has made a most welcome invasion on the English spine. That spine is no different from my spine; but it needed, perhaps, to be fertilized by a change of rhythm. And that is all to the good. [P. 77]

The English communist gets offended by Kitchner's comic play because his Eurocentrism will not allow for an alternative representation of world events. Because he assumes that history can only be conveyed through a logical narrative, the communist fails to see the essential historicity that underlies the calypsonian's farce. By rejecting a logical relationship between things in time and place (essentially by linking the Sputnik with the "discovery"), Kitchner uses his comedy to subvert Western history at its weakest, that is, at its insistence on reason and temporal progression. On the other hand, by fertilizing the Western narrative with a Caribbean imagination, Kitchner gains entry into world events and at the same time devalorizes a Western myth (in this case technological superiority). The calypsonian also debunks the differentiation between present and past which, according to Michel de Certeau, organizes the contents of history in the Western tradition.[44]

In his influential study of the problematic nature of writing in Western historiography, de Certeau has pinpointed the paradox that legitimizes "modern Western culture" and its dominance over the "other" in terms Lamming would find familiar: first, intelligibility in the structure of Western historiography is impossible without some relation with the other (the movement of history is the changing of what the West makes of the other); second, the interpretation of history depends on the silencing of the other.[45] In effect, Western historiography needs the other, but this other only has value when it is silenced. As I argue in my Introduction, the "changing" of the other into a self without genealogy and communal memories, and the ultimate silencing of this self in colonial discourse, is an important prerequisite for enslavement. Therefore, in order to rewrite colonial discourse in reverse, Lamming is compelled to question the structure of Western

44. Michel de Certeau, *The Writing of History*, trans. Tom Conley (New York: Columbia University Press, 1988), p. 4.
45. De Certeau, p. 3.

historiography, its modes of exclusion and intelligibility. He thus begins by emphasizing a simple fact: in spite of their exclusion from the discourse of history, African slaves in the New World still found means of representing themselves in an unmarked space and time.

The vodun Ceremony of Souls with which Lamming opens *The Pleasures of Exile* is such a temporal site: the vodun tradition, the author argues, has invented this ceremony so that unofficial truths—those which the living have been prohibited from uttering—can be asserted. Thus, if the central problem of a postcolonial hermeneutics is how to return to the source and become a modern at the same time, the dead in the Ceremony of Souls have simultaneous access to both past and present, which, against the grain of Western historiography, they refuse to differentiate:

> This ceremony of the Souls is regarded by the Haitian peasant as a solemn communion; for he hears, at first hand, the secrets of the Dead. The celebrants are mainly relatives of the deceased who, ever since their death, have been locked in Water. It is the duty of the Dead to return and offer, on this momentous night, a full and honest report on their past relations with the living. . . . It is the duty of the Dead to speak, since their release from that purgatory of Water cannot be realised until they have fulfilled the contract which this ceremony symbolizes. The Dead need to speak if they are going to enter that eternity which will be their last and permanent future. [P. 9]

As Taylor has noted in his study of popular culture in the Caribbean, this fusion of temporal horizons in vodun ritual is an important strategy for releasing meanings from the prisonhouse of colonialism and for bringing racial history up to the contemporary moment: "The ritual drama is a text in which a story is told, and it is this narrative that members of the community interpret in terms of the current events and social dramas they are experiencing."[46] For Lamming, the dead, by being able to speak of "matters which it must have been difficult to raise before" and to transmit their secrets through a medium, acquire a significance well beyond the certainty of meanings we associate with a final silence; they provide an authority of interpretation in which present experiences are informed by a past tradition that has survived slavery. And thus it is through the ritual enactment of death that the slaves overcome that social death that, according to Orlando Patter-

46. Taylor, p. 100.

son, deprives them of "any conscious community of memory" around which they can anchor their present.[47] Lamming's theme here is the need to come to terms with the past, but he is also involved in the quest for an authoritative moment from which the colonized can recuperate meanings that have been silenced with power and violence. Indeed, in a famous interview with George Kent, Lamming asserts that the Ceremony of Souls mirrors the journey of "Caliban-like figures" who are driven into exile by the necessity "for whatever is dead, whatever has passed on, to be summoned back for some kind of dialogue." If the past is to be "mastered," he adds, "if the factors which create it are to be healed, this past must be gone into. In ways, this is the key about the coming back of the dead in the ceremony—that they have to go into matters which they did not, for one reason or another, when alive."[48]

Exiles are involved in the same quest as the dead; in their quest for "whatever is dead," they posit their displacement as something equivalent to the Freudian return of the repressed. Under this concept, according to Tom Conley, "historiography must exhume what it cannot know, or dig up whatever it can muster, to have a fleeting grasp of the present. The past will always enter the flow of current life because it is an absence on which the visible evidence of truth is based."[49] Like the repressed, the Caribbean self enters the flow of "modern" life through writing where it shapes and reshapes itself. In the process, suggests Lamming, the dialectic of self and other is questioned. "This book is based upon facts of experience, and it is intended as an introduction to a dialogue between you and me," asserts Lamming in a preliminary address to the colonizer. "I am the whole world of my accumulated emotional experience, vast areas of which probably remain unexplored. You are the other, according to your way of seeing me in relation to yourself" (p. 12). Here the writer claims subjectivity (hence the emphasis on accumulated emotions) and casts the colonizer as the other, reversing the terms of the master/slave dialectic.

But we cannot understand the full extent of such acts of reversal, or even the whole range of Lamming's project (both as a critique of colonial modernism and as a desire to modernize the old language) until we examine the central role rereading plays in displacing the

47. Orlando Patterson, *Slavery and Social Death: A Comparative Study* (Cambridge: Harvard University Press, 1982), p. 5.

48. George Kent, "Caribbean Novelist," *Black World* 22 (March 1973), 94.

49. Tom Conley, Introduction to de Certeau, *The Writing of History*, p. xix.

colonial text and shunting Eurocentric authority. On several occasions in his discourse, Lamming takes up Shakespeare's *The Tempest* and gives it an uncanonical interpretation that deprives it of its sacred claims. Apart from rereading the text as a commentary on his own colonial situation ("*The Tempest* is a drama which grows and matures from the seeds of exile and paradox . . . it contains and crystallises all the conflicts which have gone before" [p. 95]), Lamming places it in relationship to marginalized Caribbean texts, such as James's *The Black Jacobins*, to challenge the authority attributed to Shakespeare in the colonial school. In fact, Lamming takes this act of textual revisionism a step further when he makes the Haitian Ceremony of Souls the preamble to Shakespeare's text: both become ways of "presenting a certain state of feeling which is the heritage of the exiled and colonial writer from the British Caribbean" (p. 9). Like *vèvè* signs in vodun rites, *The Tempest* is shown to be an erasable text or a text of desire, one in which meanings are the products of reading rather than writing.

I do not intend to examine Lamming's reading of *The Tempest* in detail here. There are several excellent studies of Lamming's appropriation of the play and his reading of it as a manifesto of decolonization and as a discourse that transgresses its own intentions.[50] My primary concern is the way Lamming rereads Shakespeare's text to correct or revise previous interpretations that repress the issue of Colonialism in *The Tempest*. Lamming's relationship to the English language in general and Shakespeare in particular reminds the reader of those kabbalistic gestures that interpret "a central text that perpetually possesses authority, priority, and strength."[51] As a colonized reader of a canonical text, Lamming wants to see Shakespeare's play (and the process of dispossession and colonization it signifies) as worthy of priority and attention; at the same time, he wants to correct or redirect the authority of this text.

He asserts, for example, that "Time, Magic and Man are the inseparable trinity of *The Tempest*. It is the ocean which made Prospero aware of Now; it is the supernatural privilege of his magic which made him feel that he might climb to the sky" (p. 15). Prospero evokes universal figures (Time, Magic, Man) and appeals to supernatural authority (magic), thereby initiating an ideological process that veils the concrete conditions that buttress his authority. To reread the canonical

50. See Rob Nixon, "African and Caribbean Appropriations of *The Tempest*," *Critical Inquiry* 13 (Spring 1987), 557–78.
51. Harold Bloom, *A Map of Misreading* (New York: Oxford University Press, 1975), p. 4.

text, then, one must appeal to the issues it tries to repress, especially the question of enslavement. Thus, rereading involves a chiasmic maneuver that, by reversing terms and categories, creates a new space of representation. For Lamming, it is the term *man* that invokes Prospero's "sense of decency," but *man* does not resonate with its usual universalist and essentialist (and certainly patriarchal) claims; rather, it is informed by unexpected ironies and disconnections. Lamming argues that "it was Man, the condition," which recalled Prospero to his decency, "Man in the form of Miranda, his own creation, the measure of his probable mismanagement; Man in the terrible apparel of Caliban, his slave, his long and barely livable purgatory. For Caliban is Man and other than Man" (p. 15). Earlier represented as a fixed and universal category in Prospero's dialogue, the term *man* has now been extended to include women and slaves; with such pluralized meanings, it cannot be invoked to support one order of things over another.

Having pluralized the term *man*, Lamming can now rewrite and revise the master/slave relationship:

> Caliban is this convert, colonised by language, and excluded by language. It is precisely this gift of language, this attempt at transformation which has brought about the pleasure and paradox of Caliban's exile. Exiled from his gods, exiled from his nature, exiled from his own name! Yet Prospero is afraid of Caliban. He is afraid because he knows that his encounter with Caliban is, largely, his encounter with himself. [P. 15]

Lamming's allegory of reading thus moves in two directions: he adopts the rhetoric of transgression (hence the stress on Caliban's capacity for transformation) but plays up the tones of persuasion: Caliban and Prospero have entered a contract, initiated through the gift of language, "from which neither participant is allowed to withdraw" (p. 15).[52] In short, both Prospero and Caliban are bound by their condition of exile rather than by the domination one claims over the other. In fact, in Shakespeare's text itself, Lamming sees the relationship of domination positioned at a terminal stage; the drama is "the poet's last will and testament" (p. 95).

Because it triggers a revisioning of the colonial relationship, the confrontation between master and slave leads to the recognition of the

---

52. For some insightful reflections on the rhetoric of persuasion in discourse, see Paul de Man, "Pascal's Allegory of Persuasion," in *Allegory and Representation*, ed. Stephen J. Greenblatt (Baltimore: Johns Hopkins University Press, 1981), p. 2.

latter; Caliban now has the chance to claim ownership of certain "universal" terms such as *man* and *history*. In the field of historiography, for example, the rebelling slave rescues African history from the shadow of Hegelian ethnocentrism (p. 32); history is hence redefined, in what Lamming calls "an active sense," as the process that creates "a situation which offers antagonistic oppositions and a challenge of survival that had to be met by all involved" (p. 36). Binary oppositions and forms of resistance are hence stressed here because they generate the spaces in which the repressed can return.

In his discussion of the repressed which I mentioned earlier, Conley observes that "the repressed resurges as something seen as other, and recognizably different from what it conveys. Historiography is constantly being rewritten in the abyss between the idea of the repressed and the fear of its continuous return."[53] This principle seems to be borne out in "Caliban Orders History," perhaps the most pivotal section in *Pleasures of Exile*. There, in his review of *The Black Jacobins*, Lamming casts Toussaint L'Ouverture as Caliban and the Haitian Revolution as the return of the repressed, and then proceeds to evoke new meanings in the abyss of Western history. Like Prospero in Shakespeare's text, Napoleon refuses to acknowledge Toussaint as other than a projection of his own desires; James's text, on the other hand, "shows us Caliban as Prospero had never known him: a slave who was a great soldier in battle, an incomparable administrator in public affairs; full of paradox but never without compassion, a humane leader of men" (p. 119). Furthermore, Lamming shows the repressed slaves entering history, not as the objects of labor to which they had been reduced in the plantation system, but as subjects laying claim to language and consciousness as conditions for freedom. The revolution in Haiti is posited as the transformation of objects of labor into instruments of culture and desire; here Lamming uses the imagery of the plow that resists being a mere instrument of labor and, in talking back to the hand that used to control it, "achieves a somersault which reverses its traditional posture." We need, he says, "some new sight as well as some new sense of language to bear witness to the miracle of the plough which now talks" (p. 121).

This reversal of the "traditional posture" and the new sense of language it generates exemplify what I have been calling Caribbean modernism. Although exile usually implies the alienation of the writer from a tradition, and although literary modernism has often been

53. Conley, p. xix.

presented as the rejection of traditionalism in art and convention in style, Lamming, like James and Césaire before him, conceives the appropriation of the colonial language and the redesigning of European forms as a reinvention of tradition, a Caribbean tradition no longer subject to Eurocentric authority. In his discussion of how Caliban reorders history, for instance, Lamming insists that slaves have to find detours around the barriers the master erects to separate them "from a logic of a spirit" which might declare the slaves' future "on the side of freedom" (p. 121); camouflage is one of the methods slaves use against the "orders" established by the master. I see the slaves' use of camouflage to turn the plantation system upside down as analogous to the linguistic activities of the Caribbean writer in exile: in the metropolis, these writers have entered the conceptual field of the masters and from deep inside the jungle, they have sought to "christen language afresh" and to make it available to people "who are still regarded as the unfortunate descendants of languageless and deformed slaves" (p. 119). For Lamming and James, the value of the Haitian Revolution—and thus its modernity—lie in its ability to break through the contradictions of history, to trigger a new discourse on the Caribbean subject, and to refashion the dubious gift of language. "The old blackmail of Language simply won't work any longer. For the language of modern politics is no longer Prospero's exclusive vocabulary," Lamming observes (p. 158). Once the Haitian slaves revolted and reordered history, says Lamming, "language had changed its name. A new word had been spoken. Action and intention became part of the same plan" (p. 125).

My argument is that *Beyond a Boundary* and *The Pleasures of Exile* map out both the anxiety and possibility of this new word which has become part of an international plan. The West Indies, says Lamming, belongs to the marginalized peoples of the colonized world "whose leap in the twentieth century has shattered all the traditional calculations of the West, of European civilisation" (p. 36). The anxiety, as I have already suggested, arises from the difficulties inherent in using the master's language to counter the very amputation of self which that language, as an instrument of imperial power, engenders. The possibility, as Lamming asserts in the 1984 introduction to *The Pleasures of Exile*, lies in the capacity or desire of the colonized "to transform the eyes and ears of the world" through discourse; the corollary to this kind of discursive reversal is a narrative that explodes the colonial vision.

2

From Exile to Nationalism:
The Early Novels of George Lamming

> Writing cannot forget the misfortune from which its necessity springs; nor can it count on tacit, rich, and fostering "evidences" that can provide for an "agrarian" speaker his intimacy with a mother tongue. Writing begins with an exodus.
>
> —Michel de Certeau, *The Writing of History*

> Caribbean festival arts still revolve around the aesthetic of assemblage. The makers of festival arts attach items both fabricated and found in the urban environment, and natural vegetation and animal materials, to superstructure in layers, resulting in a plethora of textures, colors, and collage-like forms.
>
> —Judith Bettelheim et al., "Caribbean Festival Arts"

What I have identified as the essential feature of Caribbean modernism—the reversion of exile from a sense of loss into the necessity from which national consciousness springs—is limpidly presented in George Lamming's 1983 introduction to his first novel, *In the Castle of My Skin*, a work published soon after his arrival in England in 1953. In this introduction, which can be read as a commentary on the conditions in which Caribbean literature was produced in the 1950s, Lamming makes a basic linkage between exile (as the misfortune of the colonized writer) and the narrative of national liberation which arises to counter loss and displacement. Instead of tracing the origins of

Caribbean narrative to an ahistorical and unproblematic aboriginal or ancestral source, or what de Certeau, in the epigraph above, calls "a mother tongue," Lamming argues that Caribbean narrative has developed in reaction to the pressures of the foreign language and culture imposed on it by the European colonizer. The resulting narrative techniques, analogous to what is identified as assemblage in my second epigraph, result from the superimposition of Caribbean forms on the colonial language and the tradition of the novel as a genre.[1]

Unlike the negritude generation, which had relied primarily on poetry to mediate their relationship with the colonizer and to secure their identity in the "given" language, Lamming and his circle were attracted to the novel because they believed that narrative offered a form and strategy for restoring the West Indian character to history. With his characteristic judiciousness, Lamming would later assert that after "the discovery" and the abolition of slavery, the third important event in Caribbean history was "the discovery of the novel by West Indians as a way of investigating and projecting the inner experiences of the West Indian community. . . . The West Indian writer is the first to add a new dimension to writing about the West Indian community."[2] The novel, Lamming would add, had become the mediatory genre through which the region could be represented and the vehicle through which its repressed memories would be recollected. This relationship between narrative and history not only sets up a theme that runs through all of Lamming's writings; it also provides an ideological underpinning for his narrative strategies. As he puts it in his 1983 introduction to *In the Castle of My Skin*, "The novel has had a peculiar function in the Caribbean. The writer's preoccupation has been mainly with the poor; and fiction has served as a way of restoring these lives—this world of men and women from down below—to a proper order of attention; to make their reality the supreme concern of the total society" (p. xi).

Now, there was nothing unique in Lamming's desire to recenter the displaced Caribbean peasant in his narrative because, as he was quick to acknowledge, the subalterns, despite their long history of depriva-

---

1. See George Lamming, "Introduction," *In the Castle of My Skin* (New York: Schocken, 1983), p. xiv (further references are in the text); Michel de Certeau, *The Writing of History*, trans. Tom Conley (New York: Columbia University Press, 1988), p. 319; and Judith Bettelheim, John Nunley, and Barbara Bridges, "Caribbean Festival Arts: An Introduction," in *Caribbean Festival Arts*, ed. John Nunley and Judith Bettelheim (Seattle: University of Washington Press, 1988), p. 36.
2. George Lamming, *The Pleasures of Exile* (London: Allison and Busby, 1984), p. 15.

tion, represented "the womb" from which the West Indian writer had sprung and "the richest collective reservoir of experience on which the creative imagination could draw" (p. xi). Within the context of national consciousness and the formation of a Caribbean national culture, as numerous commentators have observed, it was imperative for Lamming to center the drama of history on the marginalized if he was to generate a narrative of liberation. Liberating narrative in the colonial situation, as Patrick Taylor has succinctly argued, sets out to disclose "the reality of human freedom in a particular historical form, the nation" and to transform the colony (the previous space of exile) into a new arena of national culture; and popular culture is imperative to this process.[3]

However, Lamming's desire to transform the lived history of the Caribbean people into the unified drama of the nation faced several problems with an indissoluble impact on his narrative strategies, especially in the early novels. Simply put, when Caribbean novelists tried to use their narratives to activate the past, or to recenter the marginalized, they were confronted by a historical paradigm informed by both blockage and possibility. In Lamming's own words,

> This world of men and women from down below is not simply poor. This world is black, and it has a long history at once vital and complex. It is vital because it constitutes the base of labor on which the entire Caribbean society has rested; and it is complex because Plantation Slave Society (the point at which the modern Caribbean began) conspired to smash its ancestral African culture, and to bring about a total alienation of man the source of labor from man the human person. [P. xi]

The result of this perverse modernization of the African was "a fractured consciousness," which raised fundamental problems of language and ideology. The Caribbean writer trying to represent this marginalized world and to turn it into the space in which nationalism might spring up would discover, in his own communities, a culture with an allegiance torn between "the imposed norms of White Power, represented by a small numerical minority, and the fragmented memory of the African masses: between White supremacy and Black imagination" (p. xi). In terms of values and ideological inclinations, then, the writer was confronted by a double retardation: on one hand, white

3. Patrick Taylor, *The Narrative of Liberation: Perspectives on Afro-Caribbean Literature, Popular Culture, and Politics* (Ithaca: Cornell University Press, 1989), p. 189.

supremacy, by defining social status in terms of color, had inflicted psychological injury on the Africans; on the other hand, the blacks were ambiguous about "the credibility of their own spiritual history" (p. xi). If the writer was to turn to nationalism to fend off exile, if the affirmation of a community of language and culture was to be realized, Lamming had to negotiate, in narrative form, such gaps, chasms, and ambiguities, or even try to reconcile his community's divided loyalties.[4]

Moreover, there is a sense in which Lamming, like many colonized writers of his generation, turned to writing as a way of dealing with certain fundamental anxieties about Caribbean nationalism and some apprehension about the colonized writer's ability to evoke a national consciousness from the fragments left behind by colonial rule. In other words, narratives on the emerging or anticipated Caribbean nation were motivated by the desire to counter disorder and fragmentation and to harmonize different racial, cultural, and linguistic entities into a national community. At the beginning of his career, Lamming sought to incorporate all the fragments and ambivalent value systems that defined the colony into a harmonizing narrative—"an imaginative record of the total society," he called it (p. xi). No sooner had this narrative desire been evoked, however, than it raised fundamental questions about representation, identity, exile, and nationalism:

> Could the outlines of a national consciousness be charted and affirmed out of all this disparateness? And if that consciousness could be affirmed, what were its true ancestral roots, its authentic cultural base? The numerical superiority of the black mass could forge a political authority of their own making, and provide an alternative direction for the society. This was certainly possible. But this possibility was also the measure of its temporary failures. [Pp. xi–xii]

The "temporary failures" in this context are the betrayal of the working class revolt in several Caribbean islands in the 1930s, when popular movements were superseded by the colonial government's attempt to develop an alliance with the black middle class.[5]

---

4. Important background to this period can also be found in Rhonda Cobham, "The Background," in *West Indian Literature*, ed. Bruce King (London: Macmillan, 1979), p. 22; and Kenneth Ramchand, *The West Indian Novel and Its Background* (London: Heinemann, 1983).

5. After the labor unrest of the 1930s, which brought nationalism to the foreground of Caribbean politics, the 1940s can be seen as an age of political compromise. Since the 1940s, notes Bridget Brereton, members of the emerging Caribbean elite in the French Antilles and the English-speaking territories have been "largely preoccupied with demonstrating their

Immense problems thus faced the writer who tried to harmonize the disparate social elements of the colonial space into a national culture and to generate a narrative that would both articulate ancestral roots and provide an alternative direction for the emerging society. Lamming was one of the many Caribbean writers "who took flight from the failure" by going to exile in England in the early 1950s. But as we saw in the last chapter, the experience and ontology of exile would denaturalize the exiled writer's previous way of seeing and representing the colonial experience by straining, and ultimately debunking, the illusion of empire; to break through the consciousness that had imprisoned him in the dogma of the colonial mother, Lamming had to begin by redefining the terms that fixed him as a colonial subject. My intention in this chapter is to show how narrative figured prominently in this act of redefinition.

"Migration was not a word I would have used to describe what I was doing when I sailed with other West Indians to England in 1950," Lamming recalls. "We simply thought that we were going to an England which had been planted in our childhood consciousness as a heritage and place of welcome. . . . England was not for us a country with classes and conflicts of interest like the islands we had left. It was the name of a responsibility whose origin may have coincided with the beginning of time" (p. xii). Even when he wrote and completed *In the Castle of My Skin*, now considered by many to be perhaps the most powerful narrative critique of the psychology of colonialism, Lamming had yet to develop a conceptual understanding of empire as "a very dirty word," one that bore any relationship "to those forms of domination we now call imperialist" (p. xii). In writing his first novel, within two years of his arrival in London, Lamming was still driven by contradictory instincts, he believes. On one hand, he was still subconsciously imprisoned "in that previous innocence which had socialized us into seeing our relations to empire as a commonwealth of mutual interests"; but, on the other hand, his experiences as a black person in the heart of the metropolis had convinced him that "there was never any such reciprocity of interests" and he needed to develop a new language for renaming his Caribbean reality (p. xiv). Ironically, though the childhood psyche was imprisoned in the fantasy of empire, it was to his childhood that Lamming would return to evoke the

command of European culture and their intellectual 'equality' with their metropolitan counterparts." See "Society and Culture in the Caribbean: The British and French West Indies, 1870–1980," in *The Modern Caribbean*, ed. Franklin W. Knight and Colin A. Palmer (Chapel Hill: University of North Carolina Press, 1989), p. 109.

"tragic innocence" of his youth: "In the desolate, frozen heart of London, at the age of twenty three, I tried to reconstruct the world of my childhood and early adolescence. It was also the world of a whole Caribbean reality" (p. xii).

This shift from the realities of exile to the limitations and possibilities of the national space seems to support Edward Said's contention that "the interplay between nationalism and exile is like Hegel's dialectic of servant and master, oppositions informing and constituting each other. All nationalisms in their early stages develop from a condition of estrangement."[6] But how does a condition of estrangement engender narrative as the form that liberates the subject from the prison-house of colonialism? To answer this question, and to clarify the relationship between Lamming's exile and the narrative strategies he adopts in his early works, we need to read colonialism as something akin to what Said calls Orientalism—a form of discourse and an apparatus of knowledge whose powers of domination derive from the defeat of narrative by vision. Like Orientalism, the colonial vision derives its initial authority from its holistic view of the colonized, who are perceived not as actors in the narrative of history but in terms of fixed Eurocentric categories such as social Darwinism and "the nature of the Negro." According to Said, the systematic categories in which the colonized are entrapped assume that colonized subjects are both static and essentially transparent, but they cannot represent themselves.[7]

A notorious Caribbean example of this kind of discourse is James Anthony Froude's panoramic view of West Indian society, *The English in the West Indies* (1888). Although the famous English historian visited the West Indies for only a few weeks, he was confident enough to write a book extolling the power of England as the lord and master of her dominions and to negate any notion of self-government in the islands. The basic problem posed by Froude's work, as John Jacob Thomas stresses in *Froudacity: West Indian Fables Explained* (1889), was its disregard of even the elementary methodological integrity Froude would have insisted on if he were writing about a non-dominated society.[8] This kind of "panoptic" discourse is, however, constantly under the pressure of history and the narrative by which history is

6. Edward Said, "Reflections on Exile," *Granta* 13 (Autumn 1984), 162.
7. Edward Said, *Orientalism* (New York: Vintage, 1979), p. 239.
8. For a discussion of Froude and Thomas, see Roberto Marquez, "Nationalism, Nation, and Ideology: Trends in the Emergence of a Caribbean Literature," in Knight and Palmer, *The Modern Caribbean*, pp. 306–8.

represented. Because of its diachronic structure, observes Said, narrative sanctions temporal transformations, institutional change, and modernity—it introduces "an opposing point of view, perspective, consciousness to the unitary web of vision; it violates the serene Apollonian fictions asserted by vision."[9] Said's conception of narrative as diachronic form brings us to the conceptual question at the heart of Lamming's early works: why is it that works written in exile, presumably to counter displacement, are characterized by fragmentation and assemblage in both narrative style and language?

The need to counter the Apollonian fiction of empire seems to explain Lamming's desire to valorize the disruptive and diachronic functions of narrative. As he notes in regard to *In the Castle of My Skin*, he uses methods of narration in which things are never as tidy as critics would like: "There is often no discernible plot, no coherent line of events with a clear, causal connection" (p. x). Indeed, rather than appeal to a holistic world that might counter the loss and displacement discussed in the previous chapter, Lamming develops narrative strategies that underscore the converse process: his novels are primarily about a destabilized world of childhood and adolescence (*In the Castle*), of emigrants displaced in the place they hoped to claim through language and tradition (*The Emigrants*), and of the failure of the nationalist dream of a national culture that transcends race and class (*Of Age and Innocence*). Such persistent themes suggest that Lamming has accepted displacement as a strategic narrative possibility that allows the writer to deconstruct the colonial vision and to introduce the narrative of Caribbean history into the text. So although Lamming's early works are intended to evoke a narrative of decolonization and liberation, as several critics have argued, such a narrative is not possible until the writer has overcome the obstacles that block the realization of a national community of language and culture and of nationalism as a state of belonging.[10] As a result, there is explicit tension between the author's desire for a grand narrative that will restore coherence to the Caribbean social body and the mechanisms of psychological blockage

9. Said, *Orientalism*, p. 248.
10. This issue and related questions are taken up in notable studies of Lamming including Sandra Pouchet Paquet, *The Novels of George Lamming* (London: Heinemann, 1982), pp. 1–12; Patrick Taylor, *The Narrative of Liberation*, pp. 187–90; Ian Munro, "George Lamming," in King, *West Indian Literature*, pp. 126–43; Selwyn R. Cudjoe, *Resistance and Caribbean Literature* (Athens: Ohio University Press, 1980), pp. 183–202; Ngugi wa Thiong'o (James Ngugi), *Homecoming: Essays on African and Caribbean Literature, Culture, and Politics* (Westport, Conn.: Lawrence Hill, 1972), pp. 110–44; Gloria Yarde, "George Lamming: The Historical Imagination," *Literary Half-Yearly* 11 (July 1970), 35–45.

generated by colonialism. If Lamming's early novels are motivated by the desire to "return a society to itself"—as he told graduating students at the University of the West Indies in 1980—then these narratives have had to seek a detour around the "hidden forms of censorship" in the dominant culture.[11]

The major criticism usually made against Lamming's novels is that the overt rhetoric the author evokes to express an anticolonial agenda never quite seems to find an appropriate narrative form, that there is always a gap between narrative desire and the strategies of representation the author adopts. For many influential critics of Caribbean literature, it often seems that Lamming cannot find an adequate mode of narration to carry out the linguistic and epistemological revolution to which his works are committed.[12] My contention, however, is that this gap between ideology and form is not a weakness; rather, the act of narration is an attempt to resolve ideological problems that predate writing itself, problems generated by the colonial situation. In effect, each of Lamming's works is marked by notable experimentation with narrative form—and form is defined in no unclear terms in *The Pleasures of Exile* as "a dialogue of conflicting methods about a commonly felt need."[13] In Lamming's early fictions, then, each "substance" seeks its "form," but the end result is usually heterogeneity in narrative stances and styles. In *In the Castle of My Skin*, a first person autobiographical method is often mixed with streams of consciousness; in *The Emigrants* internalized focalization is often broken by third person narration; and in *Of Age and Innocence* narration shifts from the third person to interior monologue and to the diary form.

In this chapter, I want to show how these shifts in narrative stance are dictated by the problems of representation which Lamming faces in his attempt to develop narrative strategies that will both assert the "commonly felt need" for decolonization and account for the conflicting impulses of colonial modernity. These problems include the need to recenter a black subject who has been constituted as an absence in colonialist discourse, the desire to construct a narrative practice that (by challenging the relationship between self and other) initiates a new episteme, and the impulse to accord the marginal writers and their versions of the metropolitan language authority in the context of the

11. Quoted by Pouchet Paquet, p. 4.
12. See, for example, Garth St Omer's review of *Season of Adventure*, *Minnesota Review* 19 (Fall 1982), 138.
13. Lamming, *The Pleasures of Exile*, p. 158.

very institutions that repress that authority. An analysis of Lamming's early works helps us understand the precarious position of a previously marginalized Caribbean writer struggling to restore the narrative of his people's "spiritual" history using the language of the other.

Writing in the Tongue of the Other: *In the Castle of My Skin*

In his 1983 introduction to *In the Castle*, Lamming has asserted—and many critics have been tempted to go along with him—that the method of narration in his first novel was conditioned by his concern with "the collective human substance of the Village" rather than any overt exploration of individual consciousness (p. x).[14] Thus while other modernists of his generation would privilege the issue of self-hood as the locus of narration in a world in which individual consciousness seemed to be under siege, Lamming would go against the grain and privilege the communal and collective entity (or more appropriately the national space) as the key to his narrative strategies. Of his first novel, Lamming would claim that there was no "central individual consciousness where we focus attention, and through which we can be guided reliably by a logical succession of events. Instead there are several centers of attention which work simultaneously and acquire their coherence from the collective character of the Village" (p. xi).

But this kind of retrospective reading is too neat: it is doubtful whether the character of the village is collective, given the class and racial divisions within it, and the absence of a coherent line of narration does not preclude causal connections. Similarly, the presence of "several centers of attention" in the novel does not diminish the important role the boy G plays both as a narrator and character in the novel. Clearly we cannot allow Lamming's narrative desire for a collective entity able to counter colonial fragmentation to conceal the problems he encounters the moment he tries to evoke a holistic Afro-Caribbean universe in the womb of colonialism. On the contrary, if the

14. For example, Pouchet Paquet argues that the central figure in *The Castle* "crystallizes the experience of the entire community. In a sense he is the village; the history of his dislocation echoes the dislocation of the village. He is a collective character" (p. 4). While I concur with the first part of this assertion (G is certainly defined in relation to the changing history of the village), he is too subjective to be described as a "collective" character.

goal of colonial power and its discourse is to negate the black self by smashing its ancestral African culture and alienating its labor, a cognizance of the problematic nature of selfhood is certainly an important prelude to writing. Lamming's basic premise that colonialism has engendered a fractured consciousness and an uncertainty of self in the Caribbean subject has important narrative implications in his first novel.

In a general discussion of the relationship between semiotics and cultural domination, Julia Kristeva makes a point that can help us understand the centrality of notions of selfhood in Lamming's novel. According to Kristeva, the writer's desire to establish a countervailing sign system demands "the identity of a speaking subject within a colonial framework, which he recognizes as a basis for that identity."[15] Lamming cannot simply repress the individual consciousness, for doing so would affirm the will to power of a colonial discourse whose authority depends on the erasure of the colonial subject. Although Lamming may find that the generation of a reflexive subject within a colonial framework is a tortuous process, the act of narration is impossible without a subject—despite its "splitting" in language, such a subject and its struggle for a consciousness of self, community, and history are the key, if not the primary theme, of narration in The Castle. In this novel, narration appears to be predicated on an almost high modernist notion "of separation and abandonment, frustration and loss, and above all, of man's direct inner experience of something missing."[16] But this modernist view of language and consciousness, which Lamming has borrowed from André Malraux, is not an end in itself; on the contrary, it is a prelude to situating the self in a larger community of meanings. The important point, though, is that for Lamming, there is no doubt that the colonial subject is defined by "the sense of a distance between the individual consciousness and a total reality as it impinges upon that consciousness, the conviction, as a fact of experience, of absence."[17]

And thus the narration of childhood, far from being the recovery of an "agrarian" ideal, becomes a return to the history that represses selfhood, an attempt to live up to the pressures of those references that

15. Julia Kristeva, Desire in Language, trans. Thomas Gora, Alice Jardine, and Leon S. Roudiez (New York: Columbia University Press, 1980), p. 18.
16. George Lamming, "The Negro Writer and His World," Caribbean Quarterly 5 (February 1958), p. 111.
17. Lamming, "The Negro Writer," p. 111.

dislocate the self from the collective experience. At the beginning of
the novel, as the boy reflects on the meaning of the rain that has fallen
to spoil his ninth birthday, he initiates a narrative process that reveals
the anxieties of selfhood and community surrounding the colonial
subject. Instead of thinking about wish fulfillment and the happiness
usually associated with a successful birthday, the boy is distracted by
"the sodden grimness of an evening that waded through water,"
crevices on a wasted roof, and "the waterly waste" of his birthdate. If a
birthday is the cultural code for the integrity of the self and the possibility of fulfilling desire, then Lamming's narrator has become a
witness to a symbolic dissolution of his own selfhood: "It was my
ninth celebration of the gift of life, my ninth celebration of the consistent lack of an occasion for celebration," he says (p. 9). The terms for
narrating a genealogical moment have been reversed, the boy's place
within a social framework that is disintegrating under the forces of
nature is put into question, and his relationship to inherited meanings
is subverted. Thus while the boy's mother reads the floods as "the
showers of blessing and the eternal will of the water's source," he sees
them as signifying death, decay, and destruction; they evoke the
"image of those legendary waters which had once arisen to set a curse
in the course of man" (pp. 9, 10).

So the inaugural moment of narration in *The Castle* is one of loss, a
loss of identity and ontological bearings. In this novel, as in other
major Caribbean texts such as Naipaul's *A House for Mr. Biswas*, beginnings are initiated by doubts about cultural references. Here, the boy
looks at his village on the aftermath of the floods and sees "a marvel of
small, heaped houses raised jauntily on groundsels of limestone. . . .
Sometimes the roads disintegrated, the limestone slid back and the
houses advanced across their boundaries to meet those on the opposite side in an embrace of board and shingle and cactus fence" (p.
10); the season of flood "could level the stature and even conceal the
identity of the village" (p. 11). An important dialectic of self and
community now develops: the narrator shifts his focus from his selfhood to his community and sees his lack of identity reflected in, and
confirmed by, the structure of his village. In effect, the boy's most
important mode of consciousness is negative—it is an awareness of
collective loss which functions throughout the narrative as the sign of
a haunting gap of memory and genealogy in his social construction.
Rather than recalling and reorganizing past experiences, memory becomes a register of the narrator's most glaring absences: "And what

did I remember? My father who had only fathered the idea of me had left me the sole liability of my mother who really fathered me. And beyond that my memory was a blank. It sank with its cargo of episodes like a crew preferring scuttle to the consequences of survival" (p. 11).

Because memory confronts him only with disabling conditions, the boy has substituted for it what he calls "inquiry"—preoccupation with the consequence rather than the causation of his crisis of identity. But any attempts to investigate family and communal history through narrative are bound to meet the issues of alienation, emigration, and exile discussed in the previous chapter. The boy cannot find ways of evading the long shadow of an absent father and, later in the narrative, the paternity represented by colonial authority. Thus he informs us, "My birth began with an almost total absence of family relations. My parents on almost all sides had been deposited in the bad or uncertain accounts of all my future relationships, and loneliness from which had subsequently grown the consolation of freedom was the legacy with which my first year opened" (p. 12). As a narrator, Lamming's subject finds he cannot anchor his story around tangible cultural references such as family, community, and history; his challenge is to turn the absences his memory uncovers into the subject of narration itself.

The boy's narrative is therefore about his failure to inherit his history and cultural tradition and about his search for alternative references. Lamming's conception of narration in a colonial situation is determined by the notion that a self that cannot be authorized by its history must invent itself and that this invention takes narrative forms. Language and narration open up the symbolic dimension, a world of possibilities in which the subject constitutes itself even when it cannot recover its identity. If the boy and his mother seem to invest much emotion in simple objects, such as pebbles and pumpkin vines (p. 16), it is because such objects have become important supplements for the self: the pebbles come to signify permanence and continuity in a world of shifting forms, while the vine is a symbol of organic growth in a world of fragmentation.

The problem of subjectivity in a colonial situation is, of course, complicated by the fact that the very institutions with which the self is supposed to identify—such as country, nation, and language—are antithetical to the narrator's interests and desires. In the circumstances, the colonial subject can only assert its repressed identity by using narrative as a means of countervailing the given or imposed cultural system. This process of countervailing, as Kristeva has noted in another context, forces the subject through "an unsettling, questionable process" which coincides with "times of abrupt changes, renewal, or revolution in society."[18] For Lamming, however, the countervailing gesture is preceded by a critical reflection on the dominant social framework. In *The Castle*, what is crucial to the act of narration is not the challenge the colonial subject poses to the colonial economy of meanings, but the strategies characters develop either to understand the colonial situation or to retreat from it. For example, in the context of the colonial school—which is, significantly, constructed on the model of a slave ship (p. 36)—the boys are educated in the ways of imperialism and empire, while slavery, the basic fact of their history and existence, is concealed from them, is indeed erased from the existing episteme. Narration becomes a process of developing a critical attitude toward what I have already called the colonial vision.

During the school parade, the schoolboys read the flags that signify British colonialism in the Caribbean as fetishes: "They understood the flags. They understood them because they did not need to question them. The flags explained their presence, and the parade and the inspector. All these things were simple. They simply were" (p. 56). In contrast, the experience of slavery, which dominates the repressed consciousness of the island (some of the old people in the village were actually born slaves), is denied significance and the power of reference: "It had nothing to do with the people of Barbados. No one there was ever a slave, the teacher said. It was in another part of the world that those things happened" (p. 57). In their search for methods of narrating the unspoken and invisible, the boys try to go beyond the realities imposed on them by the colonial system and its language.

But although Lamming's characters attempt to develop a reflective understanding of their formation as colonized people as a prelude to negating the colonial situation, their utterances are often fixed at the originating source of the myth of empire. Self-engenderment is therefore dependent on questions of colonial beginnings and their implications. For example, if William the Conqueror was closer to the colonial subjects than their ancestral experience of slavery—as the textbooks and the teachers claim—and if the institutions that actually shaped the island's history are too far back to be taught as history, what is history and where does it begin? The schoolboys, we are told, "had read about the Battle of Hastings and William the Conqueror. That happened so many hundred years ago. And slavery was thousands of years before that. It was too far back for anyone to worry about teaching it as history" (p. 58). The function of colonial history as a self-serving fabrication is apparent here: the Battle of Hastings is brought closer in time (so that it can function as history) while the experience of slavery (less than a hundred years old in actuality) is banished from time and memory. For the colonial school, the event that launches the Caribbean's perverse modernity is left in temporal suspense and then condemned to silence. Represented by the teacher as prehistory—"History had to begin somewhere, but not so far back" (p. 58)—slavery is effectively demodernized and deprived of its constitutive powers.

But in the process of reflecting on the meaning of slavery, which has been mentioned almost casually by an old woman, the boys begin the important step of seeking an alternative narrative of history. As a starting point, they discover that it is difficult to recover reality (an original experience) from the colonial text; they now know that to theorize about their context, which is defined by fetishized signs such as coins and flags, is an important step to a new, ironic relationship with hegemonic notions of colony and empire. For even as the school asserts the special relationship between England and Barbados, the boys are surrounded by signs of crisis, signs that challenge this illusionary construct of "Little England." In fact, outside the context of the colonial school—around Savory's cart, for instance—the boys discover a new community of language in which speech is no longer formalized in signs and clichés about affairs that are remote and unreal. Here language displays what Lamming considers to be its "mischievous powers."[19] Around Savory's cart, language expresses its will to power through speech: "Talk was humorous, censorious and often filled with gossip. Sometimes someone had read or heard about something published in the paper and would break the news to the others. Things were going from bad to worse, they would agree, and suddenly their talk was filled with a kind of manufactured indignation" (p. 92). In this world of orality, the colonial subject has the possibility of breaking through the formalities of the colonial vision in two ways: first, in its mastery of "talk," the subject is subconsciously linked to African traditions and thus reconnected to the culture and genealogy which the colonial school represses; second, the oral world is not

19. Lamming, "The Negro Writer," p. 109.

79

subjected to the linguistic censorship that retards the boys' quest for meanings in the colonial school.

Outside local scenes such as Savory's cart, however, the oral culture is not recognized as a source of authority; thus Lamming's characters often have to struggle to master formalized language and find ways of breaking through the veil of codified speech which surrounds their lives. In many cases, these subjects find it difficult to be fluent in the dominant language; many of them suffer from a stammer, here posited as a symptom of the uncertainty of self which compels some of them to seek solace and security in the colonial arrangement. For example, the boy Trumper speaks with confidence about his feelings, but he is often haunted by what he considers to be his linguistic retardation—he finds it difficult to say what he means "without knowing the right words" (p. 143). Because they have not mastered the duplicitous language of self-alienation which some of the adults use, the boys cannot represent themselves except by externalizing their desires, projecting their needs onto powerful figures such as their teachers, who seem to have been authorized to speak because of their cozy relationship with the colonizer. Often, the boys will hang onto any figure who seems to provide an alternative form of authority of action and language.

Consider, for example, the famous scene in the novel in which the boys encounter a fisherman on the beach and reflect about the meaning of his authority: "There was someone powerful and corrective about his figure," they immediately conclude (p. 148). Corrective in what sense? As a model to be adopted? As a stand-in for the absent male authority figures in the community? At this point in the novel, what the fisherman represents is not clear to the boys because he strikes mixed emotions in them: "We had a feeling of release and frustration when he went. We were glad to be without him there looking round, and not sure what he might say if he saw us" (p. 149). But as a spectacle, as a mirror image that expresses the boys' ambivalent posture—their desire for authority and their fear of control—the fisherman is both inviting and threatening, something to be identified with and, at the same time, to be feared.

In addition, the fisherman appears to the boys as an autonomous entity in a social situation in which adults often appear hopelessly dependent and compromised. This point becomes more poignant if we recall that before they meet the fisherman, the boys have witnessed the principal of their school kowtowing to the white inspector of schools (p. 39). The fisherman hence seems to project the kind of power and authority which is self-engendered, that is, not derived from the colonizer. For this reason, the boys would like to be recognized by him, or to place him at the center of the alternative value system they often imagine once they are out of school. When the fisherman contemptuously fishes Boy Blue from the sea, the boys see this authority figure as someone they can identify with; he is not as remote and dehumanized as their school principal: "He was only big and strong, as we would say in the village, but he was like one of us, just like one of us. A man" (p. 153). The encounter between the boys and the fisherman becomes epiphanic.

Interestingly enough, what the boys are seeking—and this is Lamming's narrative quest too—is a semiotic space and a form of linguistic practice in which self, language, and desire can be represented without being mediated by the colonizer. Although the boys are alienated by the colonial language of their education and socialization, they have come to believe that mastering this language is their only hope of overcoming marginalization. Therefore they lament the fact that although they can "talk and talk and talk" among themselves, they cannot "tell anybody what we had talked about. People who were sure of what they were saying and who had the right words to use could do that" (p. 153). "Language was a kind of passport," they are told, which can even compensate for feelings—"You had language, good, big words to make up for what you didn't feel" (p. 154).

This dependency on the language of the other is the primary source of what Lamming deems to be the tragic nature of colonial subjects. This language hampers the subjects' willed entry into history because instead of asserting the individual's coming to consciousness, it signalizes the distance between "the individual consciousness and a total reality as it impinges that consciousness"; instead of being the symbolic manifestation of "the fact of experience," language triggers the "dislocation of facts . . . and meanings."[20] Although the momentum for narration in The Castle arises from the narrator's attempt to recover the voice and memory of Afro-Caribbean people, an ancestral voice that is ultimately expressed in Pa's dreams, Lamming's indebtedness to high modernism is revealed in his conception of language as the thing that frees and imprisons at the same time. As one of the boys

20. Lamming, "The Negro Writer," p. 111.

notes, language cuts both ways: "You could slaughter your feelings as you slaughtered a pig. Language was all you needed. It was like a knife" (p. 154).

Moreover, Lamming is conscious of the ways in which the colonial language affects perception and self-knowledge. In its transitive function, language is conditioned and extended by the consciousness it seeks to express: the writer seeks to seize the world and give it form through language, but a writer does not only use language—"he helps to make language."[21] It is in this conception of language that Lamming appears closest to the high modernist views of literary expression popular when he first wrote his novel. In this tradition, as Alan Wilde has noted in a critical discussion of late modernist poetics, language is not seen as "a means of discovering or evoking some final and ultimate 'Truth,' but as a way of releasing the self and of thereby making the phenomenal world once more the scene of purposeful action—the site, even, of the New Country."[22] Indeed, a central concern in *The Castle* is how the colonized self can be released from the language that blocks self-expression while using that language to evoke a "New Country."

There are several examples of how the transitive and phenomenological functions of language affect narration in Lamming's novel, especially in the strategies his characters develop to deal with their linguistic stammers and impasses. The first example is provided by the boy G, who as he grows older finds it difficult to account for his own feelings or to represent himself without mediators. He therefore seeks to project his desires onto objects: "I didn't know myself what my intentions were, but this feeling, no longer new, had grown on me like a sickness. I couldn't bear the thought of seeing things for the last time. It was like imagining the end of my life" (p. 213). The boy selects a pebble onto which he projects his unrepresentable desires; in a drastic reversal of common notions of subjectivity, the narrator seems to believe that the integrity of the self is better preserved through objectification; by investing itself in the pebble—"I knew it, shape, size and texture" (p. 213)—the self can come into touch with its desires, and hence reflect its feelings. Such is the value of this selfhood invested in an object that when G loses the pebble, he sees this loss as a sign of "the other's interference": "There was nothing I could do but

---

21. Lamming, "The Negro Writer," p. 113.
22. Alan Wilde, *Horizons of Assent: Modernism, Postmodernism, and the Ironic Imagination* (Baltimore: Johns Hopkins University Press, 1981), p. 99.

carry the feeling of the other's interference and resign myself to the loss" (p. 214). The loss of the pebble also foretells another dimension of alienation: when G goes to the high school, he is finally detached from his childhood friends and from the village by the very education that was supposed to lead to self-realization.[23]

Posited as the very mark of modernity—that is, as the entry point to the world of the other—the school is mistakenly assumed to be the vehicle for mastering the self and its language. As G's mother says, "The mind was the man . . . and if you had a mind you could be what you wanted to be and not what the world would have you" (p. 220). But this notion of mastery is undermined significantly when we realize that the modernizing power of the school marks the apotheosis of the colonial subject's socialization away from its ancestral sources. G comments: "I remained in the village, living, it seemed, on the circumference of two worlds. It was as though my roots had been snapped from the centre of what I knew best, while I remained impotent to wrest what my fortunes had forced me into" (p. 220). But the subject has no choice but to adopt this alienation and turn it into a positive value; rather than seek recognition from either the village or the colonizer, the self strives to maintain its integrity by masking itself: "I am always feeling terrified of being known; not because they really know you, but simply because their claim to this knowledge is a concealed attempt to destroy you. That is what knowing means" (p. 261). As I noted in the last chapter, this form of masking necessitates withdrawal from the world—a state of exile which is an important prelude to writing about the self.

An alternative response to the crisis of identity and representation in the island is presented by Trumper. After a restless and futile attempt to understand what is taking place in the community, Trumper has migrated to the United States, but at the point of G's departure for Trinidad he has returned home on a visit. The American experience has changed the boy who used to have problems expressing himself: "Trumper was smiling. A big, confident, self-assured smile. His assurance puzzled me" (p. 281). Above all, Trumper's stammer has diminished: "His voice was deeper, and he spoke more slowly and

---

23. For critical discussions of the themes of alienation and colonialism in Lamming's works, see Ambroise Kom, "In the Castle of My Skin: George Lamming and the Colonial Caribbean," World Literature Written in English 18 (November 1979), 406–20; Ian Munro, "The Theme of Exile in George Lamming's In the Castle of My Skin," English Literature Written in English 20 (November 1971), 51–60; Eugenia Collier, "Dimensions of Alienation in Two Black American and Caribbean Novels," Phylon 43 (1982), 46–56.

with greater care" (p. 281). His feelings about the land, and his relationship to the landscape, are now expressed directly, no longer mediated by the other, no longer confused by divided loyalties. What has brought about this transformation? In the United States, to use Lamming's apt phrase, this black man "was forced to recognize himself as a different kind of creature" and to adopt his difference as the source of a new national identity (p. xv). In effect, Trumper is able to make the epistemological breakthrough that has eluded other characters, including the head teacher and Mr. Slime, by recognizing the difference between self and other and by stressing the differences (self/other, slave/master) which the colonial institution tried to repress through the myth of empire.

Furthermore, although Trumper recognizes the tension between the colonial self and its language, he has found ways in which this language can be nationalized, as it were. Toward this end, he deconstructs the phenomenon of language itself; he shows that language is not a natural entity that expresses a spontaneous experience, but a fabrication; if language has been fabricated to repress the identity and historicity of the colonized, it can also be used as the agent of a black narrative. So in trying to develop a discourse on race, which was previously a taboo in the Caribbean where official colonial discourse represented black people as appendages of the British colonial tradition, Trumper reflects on the differences between the words *Negro* and *nigger* in the United States and the Caribbean. When G wonders "What's the difference?" Trumper provides an answer that indicates the extent to which alienation and self-doubt have given way to national pride:

> " 'Tis a tremendous difference," said Trumper. "One single word make a tremendous difference, that's why you can never be sure what a word will do. . . . It make a tremendous difference not to the whites but the blacks. 'Tis the blacks who get affected by leavin' out that word 'man' or 'people.' That's how we learn the race. 'Tis what a word can do." [P. 297]

For Trumper, these new terms—*Negro, my people,* and *race*—have opened a new space of resistance and identity which, at the same time, forces the narrator, confronted by the inadequacy of his education and language, to be suspended in silence: "I had nothing to say because I wasn't prepared for what had happened. Trumper made his own experience, the discovery of a race, a people, seem like a revelation. It was nothing I had known, and it didn't seem I could know it till I had lived it" (p. 298). Earlier in the novel Trumper is represented as a boy incapable of either acquiring fluency in the language of the other or entering the narrative of history; at the end of the novel, he is the agent of historical transformation: "He knew the race and he knew his people and he knew what that knowledge meant" (p. 298).

But if Trumper has mastered his life through understanding (according to the narrator, "He had found what he needed and there were no more problems to be worked out. Henceforth his life would be straight, even, uncomplicated" [p. 298]), this form of mastery is not endorsed by the narrator. In fact, the nationalism that develops out of Trumper's American experience is shown to be both insightful and limited: it is insightful because it offers the subject, through the discovery of nation and race, an alternative to colonial discourse; it is shown to be limited because it is sentimental and intuitive and hence cannot be extended to other subjects. The narrator realizes that he cannot reproduce Trumper's "deepest instincts and emotions" or even his assurance. "I wasn't worried about my duty," says the narrator. "I had a lot of time to find what Trumper had already known, but a new thought had registered. Suppose I didn't find it. This was worse, *the thought of being a part of what you could not become*" (p. 299). Trumper offers possibilities of a new political awareness, but as Sandra Pouchet Paquet has observed in her reading of this scene, "This fear of being unable to meet the challenge of a black identity, this fear of incapacity, hangs ominously over the village community."[24]

I want to argue that there is a narrative consequence to this psychological incapacity. Despite the different forms of dealing with language which we see exemplified by G and Trumper, the splitting and dispersal of colonial subjects, rather than a resolution of their crisis of identity, is what initiates the autobiographical narrative and allows it to continue. So, on one hand, the act of narrating the self engenders the tracing of a process of separation and loss, but, on the other hand, the narrative foregrounds the utopian desire for isotopic integration. As in Lamming's other works, the shaping of narrative in *The Castle* is characterized by what Roland Barthes would call the dual power of narrativity—that of "distending its signs over the length of the story and that of inserting unforeseeable expansions into these distortions"; the

24. Pouchet Paquet, p. 26.

function of narrative is to include the "deviations" it engenders within its own language.[25]

We can see the kind of power Lamming bestows on the distorting capacity of his narrative even in the first pages of the novel. As I have already noted, the novel opens with doubts about origins and genealogy and with considerable hesitancy about the meaning of phenomena and G's relationship to his world. The authority of the narrative inheres in the exposition of the disjunctive function and displaced position of the narrating subject. As we have already seen, what was supposed to be an ideal scene of desire (a birthday) is dominated by figures and images that stress the contrary—crevices in the wall, flooded canals, and the weather that plays the child "false" (p. 9). Furthermore, the child narrator is attuned to absences or to reversals in conventional meanings: he rejects the mother's view of the floods as a blessing because in her interpretation there is no correspondence between signs and signifiers; instead he opts for the more apocalyptic reading of nature (of the floods as a curse) because this view allows for coherence between the image of nature he witnesses and his state of mind.

Thus as a narrator the boy must develop a rhetorical strategy that transcends his mother's religious symbols and repetitive tunes which have ossified into meaningless signs; he must also find a detour around her amnesia, which has blocked his memory and hence postponed any possible link with the missing past, in the same way the colonial school represses communal histories. Compelled to be a narrator in a social scene in which the self and its language are not authentic representations but the effects of others' desire, the boy must design a language of narrative built on a metonymic displacement of preexisting meanings. This process involves rejecting the integrative nature of narrative and seeking value in the fragmentary and parodic. More important, meanings are not the result of an original inquiry (although the boy desires this), but of repetition, itself an important feature of Lamming's text. Repetition is a strategy not only in those sections of the book which are narrated by the author (in which it serves a parodic function); it is also pronounced in the chapters the boy narrates.

Here we need to pose an elementary question: why does the subject

---

25. Roland Barthes, "Introduction to the Structural Analysis of Narratives," in *A Barthes Reader*, ed. Susan Sontag (New York: Hill and Wang, 1982), p. 288.

prefer a strategy (repetition) that seems to retard the movement of the narrative, to hold back temporal development, which in the traditional *bildungsroman* is the movement toward knowledge and closure? Repetition, it must be stressed, is not the narrator's original strategy of dealing with his crisis of representation; rather, it mirrors the temporal situation in the village. In chapter 2, for example, the women tell the story of the floods over and over again: "They sat in a circle composed and relaxed, rehearsing, each in turn, the tale of dereliction told a thousand times during the past week" (p. 24). Repetition has become one way of controlling events and managing representation: the flow in the history of the floods, notes the boy, has acquired a pattern that "was undisturbed by any difference in the pieces, nor was its evenness affected by any likeness. There was a difference and there was no difference" (p. 25). The boy would rather have a strategy that moves him toward real difference, as Trumper's discourse at the end of the novel promises to do, but the fact that immediate history can be deprived of its referential status and then be retold as if there was "no difference" is a mark of the extent to which rewriting can confer authority on the already known, the already written. For the poor village people, stories retold acquire the authority of legends.

Lamming seeks the same kind of authority in his deliberate dispersal, distortion, and irradiation of narrative units. These examples of what Barthes, among other theorists of narrative, has called "dystaxia"—which occurs "when the signs (of a message) are no longer simply juxtaposed, when the (logical) linearity is disturbed"[26]—occur frequently in Lamming's narratives, but nowhere as prominently as in chapter 3 of *The Castle*. There the author presents a series of lexical units which mirror what he considers to be the contradictory impulses of narrative form. The first fragment of the chapter opens with what seems to be an authoritative description of the colonial school. But what appears, on one level, to be an objective representation is subtly undermined by qualifiers: the pebbled area "was called the school yard"; the church "seemed three times the size of the school"; the school was "supposed to be of Anglican persuasion" (p. 35). To the extent that this kind of representation foregrounds the narrator's hesitancy, rather than his authority, we may conclude that what we have here is indirect focalization in which a phenomenon is reflected through the boy's consciousness. But then how do we explain the

26. Barthes, p. 288.

obviously ironic conclusion to this lexia—the description of the school, the church, and the head teacher's house as "three shrines of enlightenment that looked over the wall and across a benighted wooden tenantry" (p. 35)? Are these the words of the child or the adult narrator?

Lamming's narrative strategy here is predicated on a deliberate confusion of the identity of the speaking subject. Indeed, in the second fragment of the chapter, where the school system is burlesqued (pp. 36–37), the speaking subject has been erased and the narrative becomes detached and impersonal as the narrator reflects on the equally fetishized symbols of colonial authority: "There were small flags and big flags, round flags and square flags, flags with sticks and flags without sticks, and flags that wore the faces of kings and princes, ships, thrones and empires" (p. 36). If the narrator cannot be depended on to produce determinate meanings, then language itself must be reinvented to become the source of value. But because the language spoken in the world of this novel, and the language the author uses, are colonial languages, they cannot be affirmed as they are; the ironic battery of language becomes the source of oppositional value. By the time the "red, white, and blue" colors of the flag have been repeated several times, Lamming has reduced the authoritative figures of empire to la bêtise.[27]

However, this emptying of the colonial language of its content and meaning cannot in itself provide an oppositional perspective. In another fragment, the boys struggle to produce an alternative view of things using dialogue and speech (rather than the formulas and clichés used in the school), but their discourse skids about aimlessly, seeking—but not quite finding—a center of authority. Significantly, this discourse (pp. 43–58) is both about issues of paternal and maternal authority and about the economy of representation in general: can colonial symbols be appropriated by the colonized and be reproduced? The boys take out the coins given to them at the school parade and "speculated whether it was possible to reproduce them, and made various attempts to represent them in pencil drawings" (p. 52). What is the value of this reproduced fetish, this illusion of an illusion? Can the boys ever have access to their original experiences? At the end of the

27. On the uses of irony and la bêtise as a discursive and narrative strategy, see Jonathan Culler, *Flaubert: The Uses of Uncertainty* (Ithaca: Cornell University Press, 1974), pp. 185–206, and Richard Terdiman, *Discourse/Counter-Discourse: The Theory and Practice of Symbolic Resistance in Nineteenth-Century France* (Ithaca: Cornell University Press, 1985), pp. 202–4.

discourse, the boys can only conclude that the figure of the king on the coin, the figure that authorizes the value of the pennies, is just a shadow: "The shadow king was a part of the English tradition" (p. 55).

At the end of this chapter, the distinction between the boys and their teachers, as narrators, is collapsed: both groups are unable to narrate their way out of the closed world of the fetish and the cliché (pp. 74–75). By the end of the novel, we have heard a multiplicity of voices and experienced several modes of focalization: we have listened to G's version of things, to the head teacher's interior monologue, and to Pa's ritualized forms of history (chapter 10); we have even read sections of G's diary (chapter 14). But we are never assured by the presence of a narrator who can pull all these experiences together. Is this then a narrative of dispersal, without a focalizing center? Whichever angle we choose to enter the narrative, things are never going to be tidy; Lamming's basic assumption is that the tension between the self and "the logical succession of events" (p. x) is what necessitates narrative. In this case, the narrative of assemblage is one in which the writer "takes historical moments and historical institutions and shifts them about to create one's mosaic."[28] Similarly, Lamming resists narrative closure because the narrative of history which his novels activate is continuous and open-ended; in this kind of narrative, he says, "there is really no closing of the drama. This experience will be a creative legacy, the soil of some other movement in life."[29] However, each of Lamming's subsequent novels takes up the issues of displacement and exile, nationalism and identity, dramatized in his first novel.

Empire, Exile, and Narration: *The Emigrants*

Our inevitable failure to grasp concrete meanings in Lamming's open-ended narratives has not always been accepted as the creative legacy he would like it to be. For although such texts have often promised to provide the reader with a thorough investigation of the colonial condition, they are notorious for rejecting ideological closure and providing indeterminate meanings. In other cases, readers have felt that Lamming's concern with narrative strategies and language has been too abstract and has not always provided the reader with a

28. George Kent, "Caribbean Novelist," *Black World* 22 (March 1973), 14.
29. Kent, p. 88.

concrete knowledge of the Caribbean historical experience. This complaint is encapsulated in a review of *Season of Adventure* written by the Jamaican novelist Garth St Omer. According to St Omer, Lamming's narrative is destroyed by its "burden of knowledge and analogy"; the author's ideological allegiances "intrude in the world of the novel" at the expense of the historical situation and character; and his "indirect manner of narration does not make the book any easier to read. Again and again the reader is required to make inferences, draw conclusions from a narrative that seems intended more to surprise than to reveal and expose."[30]

St Omer's criticism is heard often from readers encountering their first Lamming text, but the challenge these texts pose should not to be construed as a failing in narrative strategies, but as an inevitable consequence of the themes of alienation and displacement and linguistic incapacity which recur as his characters struggle for knowledge against the pressures of colonial domination. Like these imprisoned colonial subjects, the reader has to struggle to recuperate Lamming's meanings because his narratives are predicated on the traditional uncertainty of modernism and modernity: the author knows how to subvert the old, but not how to will the New Country—what Wilde calls the "socially, politically, and psychologically unified realm"—into being.[31] Moreover, the narration of the political and psychological transition from colonialism to national independence cannot be posited as the replacement of one set of values with another, or as the simple recovery of previously repressed individual and communal desires. As Lamming tells George Kent, "Just because the so-called colonial situation and its institutions may have been transferred into something else, it is a fallacy to think that the human-lived content of those situations are automatically transferred into something else, too." The colonial experience is a psychic process that has to be dealt with "long after the actual colonial situation formally 'ends.'"[32]

In the absence of a clear transition from the colonial to the postcolonial value system, Lamming would agree with Gilles Deleuze and Félix Guattari that the (colonized) unconscious "poses no problem of meaning, solely problems of use. The question posed by desire is not 'What does it mean?' but rather *'How does it work?'*."[33] Lamming's

30. St Omer, p. 138.
31. Wilde, p. 99.
32. Kent, p. 92.
33. Gilles Deleuze and Félix Guattari, *Anti-Oedipus: Capitalism and Schizophrenia* (Minneapolis: University of Minnesota Press, 1983), p. 109.

primary concern is how the trajectory of the colonial subject is retarded by the colonized unconscious and the problems of language and action it poses. For this reason, as we see very clearly in his second novel, *The Emigrants*, Lamming has adopted narrative strategies that emphasize displacement, discontinuity, and fragmentation. In the "space of uncertainty" created by these narrative modes of ironic distancing, Lamming seeks to signify the ultimate repression of the colonial subject and its failure to find representation in the colonial space.[34] Moreover, the journey the emigrants undertake from their Caribbean islands to England is intended to function as a metaphor of the ultimate quest for the fantasy of empire—the colonized peoples go to the mother country to fulfill the identity promised by their education and acculturation. In the process of narration, however, and through the experience of exile, these subjects can relate to the metropolis only in terms of displacement and denial; the "mother" country becomes the ironic confirmation of previous states of fragmentation and failure which they had thought to escape by going abroad.[35]

Toward the end of *The Castle*, the narrator informed us that he was haunted by the thought "of being a part of what you could not become"; in *The Emigrants*, narration is predicated on the actualization of this fear. Indeed, what strikes us most about the emigrants' journey to the colonial metropolis, which is the central theme in this novel, is how often they are pushed into processes of self-alienation so that their life stories can be narrated, and how often reality takes on the power of spectacle and hence distances the subjects not only from their immediate experiences but also from the objects of their desires. Thus in the port city that constitutes the beginning of the emigrants' voyage, the first person narrator presents us with an image of "home" as a wild site of alienated desires; the Caribbean city can only be represented as a strange spectacle, even a nightmare: "The city was like a circus that had made its residence permanent beside the sea. The passengers couldn't believe it. Compared to what they had known or seen in Trinidad and Barbados this spectacle was wildly fascinating; a flame held in the hand, charged with the color and spark of fire, but unconsuming."[36] In this landscape, we don't find the kind of grasping

34. See Culler, p. 206.
35. See Pouchet Paquet, pp. 30–36. Ngugi wa Thiong'o has argued that the loneliness of the individual and his or her awareness of exile are not enough—"For Lamming a sense of exile must lead to action, and through action to identity" (p. 142).
36. George Lamming, *The Emigrants* (London: Allison and Busby, 1980), p. 10. Further references are in the text.

for coherent meanings we saw in *The Castle*; on the contrary, the speaking subject has given in to his imagination; his representations have become projections of his neurosis, of his fear of the historical referent, of the past from which he is trying to escape, and of the future that awaits him. Rather than clarifying the status of the self, narration only provides the space in which the narrator can project himself into a world of shifting and unseen forms. This world, which appears as an imaginary gulf or valley, signifies the gap that stands between the narrator and the metropolis—"the thing beyond, which had its own secret of attraction and persuasion. A secret that urged identity" (p. 12).

Furthermore, the narrating subject delights in his capacity to represent himself in invented language as a way of creating the impression that he has mastered the "secrets of my identity" (p. 12). There is no longer the secret hankering for a natural ("agrarian") language that might help the self discover a phenomenal world. In fact, the linguistic spectacles this narrator creates around himself are marks of individual and social division and separation; the narrator displaces himself in the language he uses in such a way that the reader is no longer sure when and where to make the distinction between fact and fantasy, between experience and invention. In truth, Lamming presents us with a world in which representation has been emptied of significant meanings. For example, at the end of a long discourse on Good Friday in Guadeloupe, after an avalanche of phrases and descriptions with no relationship to any referent, the narrator is forced to question his own notions of reality—"suddenly it was no longer Good Friday and we might not have been at Guadeloupe" (p. 23). Even when the speaker poses as an authoritative source, his linguistic excesses force us to question his motives and the resulting "meanings." If the narrative impasse in *The Castle* is caused by a stammer, here it is caused by what the narrator calls "fluency."

Interestingly, the consequences of this fluency are not very different from the linguistic stammers we saw in Lamming's first novel. The first person narrator in *The Emigrants* uses a language that flows well but has little depth; this language is hence incapable of generating any authoritative meanings. To compensate for this lack of authority, Lamming shifts his focus from the "omniscient" narrator to a group of characters who represent a multiplicity of perspectives and can ostensibly provide the reader with a different path to reality and the truth amid the schizophrenia engendered by exile. Nevertheless, these characters are also entrapped by their own illusions and desires. Because they are victims of the language they have fashioned to express a false sense of self, or to deflate selfhoods that don't seem to live up to the images promoted by the empire, these subjects cannot represent external phenomena or themselves outside the paradigms delimited by their own fears, neuroses, and desires (see, for example, pp. 33–34). As a result, the reader has no access to an original experience in which the self has primacy over the language it uses; indeed, we are caught in a hermeneutical tug-of-war between a self groping to understand its existential situation and a world of forms beyond the control of this subject.

But the tension between the self and predetermined forms is central to Lamming's analysis of the colonial situation. In one of his earliest essays reflecting on the identity of the black writer in a colonial situation, Lamming had argued that the Afro-Caribbean writer already encountered predetermined categories and definitions which he or she carried "like a limb":

> A Negro writer is a writer who, through a process of social and historical accidents, encounters himself, so to speak, in a category of men called Negro. He carries this definition like a limb. It travels with him as a necessary guide for the Other's regard. It has settled upon him with an almost natural finality, until he has become it. He is a reluctant part of the conspiracy which identifies him with that condition which the Other has created for them both. He does not emerge as an existence which must be confronted as an unknown dimension; for he is not simply there. He is there in a certain way.[37]

Lamming's basic assumption that the black self encounters a predetermined identity against which it must struggle if it is to "touch" its true consciousness affects representative strategies in *The Emigrants*. Identity in this novel is determined not only by the inevitable tension between self and other, as they both seek "the unknown dimension" that might point the way out of the mutual prison of imposed identities, but also by their urgent quest for a point of interpretation beyond given meanings.

Unfortunately, says Lamming, selves with imposed identities are victimized by "a state of surprise and embarrassment" which leads to shame, "the shame that touches every consciousness which feels that

---

37. Lamming, "The Negro Writer and His World," p. 109.

it has been seen."[38] For example, early in the emigrants' voyage Collis tries to become acquainted with Dickson in a bid to penetrate the psychological defenses the latter has built around himself. Almost subliminally, however, the tension that defines the relationship between self and other is foregrounded—Collis becomes a threat to Dickson by his very presence. But since this threat is not based on any tangible action (it is really a reflection of the sense of insecurity which all the colonized share, in particular the fear of being seen or known), there is no way any mode of reconciliation between the two can be effected. Indeed, Collis's attempts to overcome the "suspicion in Dickson's knowledge" lead to a fight (p. 35). The situation is further complicated by the fact that there is nothing Collis can do to explain or rationalize the situation: "To say that he had asked a simple question of the man, was refused an answer, felt he had offended and tried to apologise: that would have made no sense" (p. 35).

The point Lamming is making here is simple: in a world in which relationships have broken down and neurosis has nullified meanings, representation can no longer appeal to the authority of the speaking subject nor can narrative be predicated on the subject's ability to interpret its conditions of existence. Here Lamming's narrative project is closer to that of the late modernists: his characters have no access to, nor do they strive for, phenomenological meanings as they did in *The Castle*. These are the kind of characters who inhabit the late modernist texts of the 1950s, characters removed from reality and confined by what Alan Wilde aptly calls "a sort of cultural or psychological dyslexia, which blurs vision itself."[39] To recognize the importance Lamming attaches to this failure of vision, we have to remember that *The Emigrants* is cast in a structural mode that is essentially ironic. The voyage motif that underlies the novel's structure promises coherence and discernible meanings at the end of the process; as we have already seen, colonized subjects believe that the metropolis is the site in which they can engender themselves. As the novel progresses, however, it becomes apparent that the voyage frustrates the characters' quest for intelligibility and identity; the closer to its destination the ship moves, the more difficult it becomes for the subjects to organize their experiences in order to make sense out of them.

The voyagers assume that the journey is a mechanism for overcom-

---

38. Lamming, "The Negro Writer and His World," p. 109.
39. Wilde, p. 109.

ing the gap between their Caribbean reality and metropolitan desire, and for reuniting the sign (the idea of the mother country) and the signifier (the real England). Of the voyagers, we are told, "no one knew the place they were going to, but everyone talked about the place he was leaving" (p. 52); and yet the more they hear about experiences of life in England, as related to them by those who have previously lived in that country (Tornando and the Governor), the more they are forced to reconsider the terms of their interpretation. They see the paradox that underlies their experience: "We others don't know the place and yet we're anxious to arrive" (p. 52); "perhaps we were all living without looking" (p. 53).

The basic problem confronting both the subject and the reader of Lamming's text can be reduced to a simple interpretative question: how do we make sense of a world of fetishized illusions? Or as Jonathan Culler has observed in terms of the semiotics of the novel as a mode of representation, "How are they to organize and relate to this strange world? What sort of connection can be made between the inner and outer, between the psychological drama and the historical and political circumstances?"[40] For Lamming, the world of the emigrant is already estranged and estranging; it is made up of people "who always saw their fulfillment elsewhere, outside of the society."[41] Represented by the other through the fetishistic symbols of empire we saw parodied in *The Castle*, the colonized live in a world that shrouds and embalms them in the very mythologies from which they thought they were escaping. In *The Emigrants*, Lamming is seeking narrative strategies the colonial writer can use to reproduce the colonial mentality, to show how it begins to disintegrate as it encounters the metropolis, and to indicate how this disintegration raises the possibility of a Pan-Caribbean identity.[42]

Indeed, as the encounter between the Caribbean emigrants and England draws closer, the main characters in the novel shift from their previous concerns with self-engenderment and begin reflecting on the possibilities of penetrating the ideological veil that conceals their real relationship with the colonizer. Their quest now is not for objects of vague desire awaiting them at the other side of the gulf, but for rules of understanding, a grid in which knowledge of the other can be transformed so that the self can touch its consciousness. Narration thus

40. Culler, p. 213.
41. Kent, p. 95.
42. Pouchet Paquet, p. 32.

becomes the movement toward a decolonized point of interpretation; as one of the emigrants puts it aptly, "The Interpretation me give hist'ry is people the world over always searchin' an' feelin', from time immemorial, them keep searchin' an' feeling" (p. 68). The interpretation of history and the historicization of interpretation form one way of countering the mythology of empire.

Once the necessity of historicization has been established, the narratives of emigration are no longer replays of colonial fantasies; in the new slave ship and reversed "middle passage," the emigrants seek ways of evolving a counter-narrative of empire. Now the emigrants reflect on the possibility of negating the narrative of empire by embracing the popular forms of Caribbean culture, forms they might previously have seen as causes of shame and embarrassment. Such popular forms are important because they challenge the very foundations of Eurocentric cultural codes and suggest an alternative hermeneutics. Thus, the calypso dance in the middle of part 1 prefigures a world in which the body is the source of its own designs, of "its own logic of receptivity and transmission, a world that could be defined only through the presence of others, yet remained in its definition absolute, free, itself. The body was part of the source of its being and at the same time its being" (p. 94). Figuratively, the Caribbean body becomes a space free of a contaminating foreign culture. At the same time, however, the overwhelming reality—the cause of anxiety and uncertainty—for the emigrants is that their identities are still fixed by the colonizer and their experiences are still mediated by the discourse of empire. Thus the desire to rediscover Caribbean popular culture comes up against the powerful machinery of empire, setting off numerous contradictions that destabilize the self. As the ship approaches the dock in England, the emigrants see the deck "hidden under a black lack of cause or choice, a veiled contradiction that would only receive some arbitrary meaning from an imaginative presence" (p. 95). So the quest for a counter-narrative is, paradoxically, underwritten by a pronounced modernist angst.

Nevertheless, the narrative seeks to negotiate the emigrants' desire to recover an autonomous but denigrated form (the calypso) and to recenter it in the "imaginative" presence of empire, which has hitherto defined them as a people without a culture. In a curious way, however, the emigrants' response to the crisis of what Lamming calls vision presents a problem—for narration to proceed, the self must be erased as a source of meaning and significance. In the case of the calypso, the body can only maintain its integrity in its biological form; because calypso is not authorized by colonial culture, the bodies it proffers are not recognized by the other, and in its function as a desiring machine, the body in the calypso dance does not seem to have cultural meaning. Indeed, its freedom depends on "the physical discharge of itself" which "constituted an open secret which everyone saw but could not read"; in showing itself, the body is "exhausted and broken by its own desire" (p. 94). But if the body yields to the presence of empire and gives in to the delirium of the other which it cannot grasp nor represent, it is hence nullified (pp. 118–24). In both cases, the self exists only as a phantasm, as what psychologists J. Laplanche and J. B. Pontalis define as "an imaginary scene in which the subject is a protagonist, representing the fulfillment of a wish . . . in a manner that is distorted."[43]

For Lamming, though, it is this erasure of the colonial self which generates a narrative that in turn inscribes the contradictory and reified site in which the colonial subject is produced. As he observes in "The Negro Writer and His World," to speak about the situation of the black writer and of the writer in general, within the "contemporary situation which surrounds men with an urgency that is probably unprecedented," is to speak of "the universal sense of separation and abandonment, frustration and loss, and above all, of man's direct inner experience of something missing."[44] The centering of absence here is a significant shift in Lamming's response to the key and inescapable problem of representing the colonial subject. For if narration in The Castle was shown to be impossible unless its author confronted the issue of subjectivity and the place of the speaking subject in the narrative, now the absence of the subject is the key to writing about exile and alienation.

We have a good example of how absences determine the nature of a narrative in the second part of The Emigrants: here the story centers around neither the self nor its other, but is generated by a hiatus between the two entities. This hiatus is manifested by the failure of the colonizer and the colonized to initiate the dialogue that Lamming had earlier hoped could reconstitute the relationship between Prospero and Caliban. Brought together by historical necessity or accident, the

---

43. J. Laplanche and J. B. Pontalis, The Language of Psycho-Analysis, trans. Donald Michol-son-Smith (London: Hogarth Press, 1973), p. 314.
44. Lamming, "The Negro Writer and His World," pp. 110–11.

Englishman Pearson and the Trinidadian Collis are confronted by the gulf between them and discover the need for silence where there should have been dialogue: "It seemed right that there should be silence" (p. 144). Even among the emigrants themselves, speech is no longer spontaneous and they often resort to linguistic masks to conceal the self not only from the other, but also from itself. Repression of selfhood has become the condition of exile. Whereas they were earlier associated with regional pride and "national" (or island) traits, and with a determination to assert their distinctive cultural and social identities, the emigrants have now become substitutable; the reader no longer bothers to tell the difference between them because they seem to have little individual identity.

Even the significance of the metropolis, initially conceived as the source of the emigrant's identity, has been deprived of its cultural and psychological value—"England was simply a world which we had moved about at random, and on occasion encountered by chance" (p. 229). The function of narrative, it would seem, is to sustain displacement because this is the reality of the colonial condition. Lamming does not present displacement as an end in itself, however; instead, it is posited as a prelude to the characters' need to eventually reinvent themselves in their quest for a more meaningful identity. For example, once in England Una Solomon can kill her former self, Queenie, and acquire a new identity; "it didn't matter" who she was now "because I didn't really belong to it" (p. 239). However, this kind of self-alienation is motivated by what Lamming has identified as a greater utopian desire—"the desire for totality, a desire to deal effectively with that gap, that distance which separates one [person] from another, and also in the cause of an acute reflective self-consciousness, separates [people] from [themselves]."[45] The gap between the nationalist desire for totality and the nightmare of colonial history is the subject of *Of Age and Innocence*.

The Drama of Politics: *Of Age and Innocence*

In discussing the relationship "of the artist to the drama of politics" as a basic theme in his works, Lamming has been keenly aware of the special difficulties confronting writers who are products "of a society

45. Lamming, "The Negro Writer and His World," p. 112.

in a state of transition and which is at the same time an explosive society."[46] Fictions that offer blueprints for national formation, or seek to realize the desire for national consciousness in narrative terms, often have to contend with two basic historical problems: (1) the nationalist movement draws its strength from its basic opposition to colonialism, but it does not yet have a language to harmonize the disparate elements that constitute the emerging nation; (2) political developments in the postcolonial situation seem to indicate that the new nations in the Caribbean replay the errors of colonial history anew.[47] Lamming's political narratives are hence informed by a paradox: they seek to will a new Caribbean nation into being, but they also deconstruct the premises of nationalism, especially its dependence on the matrix of modernization. As he told George Kent, *Of Age and Innocence* presents the society in *The Castle* "now extended to the whole area in its last stages of colonialism."[48] This extension has important ideological and narratorial implications.

In her incisive critique of the narratives of national formation in the so-called Third World, Jean Franco has explored this paradox in terms I find pertinent to the politics and poetics of Lamming's novel. According to Franco, the narratives of national formation, especially those written during the period of transition from colonialism to national independence, are propelled by the writer's inability to sustain the illusion of the new nation as a harmonization of national ideals. Unable to will the new nation into being, writers of such narratives proffer "a skeptical reconstruction of past errors" and try to make "visible that absence of any signified that could correspond to the nation." These novels enact "a motley space in which different historical developments and different cultures overlap" and dramatize "the unfinished and impossible project of the modernizing state."[49] Now, the target of Lamming's criticism is not merely the colonizer, but those Caribbean politicians and activists who, in seeking to nationalize, and hence appropriate, the colonizing structures forget to tap the roots of West Indian culture to create a more harmonious culture. At the dawn of independence, the differences nationalists had repressed in order to

46. Ian Munro and Reinhard Sander, eds., *Kas Kas: Interviews with Three Caribbean Writers in Texas: George Lamming, C. L. R. James, Wilson Harris* (Austin: African and Afro-American Research Institute, 1972), p. 12.

47. I borrow this phrase from Jean Franco, "The Nation as Imagined Community," in *The New Historicism*, ed. H. Aram Veeser (New York: Routledge, 1989), p. 205.

48. Kent, p. 96.

49. Franco, p. 205.

present a common front against the colonizer begin to emerge and threaten the new nation. In the process of narrating the problems of the emerging nation, Lamming's novel marks the dissolution of what Franco would call the once totalizing myth of the nation "which is now replaced by private fantasies lived out amid public disaster. And the novel, rather than an allegory, has become the terrain of conflicting discourses."[50]

Lamming expresses this theme of the failure of the nationalist quest for a totalizing narrative and the ascendancy of conflicting discourses in several ways: by constantly representing a triple discursive conflict between what the narrative enacts, what characters assumed were original experiences, and the popular meaning of such experiences; and by expressing recurrent stammers in the linguistic structures his characters formulate in their often futile attempts to create a singular meaning for the nation. These stammers call our attention to the absence of a signified that might correspond to the nationalists' dream of liberation. Indeed, both strategies coalesce in the struggle between "things" and "words" which marks most of the novel. For example, at the beginning of the novel, as the plane carrying the emigrants returning home to San Cristobal prepares to land, Mark "could not receive what his eyes were seeing"; the pages of his diary—a document intended by its very generic configuration to capture authentic experience—remained "a familiar contrivance of words and paper which ignored all desire."[51] Because Mark is returning to his native land at the end of the colonial era as a witness to both the death of colonialism and the birth of an independent Caribbean nation, words are an important instrument for rewriting the history of the country and the self. Such an act of rewriting, as I have argued earlier, is one way of overcoming the anxieties of exile. For if Mark, who has no prior knowledge of his native island except what he has read in books, can represent his people directly—that is, without mediating them through the values and concepts previously set by the colonizer—then he can generate a narrative of the nation in which public and private histories can be harmonized. Indeed, Mark's ultimate desire is to legitimize the new nation, and his place in it, through narrative.

But as Mark writes, he finds that words will not simply function as

50. Franco, p. 208.
51. George Lamming, *Of Age and Innocence* (London: Allison and Busby, 1981), p. 11. Further references are in the text.

signs of his desires; the old language refuses to be mastered by his will, and the production of a new idiom faces numerous obstacles. His struggle to capture his experiences in writing foregrounds the "absence of things outside; and that absence, transparent and impenetrable had taken meaning from his mind" (p. 14). The same linguistic blockage affects other characters in the novel. For example, when Mark's wife, Marcia, tries to "collect" words in her head as a way of dealing with a situation of crisis (the possible crash of the plane), she realizes that words don't provide the clarity and coherence she needs; rather, they are "vague and vagrant," resisting the command of her desires, refusing "to obey their normal use." The words "slipped from their meaning, sailing briefly like feeble noises that stumble for a while before returning to the silence which contains them. The signs did not cohere. The ends would not meet in a meaning which would help her memory" (p. 13).

What these examples illustrate is a situation already hinted at in Lamming's earlier texts—attempts to capture the self and its historical conditions in writing inevitably lead to self-alienation, and it is this alienation that ignites and fires Lamming's narrative. In *Of Age and Innocence*, the subjects' quest for elusive meanings dramatically foregrounds the close link between language and the crisis of identity Lamming has isolated as one of the key issues in the colonial situation. In his many discussions of linguistic practice under colonialism, Lamming has argued that his primary desire is a form of rational language which the colonial subject can command. He has categorically stated that language, for colonized peoples, functions as "symbolic interpretation," as an "instrument of the exploring consciousness."[52] But to trace this language of interpretation—to read Lamming through his discourse on language, writing, and reading—is to fall into what Louis Althusser once called "the mirror myth of knowledge as the vision of a given object or the reading of a given text."[53] Even a critic like Pouchet Paquet, possibly the most insightful reader of Lamming's novels, falls into the trap of transparency when she says that in *Of Age and Innocence*, "Lamming offers a detailed social analysis based on the specific relationships between representative, and therefore typical, characters, and between these characters and their environment."[54]

52. Kent, p. 88.
53. Louis Althusser and Etienne Balibar, *Reading Capital*, trans. Ben Brewster (London: Verson, 1970), p. 19.
54. Pouchet Paquet, p. 64.

Lamming may certainly desire such a close correspondence between subject and history in his discourses on reading and writing, but my contention is that narration in his third novel is predicated on the impossibility of such a relationship. In multifarious ways, the novel invites a reading that traces the dislocation inscribed in its narrative and linguistic structures, a dislocation that is the most manifest symptom of the division between the dream of the nation and its realities. On the most elementary level, this dislocation is obvious in the subjects' anxiety about their selfhood and capacity to represent themselves in language or even to communicate their intentions. Thus Marcia knows why she and Mark are leaving England for the Caribbean, but she cannot verbalize this reason: "She understood only for herself; she could not communicate what she understood, just as the dialogue she had read was at once final and incomplete" (p. 35). Mark's diary—which she had assumed would contain the motives for his decision to return to the Caribbean—only complicates the process of understanding; "it seemed the diaries followed no regular order in time" (p. 36). Even Penelope's decision to leave England "existed without reference to any logic of thinking or feeling" (p. 41).

Lamming's characters hence function in a world in which words float around without referents. Clearly, the new nation does not provide a cultural or political project these characters can identify with; at the moment of independence, characters still experience what Lamming considers to be a dislocation of facts, historical sense, and meanings. Nationalism was supposed to lead to the rehabilitation of the nation through the revalorization of its history and the reinstitution of its national culture. But in Lamming's deconstructive moments, the circumstances in which the new nation emerges (according to Lamming, "the tactical withdrawal which the British now proudly call decolonization simply made way for a new colonial orchestration" [The Castle, p. xiv]) have led to the disappearance of the nation-state as a valid framework for a new Caribbean identity.[55]

Nowhere is the disappearance of the nation as a framework for coherent meanings as clearly demonstrated as in the "mad" discourse of the nationalist, Shepherd. Here we have a discourse of the unconscious which in the end functions as a mirror image of the historical displacement of the island of San Cristobal, its reduction to an unknown and unformed place of conflict and struggle. According to Shepherd:

55. See Pouchet Paquet, p. 116.

You do not know San Cristobal, coming up by accident one morning from water, the tiny skull of a mountain top which was once asleep under the sea. Here Africa and India shake hands with China, and Europe wrinkles like a brow begging every face to promise love. The past is all suspicion, now is an argument that will not end, and tomorrow for San Cristobal, tomorrow is like the air in your hand. I know San Cristobal. It is mine, me, divided in a harmony that still pursues all its separate parts. No new country, but an old land inhabiting new forms of men who can never resurrect their roots and do not know their nature. [P. 58]

Unlike Mark, a returned exile seeking validation through a national allegory in which everything is knowable and representable through harmonizing national symbols, Shepherd sees the island as a reflection of himself, divided and alienated from its roots and traditions. Shepherd's alienation in language, and his separation from nature and culture, allow Lamming to make visible the vestiges of colonialism in the Caribbean nation about to be born.

In significant ways, then, Lamming's novel confronts the issue of representation on a more problematic level than the symbolic one that Pouchet Paquet's reading promotes. Lamming's premise is that the novel, as a document legitimizing the claims of the new nation, is the medium through which—in Fanon's apt phrase—"the Past is given back its value."[56] But for this past to be revalorized in a new national narrative, the writer must bring together the scattered elements of ethnic (or national) history and give it a new meaning against a colonial mentality trained to resist anything that comes from Africa or Asia. The paradox of the new national culture, as Shepherd notes in the above quotation, is that the new inhabitants of a territory constructed by the colonizer cannot fully resurrect their old roots nor completely recover their precolonial nature.

In writing on the colonized intellectual's "passionate search for a national culture which existed before the colonial era," Fanon argues that this quest is motivated by the anxiety to "shrink away from that Western culture in which they risk being swamped." "Because they realize they are in danger of losing their lives and thus becoming lost to their people," says Fanon, these men, hotheaded and with anger in their hearts, relentlessly determine to renew contact once more with the oldest and most pre-colonial springs of life of their people."[57] As

56. Frantz Fanon, *The Wretched of the Earth*, trans. Constance Farrington (New York: Grove Press, 1968), p. 211.
57. Fanon, pp. 209–10.

Shepherd suggests in his speech, the same kind of romantic anxiety engenders Mark's discourse of return. This discourse is limited because it isolates the speaker from a past that is contentious and contested and more complex than it appears, because it fails to come to terms with linguistic and cultural differences, and because it seeks old forms to express new social constructs. Indeed, if the problem of representing history "is essentially a narrative problem, a question of the adequacy of any storytelling framework in which History might be represented," as Fredric Jameson has argued in another context,[58] Lamming's narrative takes up a similar problem: Can the history of an emerging Caribbean nation ever find an adequate framework? Can an old land inhabited by new people use old forms to express its resurrected history, or was Fanon right in saying that "the crystallization of the national consciousness will both disrupt literary styles and also create a completely new public"?[59]

The innate limitation of old ossified forms is exposed in Shepherd's mother's folktale version of the island's history. In her story, Ma Shepherd inscribes her authority by appealing to nature and tradition and by trying to transcend her temporal limitations: her claim is that the measure of time is "too great" to be restrictive. Her version of events will be authoritative not only because she witnessed some of them (the fire and the floods), but also because by destroying "paper, an' records men make for rememberin'," these natural disasters left her memory as the only record of the past (p. 67). It is noteworthy, however, that history appears to the old woman not as a process but as a spectacle, the projection of her own fears, her apocalyptic vision and apprehension of the world. Thus her historical "revelations" are steadily questioned by the rest of the narrative, and when she becomes the key state witness in the trial of nationalists arrested for sedition, then her "historical" discourse is shown to be compromised. But if we cannot trust Ma Shepherd's recollection and representation of history through old forms, neither can we trust the official version. The history of San Cristobal appears "broken" to Penelope because she cannot find documents to verify local legends (pp. 87–88), but the reader is already aware that even if such documents existed, they could only denote a partial and ideologically slanted view of the island. Does this mean that the history of this Caribbean island has been destroyed beyond

58. Fredric Jameson, *The Political Unconscious: Narrative as a Socially Symbolic Act* (Ithaca: Cornell University Press, 1981), p. 49.
59. Fanon, pp. 239–40.

recovery? Can narrative recover a history that has no documents or reliable memories?

Lamming suggests that there are two possible narrative ways of reconstructing history: we can excavate fragments and ruins from the past and strive to fill the gaps in existing local histories, thereby establishing vital connections; or we can valorize the gaps and fragments of this history and turn them into actual sources of imaginary value. Both alternatives come into play in clearly connected ways. Mark, for example, believes that historical gaps can be plastered by privatizing history, appealing to the power of the individual experience, so to speak. His diaries are hence textual instruments for transforming absences and gaps into meanings that originate in the self. When he tries to describe an ordinary scene, Mark notices an absence of relationships between the resulting discourse and its objects; but he says that it is "precisely this absence which seems to restore each thing to its completeness. A certain lack of connection had endowed the pebble with a formidable and determined power of its presence. It was there, independent, obstinate, decisive" (p. 72). Indeed, Mark is no longer worried about his inability to recover his authentic self from the debris of Caribbean history. Instead, he adopts his failure to recover an essentialist experience as the source of the authority of his discourse. Unable to embark on an archeological quest for the past and recover some truth from what he aptly calls "the dreary pile of history," he notes that although what he sought was the "original" version of things, he is condemned to repetition: "Each account can only be a fresh corpse which we assemble in order to dissect again. Nothing was lost when I burnt the last pages of the pirate's biography. I had only burnt a little corpse whose original I could never know" (p. 107).

But the central problem of Caribbean modernism, as we have already seen, has to do with fear toward, and confusion about, beginnings. Lamming's novel poses a simple question in this regard: where does colonialism end and where does the postcolonial situation begin? Indeed, what is the decolonized subject's point of entry into Caribbean history? Addressing a nationalist crowd at a political meeting, Mark chooses the legend of the Tribe Boys as his point of entry into what he hopes is a rational dialogue between himself and the people of San Cristobal, but in the end his speech becomes "a fragment of a monologue between Mark Kennedy and himself, and the theme was his identity" (p. 179). At the end of the novel, the three boys who have become symbolic embodiments of the island's main ethnic groups have committed themselves to defend nationalism, to rise in revolt like "the Tribe Boys do," but their resistance is just a repetition of the past, not a new beginning: "It was a moment which entered them like steel, one accident of time exploding from the whole accumulated muddle of their past. It opened the earth under their feet to honour their fantasy and their hope" (p. 412).

Lamming, then, seems to express doubts about those attempts at new beginnings in the Caribbean which confuse the new with the original: what is original in the Caribbean, what begins with the "discovery," which I have been using as the inaugural moment of Caribbean modernism, can never be an ideal beginning; it is rather like that corpse Mark Kennedy dissects every time he tries to recover the origins of his pirate subject. And so modernity, and the discourse on national identity which it nurtures, still remain incomplete projects in Lamming's early works, to be taken up in his later novels, in the works of his contemporaries Samuel Selvon, Alejo Carpentier, and Paule Marshall, and in those of a younger generation of Caribbean writers such as Merle Hodge, Zee Edgell, and Michelle Cliff.

3

Beyond the *Kala-pani*:
The Trinidad Novels of Samuel
Selvon

It is through the effort to recapture the self and scrutinize the
self, it is through the lasting tension of their freedom that
men will be able to create the ideal conditions of existence
for a human world.
> —Frantz Fanon, *Black Skin, White Masks*

The great modernisms were . . . predicated on the invention
of a personal, private style. . . . This means that the modernist aesthetic is in some way organically linked to the conception of a unique self and private identity.
> —Fredric Jameson, "Postmodernism and Consumer
> Society"

In 1950 George Lamming and Samuel Selvon arrived in England
from Trinidad on the same boat, determined to become writers in the
heart of the metropolis and subconsciously obsessed with similar
questions about their colonial identities and anxieties. Ten years later,
reflecting on "the decade in which the West Indian acquired recognition as a writer," Lamming paid Selvon and Victor Reid a compliment
that has important implications for any discussion of the West Indian
novel and its formal modalities:

Writers like Selvon and Vic Reid—key novelists for understanding the
literary and social situation in the West Indies—are essentially peas-

ant . . . they never really left the land that once claimed their ancestors like trees. . . . The peasant tongue has its own rhythms which are Selvon's and Reid's rhythms; and no artifice of technique, no sophisticated gimmicks leading to the mutilation of form, can achieve the specific taste and sound of Selvon's prose.[1]

This compliment is not remarkable because of its accuracy or the spirit in which it was made; it is remarkable because in commenting on Selvon's work, Lamming had acknowledged an alternative route to Caribbean representation and identity, a route different from his own. For although Lamming's novels had achieved their resonance and force by mutilating the forms and designs embedded in the colonial language and through sophisticated narrative gimmicks, he was cognizant of the extent to which Selvon's "peasant idiom" and sensibility could provide the writer with a point of entry into Caribbean oral culture and hence provide native sources of meaning and expression for the emerging nations of the region. Furthermore, Lamming was attracted by Selvon's work because he saw, in its language and ideology, resolutions to questions of national formation which he had left suspended in his early works.

In the preceding chapter I argued that Lamming's early novels begin with the intention of developing a social critique of colonial society but end at an indeterminate point at which the narrator is concerned with the limits of the discourse of national identity. Because Lamming posits the drama of colonialism and decolonization as ongoing, his early novels eschew closure; they leave the relationship between modernity and the discourse on national identity incomplete, awaiting a future in which history will resolve the issues colonialism has raised. In spite of this absence of closure, each of the three novels I discussed in the previous chapter raises fundamental questions about the colonized subjects' horizons of expectations and the sites and ways in which new identities might be evoked in the emerging Caribbean

---

1. George Lamming, *The Pleasures of Exile* (London: Allison and Busby, 1984), p. 45. See also F. Gordon Rohlehr, "The Folk in Caribbean Literature," in *Critical Perspectives on Sam Selvon*, ed. Susheila Nasta (Washington, D.C.: Three Continents Press, 1988), pp. 29–43. Lamming's characterization of Selvon's language as "the people's speech, the organic music of the earth" is debated in several essays collected in *Critical Perspectives*: Bruce F. MacDonald, "Language and Consciousness in Samuel Selvon's *A Brighter Sun*" (pp. 173–76); Frank Birbalsingh, "Samuel Selvon and the West Indian Literary Renaissance" (pp. 142–59); Harold Barratt, "Dialect, Maturity and the Land in Sam Selvon's *A Brighter Sun*: A Reply" (pp. 187–95); Michel Fabre, "From Trinidad to London: Tone and Language in Samuel Selvon's *A Brighter Sun*" (213–22).

nation. Consequently, two basic positions on modernity and the construction of identities emerge from Lamming's works.

First, Lamming suggests that given the multiplicity of their cultures and traditions, Caribbean peoples need to come to terms with their differences even as they seek a new national identity in the decolonized zone. For if colonial discourse represses such differences in order to subject the colonized to the totalized myth of empire, deconstructing colonial mythologies demands the representation of the different but interrelated histories of the peoples who inhabit the islands. In *The Castle*, it is the recognition of difference as a constructive category that allows Trumper to "become a Negro." As he tells the narrator, "You ain't a thing till you know it, an' none o' you on this island is a Negro yet."[2] Trumper's new realization is that differences of race, class, and culture have always structured colonial society, but such differences have been masked in the name of a homogeneous English tradition. Thus, comments the narrator, "Whatever we had known we hadn't known this difference" (p. 299). Clearly, the recognition of difference is an important prerequisite for both a private and a public identity.

Second, the decolonized subject's identification with the Caribbean landscape, however problematic it might be, already portends a new narrative of history. Here Lamming seems to share an assumption, more recently articulated by Glissant, that for African slaves in the islands, the Caribbean landscape was never a source of joy or pleasure; since the slaves could not claim the right of possession, the plantation landscape was not a site of identification (a nation) but a place from which one escaped in search of freedom.[3] Writing in the nationalist period when the colonized set out to claim the land as the source of their new identity, Lamming has his characters turn to the landscape as the point of entry into Caribbean culture, but in the process they also confront difficult questions about Caribbean identity and heritage. The problematic relationship between landscape, nationalism, and identity is succinctly expressed in *Of Age and Innocence*: "Nationalism is not only frenzy and struggle with all its necessary demand for the destruction of those forces which condemn you to the status we call colonial. The national spirit is deeper and more enduring than that. . . . It is the private feeling you experience of possessing and

2. George Lamming, *In the Castle of My Skin* (New York: Schocken, 1983), pp. 297–98.
3. Edouard Glissant, *Caribbean Discourse: Selected Essays*, trans. J. Michael Dash (Charlottesville: University Press of Virginia, 1989), p. 130.

109

being possessed by the whole landscape of the place you were born."[4] But the emerging new nation of San Cristobal is also referred to as an entity "divided in a harmony that still pursues all its separate parts" (p. 58). Given this unreconciled opposition between the desire for unifying national symbols and the realities of difference, the central question that Lamming leaves suspended in his early works, as I argued in the last chapter, is this: how can cultural differences be simultaneously sustained and submerged in the ideal of the nation?

A similar preoccupation with the unexpected convergence of difference and reconciliation pervades Selvon's Trinidad novels, which I read as narrative responses to the question Lamming left suspended. But Selvon's frantic quest for forms of closure which might bring the narrative of colonialism to an end is also mediated by his East Indian identity. For the legacy and tragedy of East Indian indentured laborers and their descendants has been their historical placement outside the Manichaean zone of colonialism, marginalized in relation to both colonialism and the African culture of the slaves. In other words, if white colonizers perceived East Indian laborers as a convenient replacement for slaves—inheriting slave quarters and working conditions, hence deserving of treatment previously meted out to the newly emancipated Africans—for the former African slaves, as David Dabydeen has aptly observed, "Indians were perceived as a threat to African security, a threat to adequate wages and other material resources."[5] And in reality, notes Bridget Brereton, "indentureship was no different from slavery. . . . Indians on the estates performed the low prestige jobs like weeding, digging, and transporting cane, which Africans chose to avoid. So the indenture status itself contributed to the unfavourable image of the 'coolie.' Africans, once at the bottom of the social scale, now had an easily recognisable class to which they could feel superior."[6]

In the contemporary period, as Taylor suggests at the end of his

---

4. George Lamming, *Of Age and Innocence* (London: Allison and Busby, 1981), p. 174.

5. David Dabydeen, "Preface," *India in the Caribbean*, ed. David Dabydeen and Brinsley Samaroo (London: Hansib, 1987), p. 11.

6. Bridget Brereton, "The Experience of Indentureship: 1845–1917," in *Calcutta to Caroni: The East Indians of Trinidad*, ed. John la Guerre (London: Longman, 1974), p. 37. See also the essays by J. C. Jha, "The Indian Heritage in Trinidad" (pp. 1–24); Kelvin Singh, "East Indians and the Larger Society" (pp. 39–68); and Brinsley Samaroo, "Politics and Afro-Indian Relations in Trinidad" (pp. 84–97). Important historical and cultural background to East Indian indentureship in the Caribbean can also be found in two essays by Brinsley Samaroo in *India in the Caribbean*: "Two Abolitions: African Slavery and East Indian Indentureship" (pp. 25–42); and "The Indian Connection: The Influence of Indian Thought and Ideas on East Indians in the Caribbean" (pp. 43–60).

book on Caribbean literature and popular culture, East Indians have become victims of the allegory of the nation and the totalized history of the nation-state. According to Taylor, "One myth that was introduced in the postemancipation period, and is all too existent today, is the myth of a black history divorced from that of East Indian, Chinese, and other nationalities brought into plantation colonies to replace slave labor and keep wages low. These oppressed and exploited groups likewise had to confront colonialism, face the problem of cultural delegitimation, and recreate their own."[7]

Selvon's Trinidad novels deal with the transformation of East Indian cultures in the colonial and postcolonial Caribbean, the attempt of East Indians to redefine their value system against the pressures of modernity and modernization, and the quest for individual identities against the claims of old Indian traditions. Because he is concerned with the place of East Indians in an emergent Trinidadian national culture and their recognition as part of the mosaic of the nation, Selvon uses his narratives as agents of national consciousness. In particular, he posits social creolization as a temporal movement that will propel East Indian peasants from sites fixed by the colonial economy (the sugar cane plantation) and Hindu culture to a new totality defined by a consciousness of a mutually shared Caribbean "creole" nationhood.[8] Indeed, few Caribbean writers have posited creolization as a metacode for West Indian society and as a commentary on their own writings as much as Selvon. Instead of seeking the sources of his writings in the rich Indian heritage that East Indians in Trinidad have sustained in the plantation, Selvon has relegated such traditions to background and local color, moving beyond them to assert the liberating potential of creolization. When he was growing up in Trinidad, as he said in a 1979 lecture at the University of the West Indies, Selvon conceived himself as the product of intermingled cultures in transition; hence he had no desire to isolate himself from "the mixture of races that comprised the community," even when this meant negating cultural positions that were considered pure or exclusive to one group:

> If I say that the ritual of a Hindu wedding meant nothing to me because I did not understand it, then I have to say in the same breath that a

7. Patrick Taylor, *The Narrative of Liberation: Perspectives on Afro-Caribbean Literature, Popular Culture, and Politics* (Ithaca: Cornell University Press, 1989), p. 230.

8. Selvon reflects on issues of national consciousness and identity in Michel Fabre, "Samuel Selvon: Interviews and Conversations" (p. 73), and Peter Nazareth, "Interview with Sam Selvon" (pp. 93–94), both in Nasta, *Critical Perspectives*.

Shango ceremony was even more of a mystery. It was almost as if these two events, for example, were outside the day-to-day social rounds we led. . . . At this time I was putting down the roots of the mixture of characteristics, attitudes and mannerisms which comprise the Trinidadian.[9]

Instead of positing old African or Indian traditions as the basis of a new Caribbean national culture, Selvon believes that the process of creolization has created a new people and culture.

Creolization, however, is a very problematic term in Selvon's writings; it often seems to be confused with modernity (especially in its more restricted definition as a rejection of tradition) and westernization, more specifically the adoption of cosmopolitan or urban values. Thus Selvon assumes that the creolizing process "was the experience of a great many others of my generation," but it was also a source of "a certain embarrassment and uneasiness"; creolized peoples were hostile toward "Indian habits and customs" as if "it were a social stigma not to be westernised."[10] Because of this equation of creolization with modernization or westernization, the term *creole* poses a double paradox for Selvon and the East Indian characters who inhabit his novels. First, creolization is posited as liberating because it allows the West Indian subject to borrow and merge many cultural elements from the ethnic groups that constitute the Caribbean; but having borrowed from the parts that make the whole, these subjects no longer seem to owe allegiance to any particular tradition. The second paradox has to do with the confusion, in the minds of Selvon's characters and possibly the author himself, between creolization and modernity. When it is associated with cosmopolitanism, as we see in the Tiger novels, creolization allows the subject to reject narrow ethnic loyalties that might hamper the constitution of a national culture, but it also leads to snobbishness and the rejection or negation of popular culture.

Moreover, for East Indians in the Caribbean, creolization suggests meanings different from those proposed by Afro-Caribbean writers such as Glissant. For Glissant, as we saw in the Introduction, creolization is not "the glorification of the composite nature of a people," nor is it the valorization of a culture between two "pure" extremes, but the basic condition of a cross-cultural process. If we speak of creolized

9. Samuel Selvon, "Three into One Can't Go: East Indian, Trinidadian, West Indian," in Dabydeen and Samaroo, *India in the Caribbean*, p. 15.
10. Selvon, "Three into One," p. 15.

cultures, says Glissant, "it is not to define a category that will by its very nature be opposed to other categories ('pure' cultures), but in order to assert that today infinite varieties of creolization are open to human conception, both on the level of awareness and on that of intention."[11] For East Indians, on the other hand, there is a definite anxiety toward creolization and a certain hesitancy to adopt it as a process that leads to awareness and subjectivity. There are two basic reasons for this anxiety. First, East Indian cultures in the Caribbean evolved in a historical condition fraught with contradictions: their indentureship was supposed to be temporary but became permanent; East Indian laborers were legally defined as free, but they lived under conditions of virtual slavery. Furthermore, indentured laborers were determined to hold on to their Indian culture while "advancing" with the modern economy represented by the plantation. For these laborers, notes Dabydeen, crossing over *Kala-pani* (the dark waters) was also a form of cultural crossing underwritten by social ambivalence: on one hand, indentureship was considered to be a form of caste defilement leading to social ostracism; on the other hand, however, the physical and spiritual journey was justified by the dream of modernity—"the prospect of a new beginning in new lands" and "promises of plenty."[12] Once in the Caribbean, however, these laborers would find such expectations unfulfilled; under the economic hardships of the sugar plantations, they would yearn for their ancestral traditions and struggle to maintain the "purity" of Indian cultures against a modernity that was now conceived as a threat to the Indian self.[13] In this historical and social context, Selvon's characters strive for creolization and modernity against the pull and censure of this "pure" Indian tradition.

There is a second reason for what Selvon construes to be East Indian resistance to creolization: in the mythologies both of empire and of nation, East Indian subjectivity is not sustained by the binary opposition between self and other, especially where this self is presented exclusively as Afro-Caribbean and its opposing other as the white European. Until the 1940s and 1950s, East Indians existed in a state of limbo in relation to the social and historical forces that were shaping the new Caribbean nations. They were even denied access to important colonial institutions, such as the educational system and the

11. Glissant, p. 140.
12. Dabydeen, p. 9.
13. Singh, p. 60.

English language, which were becoming both the training ground and the mechanism of Caribbean nationalism. When the East Indians ultimately had access to education and the English language, as Kelvin Singh has noted, this access led to "a corresponding erosion of the linguistic base of the traditional Indian culture, leading to the increasing meaninglessness of that culture among the younger Indians, a generation gap between parents and children in the rural areas, and intrafamilial conflicts over such emotionally vital problems as romance, selection of mates and life styles."[14] Even in the great nationalist period, contends Selvon, East Indians in Trinidad were already fixed in a situation of displacement: "As for the Caribbean man of East Indian descent, he was something else. He wasn't accepted by those from India, and he wasn't wanted by the others because he wasn't a black man so he couldn't understand what was going on."[15]

In the circumstances, Selvon shares V. S. Naipaul's anxiety about place and culture, but the two writers' terms for representing this East Indian angst are radically different. As I will show in a close reading of his Trinidad novels, Selvon does not assume that loss and alienation can be written about as if they were the sources of authority and superiority; instead, they are shown to be symptoms of repressed desires. To be an East Indian creole in Trinidad is to become cognizant of how modernity promotes colonial values but, at the same time, blocks the colonized people's access to colonial culture. Like the gift of language, modernity is seen as both a gift and a curse; it tells colonized peoples that they can appropriate colonial institutions and nationalize them for their own identity, but only to a point. In their quest for self-awareness, Selvon's subjects are involved in a process of questioning previous notions of self and other, but they are not always sure whether to turn to "pure" Indian traditions or to embrace creolization as a way of dealing with the anxieties of modern life. Thus, even in the moment of nationalist awakening, "people are finding out that they have been thinking the wrong thoughts, living in the wrong place, christened with the wrong name, following the wrong creed, and want to metamorphose themselves."[16] These, then, are the basic hermeneutical problems faced by East Indian subjects in the West Indian space: First, on what social sphere and historical horizon will their cultural metamorphosis take place, and can it escape the curse of

14. Singh, p. 60.
15. Selvon, "Three into One," p. 18.
16. Selvon, "Three into One," p. 19.

repetition, given Selvon's remark that in the Caribbean "the wheel of history groans and squeaks as it repeats itself"?[17] Second, can either the colonial or postcolonial subject ever find narrative detours around the social and psychological blockage established by colonial discourse through an appeal to the uniqueness of the individual subject or its ancestral culture?

Modernity and the Colonial Subject

As I hope I have shown in previous chapters, the colonial subject's quest for aboriginal cultural sources, like its desire for modernity, is an act determined by a totality organized by the colonizer. Therefore, the quest of the colonial subject—the need to master colonial culture and its institutions and to use them to generate a new consciousness of self and nation—is often determined by a clearly Freudian process of desire and signification. In this process, as Kaja Silverman skillfully notes in her influential work on semiotics, the unconscious is "established simultaneously with the desires it houses—desires which are on the one hand culturally promoted and on the other linguistically blocked."[18] This blockage of desires, which in Selvon's novels is manifested in the colonial subject's inability to be gratified in either its traditional culture or the colonial realm, ignites what Silverman calls "a series of displacements, which continue throughout the entire existence of the subject and structure that subject's psychic reality."[19] Selvon's narratives are organized around such a series of psychological displacements which in turn pose questions that are at the very heart of Caribbean modernism: How can the colonized self free itself from the hold of colonial history and attain its "authentic" image? Can the attainment of self-understanding lead to a mastery of the historical process that triggers displacement?

Many of Selvon's Trinidad novels, notably the ones I'm concerned with here (*A Brighter Sun*, *Turn Again Tiger*, and *The Plains of Caroni*), are constructed around a process of loss, separation, and self-displacement which foregrounds the cultural crisis of the self. In each of these novels, the colonized East Indians attempt to subjectify themselves against a background of ideological and linguistic contestation: each

17. Selvon, "Three into One," p. 19.
18. Kaja Silverman, *The Subject of Semiotics* (New York: Oxford University Press, 1983), p. 77.
19. Silverman, p. 77.

quest is framed by two opposed semiotics—the regimented, formal language of colonial discourse and the subversively ironic or parodic "calypso idiom." Consider the opening of *A Brighter Sun*, for example: Trinidad in 1939 is introduced to us in dead prose that deprives even dramatic historical events of their significance; the reader is immersed in a chaotic world in which Trinidadians with money are attending the races, a group of Jewish refugees has arrived from Europe, war is declared with Germany, but life goes on in its mundane rhythms. "Emergency regulations were introduced, mail and telegrams censored, the churches prayed for peace, and the adjacent territorial waters were proclaimed a prohibited area. A man went about the streets of the city riding a bicycle and balancing a bottle of rum on his head."[20] Language dazzles rather than clarifies as we try to establish connections or oppositions that might stabilize meanings. What, surely, is the relationship between the state of emergency and the solitary man riding his bicycle?

This mixture of disparate elements, of course, reflects Selvon's indebtedness to the calypso aesthetic, especially its melodic lines, which come loaded with words and phrases that appear to be unrelated and to have no value in themselves. In such disparity, the calypsonian encodes cultural and social differences and hence signifies an "emerging nationhood."[21] This juxtaposition of unrelated elements has what semioticians call syntagmatic value. "In the syntagm," says Ferdinand de Saussure, "a term acquires its value only because it stands in opposition to everything that preceded or follows it, or both."[22] In the above description, for example, the two events (the important official pronouncement and the private activities of the rider) elicit indifference from the reader who fails to see their significance; in the process, both events are reduced to the same level of meaning. Moreover, the emergency, a drastic act with important implications for the colony, is represented in a nonchalant tone, one underscored by its apparent pairing with a tedious, ordinary episode.

20. Samuel Selvon, *A Brighter Sun* (London: Longman, 1955), p. 3. Further references are in the text.

21. In the Trinidad of the 1950s the calypso was often seen as what Rohlehr calls "a sign of emerging nationhood"; Albert Gomes, a leading nationalist writer, could hence argue that "the calypso singer has begun to announce in his songs that our ethnic 'potpourrie' is a reality, and that its many pots have begun to pour one into the other" (quoted by Rohlehr, "The Folk in Caribbean Literature," p. 36).

22. Ferdinand de Saussure, *Course in General Linguistics* (New York: McGraw-Hill, 1966), p. 123.

A few moments later, Selvon seems to reinforce his strategy of algebraization (rather than narrative foregrounding) by shifting his interest from the official and rational acts to erratic and prohibited events: the East Indian (who is "reputedly mad") and the black man "called Mussolini" are intended to force the reader to question the whole notion of significance in representation. Indeed, Selvon's use of the dead prose of the colonial bureaucracy should not be seen as a way of rejecting focalization as a narrative technique; rather, he wants his readers to realize that his subjects, their claims for uniqueness not-withstanding, struggle to define themselves against already existing images and modes of knowledge which repress subjectivity alto-gether. For in colonial discourse, as Homi Bhabha has pointed out, "subjects are always disproportionately placed in opposition or domi-nation through the symbolic decentering of multiple power-relations which play the role of support as well as target or adversary."[23] Also, by collapsing the traditional division between private and public events and discourses, Selvon questions one of the most cherished notions of high modernism—the notion of a unique subject function-ing as the source of its own meanings.

Moreover, by pairing historical events with the more immediate activities of ordinary people, the narrator refuses to privilege such events: "French residents pledged their support to General de Gaulle, and a man named Lafeet died in a hut far in the hills of the Northern Range, and nobody knew anything until three weeks later" (p. 4). What we have here is an ironic relationship between objects and events in which the authority of one is questioned by the other. At the same time, the author borrows the "excessive" rhetoric common in calypso songs as a tactic of exploding the constrictions of official dis-course. In the following example, Selvon adopts a *picong* (mockery) technique, common in the calypso ode, to foreground the uneasy position of colonial subjects caught between two contesting forms of language:

> There was a change in the economic and social life and outlook of Trinidadians in 1941. United States personnel arrived, and the con-struction of bases provided work at higher wages. . . . There was a new scale of increased taxation "upon those best able to bear it." A man

23. Homi K. Bhabha, "The Other Question: Difference, Discrimination, and the Discourse of Colonialism," in *Literature and Politics: Papers from the Essex Conference 1976–84*, ed. Francis Barker et al. (London: Methuen, 1986), p. 158.

named Afoo Dayday was caught urinating behind a tree in a park and was jailed. An Indian man from Gasparillo, a southern village, went about the city eating bottles and sticking pins and needles in his body. [Pp. 17–18]

At first glance, the relationship between the center and margin of colonial society seems to have been blurred: the well-managed prose and controlled euphemisms suggest, indeed enforce, an image of continuity and connection, a pattern in which things as opposed as American soldiers and East Indian peasants move to a common drum, constitute a linguistic community. But even as he falls back on official clichés, Selvon introduces elements of the uncanny which give the rational discourse a carnivalesque air: Afoo Dayday and the man from Gasparillo have defied the logical discourse of colonial modernism; they function as forces of chaos and madness amid the official order of things. And it is against both the chaos and the official order that Selvon's subjects struggle to define themselves.

But in order to engender themselves and sustain an "authentic" image, it is not enough for these characters to define themselves against the already written. They must also develop strategies to recover their own positions of principle or origins; they must show that they are not merely mimics of the other. In the first place, these subjects must learn how to penetrate the totality that official discourse promotes and to expose the distinctions and contradictions that are repressed in the mythology of empire. These characters must develop an ironic relationship with the dominant discourse, seeking their consciousness not in the reconciliation of the difference between self and other, but by maintaining this and other divisions, including the disjunction between reality and illusion, image and ideology. Taking over from Lamming, as it were, Selvon insists that the differences that have hitherto defined the Caribbean experience be turned into the source of discursive resistance. To borrow Pierre Macherey's famous expression, the kind of knowledge Selvon's subjects seek is not dependent on the "discovery or reconstruction of a latent meaning, forgotten or concealed. It is something newly raised up, an addition to the reality from which it begins."[24] Thus, in order to subjectify himself in *A Brighter Sun*, Tiger must raise a new knowledge against the overdetermined world of both colonialism and Indian culture. His world is

24. Pierre Macherey, *A Theory of Literary Production*, trans. Geoffrey Wall (London: Routledge, 1978), p. 6.

overdetermined in the sense that it imposes three contradictory images on him, images that are not dependent on his will or desire: from the perspective of the official discourse, he is a colonized man, an appendage of the colonial culture, just another object in the catalogue of objects that inhabit the book; to his Indian parents, he is the heir to a proud Hindu tradition defined by masculinity; but to his urban friends, he is a creolized man, a product of mixed cultural values.

The pressures that arise from such given images are evident at Tiger's wedding ceremony, where the juvenile groom and his bride are asked to live up to a prescribed image of their culture; indeed, the wedding becomes the medium through which Hindu culture in Trinidad rationalizes its function and relevance (p. 4). However, the subject's relationship to old rituals is defined by indifference and distance:

> The whole affair had been arranged for him; he didn't have anything to do with it. He wondered if she could cook, but he didn't ask himself if she knew anything about what boys and girls did when they got married, because he didn't know either. He was aware of a painful exhilaration; painful because neither of them understood, exhilarating because it was something different in his monotonous life. [P. 5]

Thus Tiger is thrown into the world alone, given an image by his culture, expected to live according to its expectations, but without authority or knowledge about the contexts in which he has to define himself. He understands what is expected of him—"now he was a man. He would have to learn to be a man, he would have to forget his friends" (p. 6)—but he does not understand the social implications of such ideals of manhood. So, if Tiger's mind is "in turmoil" after the marriage, it is precisely because manhood is a sign to which he cannot as yet assign significance. Indeed, the idea of manhood, far from being the interpretant of his reality, is contradictory in itself: away from his parents and friends, in the "unknown" (p. 7), Tiger cannot live the already created image of a man."Unknowingness folded about him so he couldn't breathe" (p. 11). In many ways, Tiger begins to discover that living by his predetermined image of manhood deprives him of the very autonomy that was supposed to define his authority; determined to cern himself, he concludes that "he might as well learn to do things without the assistance of other people" (p. 13). But no sooner has Tiger asserted the need of the self to create its own meanings than he discovers that he cannot engender himself, that he must appeal to the legitimizing claims of the community whose values he is trying to reject: "He wanted to buck up his courage and say something to show them he was a man, that he could swallow rum just as they did" (p. 14). At this stage, it begins to become clear that Tiger, as a colonized subject—colonized even by his East Indian culture, which imposes meanings on him—cannot make a distinction between the given image and reflective knowledge.

In Selvon's postulation, then, the colonial subject predicates its notions of selfhood on its ability to develop conscious knowledge about experience; for this subject, a different mode of seeing and representing things is assumed to trigger a concomitant change in the self that sees and represents. It is in this connection that the relationship between image and ideology becomes crucial in Selvon's account of colonial modernism: for if the image is an effect of knowledge, it does not necessarily reflect real conditions, or even proffer authentic representations; on the contrary, the image is shown to be the effect of the subject's illusions about its selfhood. Like many of Selvon's other characters, Tiger cannot define himself without penetrating the veil of ideology which both his Indian and colonial cultures have placed between him and what he considers to be his authentic self. Young Tiger chooses to reconstitute himself not by developing a new image for himself, not even by unveiling a self that might have been hidden behind social masks, but by confirming the image expected of him by his culture. He will live the way his culture expects him to, but this will be an act of choice, and thus he will be responsible for his actions. But no sooner has he made this decision than he discovers the impossibility of reconciling the external, socially expected image and what he believes is his true self. At this stage in his quest for subjectivity, strategies of alterity become appealing; he believes he can rediscover his true self by developing a counter-image, by revolting against all the social and ideological norms that were supposed to define him as an Indian and a colonial subject.

For example, Tiger begins to detest money and the cash nexus—an important index of modernity and "East Indianness"—and to denigrate its value. Rather than seeing money as the key to opportunity, Tiger represents it as a fetish that comes between people and the value of things in themselves: "If there was any way of getting by without money, he would take it. He preferred ten pounds of rice to a dollar bill: he couldn't eat the dollar bill. And if he had his way he would trade his crops in Tall Boy's shop for flour and cooking oil and perform all negotiations by an exchange of the things he possessed for the things he wanted" (p. 34). However, Tiger's utopian desire for a pre-modern economy in which the exchange of goods is not mediated by arbitrary signs is tempered by an awareness of his inability to reverse history; he cannot have his way in the movement of time and its economies of representation. In the circumstances, Tiger's longing for a past before the fetish reflects his disillusionment with the "modern times" that he had earlier hoped would provide him with a new identity. He had invested so much value in education, as a general process by which the subject acquires knowledge about its own experiences, because he believed that if only he could master colonial culture and its conventions, then he could close the gap between the "space of experience" and the "horizon of expectation."[25] Thus, the young man had adopted experience and knowledge as means of overcoming the lack that always defines the colonial subject—the fact that despite the assimilative claims of the colonial ideology, the colonized will never have the same rights as their colonizers.

As a young man, Tiger believes that his crisis of selfhood is a direct result of his lack of reflective knowledge, or even of an ideology of self which can only be acquired through literacy. Thus, when his daughter is born, Tiger cannot understand his new role as a father because he is not experienced. "So many things exploded like a sandbox seed in his mind, shocking him, pitching him because he did not know" (p. 43). But even the experience of fatherhood (a manifestation of the masculinity he was asked to master) does not help Tiger overcome his doubts; paternity and patriarchy confront him with the limits of his own knowledge and indeed accentuate his lack: "He was not alone. He had a wife. He had a child. He put the picture of them in front of his mind to ward off all the things he didn't know, which came to choke him from the dark" (p. 44).

In view of Tiger's inability to master the colonized space and its institutions, Selvon's narrative becomes dependent on an ironic temporal movement: characters strive for the future because it promises self-fulfillment and modernity, but no sooner has this future arrived than it appears empty, so that the subjects cannot derive self-consciousness by opposing the past they have surpassed.[26] In effect, this

25. I have borrowed these notions of temporal modernity from Jürgen Habermas. See his discussion of Reinhart Kosellek's notion of modern "time consciousness" in *The Philosophical Discourse of Modernity* (Cambridge: MIT Press, 1990), p. 12.

26. For the relationship between modernity, temporality, and self-consciousness, see Habermas, pp. 5–12.

kind of ironic reversal of temporality is Selvon's way of questioning the claim, common in the discourse of colonial modernism, that knowledge and education—as the primary instruments of rationalization—liberate the self from the tyranny of tradition and open up a future in which desires can be realized. It is true, of course, that for Tiger a direct experience of things appears to enforce his image of manhood (the best example is the birth of his daughter, which is a sign of his authority as a father); but no sooner have such previously meaningless signs as manhood become symbolized, that is, represented in concrete terms, than they raise questions about their value. In this case, Tiger's manhood is questioned by the fact that his wife has given birth to a girl instead of a "more valuable" son. What becomes clear, then, is that concepts such as "manhood" have no fixed value, but are arbitrary signifiers: "To my wife, I man when I sleep with she. To *bap*, I man if I drink rum. But to me, I no man yet" (p. 45). For Tiger, a mode of knowledge that is predicated on experience must always remain incomplete, foregrounding the lack that determines his cerning as a colonial subject: "He was conscious only of the great distance which separated him from all that was happening. Things always happened to other people, but nothing happened to him" (p. 76).

At this stage in the novel, Tiger knows that the knowledge of the world he is getting from Sookdeo does not "put him right" because it does not make the "modern world"—which he hears about through the radio and newspapers—directly accessible. The assumption is that such second-hand knowledge has minimal value because it does not make distinctions between the imaginary and the real, between the ideological and the empirical. When soon afterward Tiger embarks on a slow and deliberate process of self-education, he believes that literacy will not only give him the authority and means to mediate his experiences directly, but will also enable him to overcome the ideological veil that masks the essence of things. But no sooner has he begun to "learn things" than the subject discovers that life is more complicated than living up to a set of preset images and norms (p. 81). Knowledge, previously represented as the act of reconciling the subject with "reality"—and hence desired as an instrument for suppressing the images that sustain the false illusions that had previously defined the self—now begins to appear unable to grant this self authority or autonomy. At this juncture, Selvon's text poses an interesting question: is knowledge a category distinct from image or are the two terms unified by their function as ideological effects?

A possible answer to this question has been posed by Paul Smith in another context: "Wherever the 'I' speaks, a knowledge is spoken; wherever a knowledge speaks, an 'I' is spoken."[27] But Smith goes on to make the important assertion that the I that is produced by knowledge, and the knowledge that produces a subject, are always situated at "the point of intersection between 'subject' and system."[28] Since knowledge is a product of the system, rather than an agency of the subject, it is (like the image) a form of ideological interpellation. Thus Tiger's new knowledge displaces him by drawing him deeper into the colonial epistemology and so exacerbates his crisis of selfhood. No wonder he now seeks solace in the imagined rather than the real world, in what he would have been rather than what he is (pp. 97–99). Education, the great white hope of mastering the ideologies and instruments of colonial modernism, is ultimately exposed as an agency of displacement.

Memory and the White Mythology

The theme of education as a form of displacement and repetition is crucial to the form and structure of *Turn Again Tiger*, the sequel to *A Brighter Sun*. At the beginning of this novel, readers discover with consternation that Tiger has returned to the sugarcane plantation, the site of objectification from which (or so we thought) his education and experience were intended to provide escape. At the end of *A Brighter Sun* Tiger has obviously become disillusioned with the promise of modernity, and his mastery of some of its conventions doesn't seem to have led to any form of self-improvement; nevertheless, there is nothing in his sense of disillusionment to suggest that he prefers a life of neo-slavery in the cane plantation to life in the urban space. What, then, motivates his return to an oppressed past and its restrictive traditions? Is it possible that he sees this return to the past as providing him with another space of experience in which he can develop a new relationship with (traditional) East Indian culture and its collective memory?

In truth, these questions crop up throughout the novel and never seem to be resolved. But in his "rereading" of the cane field and its

27. Paul Smith, *Discerning the Subject* (Minneapolis: University of Minnesota Press, 1988), p. 100.
28. Smith, p. 101.

culture, Tiger seems to be seeking nothing less than a genealogy of historical displacement and a topology to mediate cultural alienation: "Standing on the hill gave him a feeling of power. He hated the cane. Cane had been the destiny of his father, and his father's father. Cane had brought them all from the banks of the Ganges as indentured laborers to toil in the burning sun. And even when those days were over, most of them stayed shackled to the estates."[29] Tiger reflects on the alienating powers of the cane and realizes that he can never identify with it; the knowledge that the cane leads to social death, and not the social upliftment his ancestors expected when they came to the Caribbean, is what gives the character power over the commodity. We could even argue that although his previous experiences in the city have not endowed Tiger with any positive mode of knowledge, they have given him a certain kind of reflectiveness which allows him to enter into a symbolic relationship with the cane. However, Tiger's "turn" to the past (hinted at in the title of the novel) is motivated by the realization that he cannot acquire a new identity until he has come to terms with collective loss in all its dimensions.

But as he reflects on what has happened to him since he left the sugar belt as a young man, Tiger realizes that his reflective knowledge has not enhanced his authority: "All his life had led to this—indecision on the hill, looking down into a dark valley" (p. 2). Figures of old men who live and die in the cane fields are a constant reminder to Tiger that his image as an indentured subject—a subject outside culture, history, and tradition—has been fixed by a long history. The tragedy of the old laborers whom he encounters wherever he goes is the fact that irrespective of their geographic location, they are substitutable, like physical objects. Even Tiger's own father has no character outside his function as a laborer: "Tiger's mind drifted back to another old man he had known, Sookdeo, who taught him to read. There was a parallel, instinctively he knew. He could easily imagine that his father was Sookdeo. Old men's voices took on a certain timbre of defeat, a peculiar tone belonging to hard experience" (p. 4). Clearly, neither Tiger's experiences in the city nor his literacy can liberate him from shared collective memories. The modernist myth of a unique subject engendered by the rejection of the past and tradition will simply not do.

In the end, however, Tiger cannot exist without the negative knowl-

29. Samuel Selvon, *Turn Again Tiger* (London: Heinemann, 1979), p. 1. Further references are in the text.

edge that helps him to establish an ironic disjuncture between himself and the ancestral voices and experiences that he might easily have assumed to be the groundings for his selfhood. But the resulting *dédoublement* cannot be complete because the subject must always reinvent himself in the context of the very history and culture he would like to transcend. Reflecting on his own changes over the years, Tiger realizes that his *dédoublement* from the old men who hover around him like the shadows of death is tenuous, that his notion of difference is based on questionable investments in the imaginary which often sustain the illusion that knowledge about self changes the self's conditions of existence. For in the end, if there is a mark of Tiger's development it is not to be found in the isolated moments of narcissism in which he adopts imaginary notions of self as if they were real, but in his capacity for ironic reflection.[30]

In *A Brighter Sun*, as we have already seen, education and the mastery of the colonial language were viewed as the source of a (desired) positive knowledge that would enable Tiger to transcend the traditional "cane culture" of his parents; modernization was adopted as a strategy by which both the community and the individual would be reconstituted in radically different ways. The highway that Tiger helps build at the end of the novel was to function as a sign of temporal development. In *Turn Again Tiger*, on the other hand, the meaning of this highway has changed: "It seemed to him, watching the Highway, that it was nothing more than a symbol of the sameness of his life" (p. 8). The footprint which he had made in the asphalt (a sign of authority and the capacity for self-inscription, then) is now apprehended as a hieroglyph of doubt: "The footprint obsessed his mind for a minute: a sudden thought: Is all these irrelevancies avoidance or inability to cope with life?" (p. 8). With this example in mind, we can conclude that knowledge, far from providing the subject with a privileged point of reflection from which to master uncertainty, has become the source of uncertainty itself. Nevertheless, this knowledge does have the ironic power of the negative: Tiger is able to differentiate himself and (in Paul de Man's words) to "acknowledge his previous mystification."[31]

Indeed, Tiger's decision to return to the sugar belt, his original scene of repression, is based not on any ideological conviction, but on an

30. For a different view of Tiger's "development" see Frank Birbalsingh, "Samuel Selvon and the West Indian Literary Renaissance," in Nasta, *Critical Perspectives*, p. 155.
31. Paul de Man, "The Rhetoric of Temporality," in *Blindness and Insight* (Minneapolis: University of Minnesota Press, 1983), p. 214.

acute awareness of the gap between what colonial modernization (here represented by the experiments in cane farming) promises and what it delivers. If we seem to have a Tiger with a divided mind here, it is because the subject has developed the double language of irony which, as de Man observes in another context, "splits the subject into an empirical self that exists in a state of inauthenticity and a self that exists only in the form of a language that asserts the knowledge of this inauthenticity."[32] To sustain these two images for his subject, Selvon invokes a temporal structure that simultaneously formulates and makes ironic the very system of values within which the self seeks to differentiate itself.

Inevitably, all the values Tiger tried to acquire in *A Brighter Sun* are questioned in *Turn Again Tiger*. In the first text he aspired to manhood, but now, in spite of having a family and having acquired "masculine" experience, he is reminded that he is just a young man (p. 26); at the beginning of his quest for identity, he embraced change as the thing that would reconcile him to the objects of his desire, but now he isn't "quite sure if the change was a good thing" (p. 32); previously, he was convinced that knowledge was the key to life, but now he believes that "underneath not knowing a damn thing" is what life is all about (p. 33). Against this background of psychological blockage and linguistic censorship, Tiger discovers that neither the adoption of an image nor the inflection of an ideology contains resolutions to his crisis of identity. Ultimately, Selvon's narratives show that Tiger cannot transgress the other's regime of truth because he still believes in the efficacy of the colonial system; indeed, he seeks to master colonial strategies of representation until, toward the end of *Turn Again Tiger*, he turns against the colonial system of representation by literally burning his edition of Shakespeare, the central text in the colonial canon. Because Tiger still believes in the system that entraps him, he finds it difficult to resist the "white mythology."

For this reason, the problem of transgressing the colonial regime of meaning is better represented by a group of minor characters who seem to inhabit what Deleuze and Guattari would call "points of nonculture."[33] Such characters inscribe their selfhood not by mastering the language of the other, but by adopting their parapraxes as a strategy of struggle and identity. In the process, these minor charac-

32. De Man, p. 214.
33. Gilles Deleuze and Félix Guattari, *Kafka: Toward a Minor Literature*, trans. Dana Polan (Minneapolis: University of Minnesota Press, 1986), p. 27.

ters act as foils to Tiger's "positive" quest for identity within the colonial structure. For example, early in *A Brighter Sun*, when the newly married Tiger is struggling to define his manhood, we are forced to compare his teetering quest for identity with Joe Martin's decisive and violent break with his grandmother. By violently rejecting the authority of Ma Lambie, Joe suddenly becomes a man "capable of loving and hating deeply" (p. 26); he will reconstruct his selfhood by rejecting all institutions (including that of the family) in the same way other, minor demented characters in the novel assert their freedom through their madness.

Similarly, Tiger's initial faith in the liberating powers of knowledge and modernization is put into question when he learns of the experiences of Sookdeo, the old man who teaches him how to read. Indeed, if we read the figure of Sookdeo as the logical outcome of colonial doctrines of labor, we have to see his destruction by the cane fields as the repressive and destructive course of a modernization that relies on commodities. Sookdeo lives on "rum and memories"—one the figure of forgetting, the other the term for a compromised historical record—and presents the image of a body that has been "cracked and gnarled with labour." We are told that "his whole body gave that impression, as if he had done too much work in his childhood, before his bones had a chance to sharpen themselves" (p. 65). Sookdeo has now opted for the life of a hermit, firmly establishing a radical disjuncture between himself and the dominant culture. So if Sookdeo appears reluctant to teach Tiger how to read, it is because he is well aware of the perils of investing in agencies of westernization, such as education. Young Tiger may see self-education as a point of entry into colonial culture, but Sookdeo prefers an ironic relationship to this culture. In the last two chapters of *A Brighter Sun*, Selvon offers the reader a dramatic rendering of the contrasts between eschatological faith in the idea of progress and a transgressive rejection of temporality: for Tiger, the uprooting of the landscape to prepare for a new road is the kind of displacement that promises change (p. 146); for Sookdeo, it is apocalypse (pp. 151–52).

In the above examples, Selvon may not be directly questioning the notion of modernization itself, but he seems eager to interrogate many of its claims, especially the whole idea of rationalization, the belief that a rejection of tradition restores autonomy to the subject. He also wants to expose its close relationship to "white mythologies" about the colonial self and its culture. Thus, Tiger's struggle to be "modern" is questioned by a subtext revolving around characters who inscribe themselves through an erratic discourse that reverses preconceived notions of selfhood. For example, in *Turn Again Tiger*, Soylo has inscribed himself in a counter-modernist discourse in which "madness" fashions a discourse that haunts the logical language of development which Tiger tries to champion.

Five Rivers is an experimental station for new strains of sugar (a place where technology promises to preserve the sweetness of sugar while taking the pain and blood out of its production), but we cannot reflect on the scientific advances being made here without hearing Soylo howling like a mad dog at night, "moaning and gasping like a tortured spirit" (p. 23). Soylo has escaped into this habitation in the belief—supported by "old knowledge"—that sugar would not grow in Five Rivers; however, his "earthlore was out of date with recent agricultural development. Cane grew in the valley. Cane swept through the valley, displacing vegetable crops and a grapefruit field that was doing well" (p. 23). We have already seen how cane functions as a metaphor of modernization in Selvon's novel, but what is interesting in this instance is that it now grows against the will of nature and the desires of human beings. A new force (science) has made natural and human considerations irrelevant. Soylo's response to this new force is to estrange himself in the hope that, cut away from the sugar economy and its workers, he can sustain an Edenic mythos (p. 24). Thus in view of the overwhelming power of the system, the self asserts its autonomy by resorting to a language that alienates it; now Soylo self-consciously represents himself to Tiger as a stranger (p. 24).

What all these minor characters foreground, among other things, is the futility of Tiger's struggle to subjectify himself by mastering the languages and codes of the colonial system. These characters seem to seek their identity in the limits of consciousness itself; in the process, they evacuate what could be considered a zone of transgression. In celebrating a language that runs counter to the logical discourse of modernism—in adopting the "deep" language of madness—these characters adopt what Jameson would call "the schizophrenic way of living contradictions."[34] The example of More Lazy in *Turn Again Tiger*

34. Fredric Jameson, "Postmodernism and Consumer Society," in *The Anti-Aesthetic: Essays on Postmodern Culture*, ed. Hal Foster (Port Townsend, Wash.: Bay Press, 1983), pp. 118–20. See also Gilles Deleuze and Félix Guattari, *Anti-Oedipus: Capitalism and Schizophrenia*, trans. Robert Hurley et al. (Minneapolis: University of Minnesota Press, 1983), p. 287; and Gilles Deleuze, "The Schizophrenic and Language: Surface and Depth in Lewis Carroll and Antonin

is an apt counter to Tiger's investment in a modernist discourse that, by synthesizing traditional and modern values, hopes to reveal the truth about, or establish the identity of, the colonial subject. For More Lazy has deliberately fashioned a mode of cultural contestation which negates the essence of subjectivity itself: he is described as the man "who defies the system . . . who in the flow of human movement, is seemingly carried along towards the total and final destination of all men, but who in his lifetime is a complete nonconformist" (p. 97).

But More's disinvestment from the "the order of things" is not merely nonconformism. He has, in essence, renounced all the valued props of self-identity; for example, "parentage, important to other people, had no relevance with reality to him" (p. 97). Other people attached importance to names as signifiers of selfhood, but More had not found any value in such signs: "Somewhere in the dim past More Lazy had been christened Theodore Sebastian, but he had never really had any cause to use this name" (p. 98). And, more important, he refuses to invent an image of himself—"I don't figure nothing out. I just is, that's all" (p. 100)—and in the process leaves the villagers to recreate him according to their fantasies and desires (p. 99).

More Lazy's refusal to develop a positive image of self is contrasted with Tiger's frantic desire to recreate himself according to prescribed rules: while the former finds solace in dreams (p. 102), the latter's greatest fear is that his attempt to inscribe himself in the vast world brought home to him by the radio "was a sort of escape from the immediate realities about him" (p. 111). At this stage in the quest for an authentic image of self, Tiger has found himself in a double bind: knowledge and experience open up the vastness of the world and offer possibilities of liberation, but they accentuate the alienation of the self from its culture and traditions; an acceptance of the old image, on the other hand, entails the imprisonment of the subject in the economy of the other. This paradoxical relationship between knowledge and desire is central to Tiger's attempt to develop a modern image and ideology of self. In the first instance, as we have already seen, Tiger had invested in knowledge because he felt that it would enable him to close the gap between the appearance of things and their realities. At this stage, books were seen as signs of reality because they were

---

Artaud," in *Textual Strategies: Perspectives in Post-Structuralist Criticism*, ed. Josué V. Harari (Ithaca: Cornell University Press, 1979), pp. 277–95.

expected to yield an encyclopedic knowledge that establishes rules to be followed and goals to be attained. As several critics have argued, in the Western and colonial traditions, the metaphor of the library reflects a desire for order, totality, or truth, a form of symbolic representation which can explain reality.[35]

In his quest for this symbolic system, however, Tiger finds it increasingly difficult to reconcile what he reads in books with the realities of the cane fields. He becomes convinced that knowledge is itself an unattainable ideal, a fantasy that cannot account for the nature or meaning of things; so, if the subject is to recover his self-reflectiveness, the colonial library has to be rejected:

> He went inside and he brought out all the books he had, and he sat on the steps with them and crumpled all the pages. He threw them in a heap on the ground in front of the house and set fire to the paper. "No more books," he told himself, watching them burn, "they only make me miserable. Plato, Aristotle, Shakespeare, the lot. All them fellars dead and gone, and they ain't help me solve nothing. You study this, you study that, and in the end what happen?" [P. 112]

This burning of the books has three consequences: First, knowledge is recognized to be an elusive mirage; Tiger fails to use knowledge to create a total image of self because he discovers (to borrow Eugenio Donato's comment on the library) that "each field of knowledge reveals itself to be contradictory, unsystematic, or simply unable to give an adequate representation of the objects it is supposed to describe."[36] Second, this denigration of knowledge allows Tiger to adopt his own private desires as a more natural and spontaneous form of existence (p. 114) because the rejection of the canonical texts of Western culture is the rejection of predetermined conceptions of the colonized self. Third, an important question is raised for the reader: is there any difference between knowledge and desire, or does what appears to be rational discourse belong to the imaginary realm too?

The truth is that neither the kind of knowledge Tiger seeks (mastery of Western modes of representation) nor his desires (to be a "modern")

---

35. See Eugenio Donato, "The Museum's Furnace: Notes toward a Contextual Reading of *Bouvard and Pécuchet*," in Harari, *Textual Strategies*, p. 216; and Michel Foucault, "Fantasia of the Library," in *Language, Counter-Memory, Practice: Selected Essays and Interviews*, ed. Donald F. Bouchard, trans. Donald F. Bouchard and Sherry Simon (Ithaca: Cornell University Press, 1977), pp. 87–112.

36. Donato, p. 214.

reflect any authority; on the contrary, both knowledge and desire are mediated by a pervasive "white mythology."[37] For example, even after Tiger rejects the authority of books, he is consumed by a desire for the white woman Doreen; he is haunted by an earlier incident by the river when he had seen her naked and had run away, pursued by the set of prohibitions figured by the white woman in the colonial culture. Ironically, Tiger's cognizance of the white woman as the "forbidden fruit" makes desire the central category in the mediation of his selfhood. In other words, to restore his pride, Tiger must acquire Doreen, now a sign of what Jacques Lacan calls a "passion of the signifier."[38] To borrow Lacan's formulation, Tiger's desire is constituted by the gap that exists between himself and this signifier which, as the sign of the other's power over him, already possesses the privilege "of satisfying needs . . . the power of depriving them of that alone by which they are satisfied."[39] With a mixture of fear, lust, and anger, Tiger sexually possesses Doreen so that he can deprive her of the power she has over him as a signifier of the "white mythology": "his grip tightened and he felt that if he killed her everything would be all right. . . . That was why he held her, to kill her" (p. 146). Desire and knowledge, Tiger discovers in the end, have one thing in common—they have no value in themselves except as mediators of the colonial power relation. Neither can be the basis of a new image of self, nor a means of transcending the prisonhouse of colonialism.

The Modern Drama of Independence

A decolonized image of self remains an unfulfilled utopian impulse in Selvon's early texts; what remains at the end of the quest for the modernist ideal (*A Brighter Sun*) and a return to the past (*Turn Again Tiger*) is the threat of dissolution. In spite of Tiger's constant celebration of creolization as a topos for modernization, and hence its function as a force of differentiation—one that leads to the dissolution of traditional forms of life—the colonial subject's quest for self-identity

37. See Jacques Derrida, *Margins of Philosophy*, trans. Alan Bass (Chicago: University of Chicago Press, 1982), p. 213.
38. Jacques Lacan, *Ecrits: A Selection*, trans. Alan Sheridan (New York: Norton, 1977), p. 284.
39. Lacan, p. 286. According to Silverman, "Displacement makes possible the fulfillment of a repressed desire through a series of surrogate images since it transfers to the latter the affect which properly belongs to the former" (p. 91).

takes place within a shifting but unchanging context, that of sugar and the plantation system it engenders. If there is one special feature that defines the paradox of modernity in Selvon's text, it is Tiger's alternation between the dream of recapturing his self in a future realm of freedom and the need to recover an original, unalienated cultural source. Nevertheless, these ideals do not represent clear-cut alternatives. In *A Brighter Sun*, Tiger seeks his identity by rejecting the culture of the cane; in spite of the problems he encounters in trying to define himself in Barataria, any return to the plantation is considered regressive and unthinkable: "He considered going back to the canefields in Chaguanas, but the thought of it made him laugh aloud" (p. 215). If a return to the past holds only the possibility of repression, why does Tiger go back to the plantation in *Turn Again Tiger*?

In an insightful introduction to the novel, Sandra Pouchet Paquet has asserted that this turn backwards is a questioning of creolization as liberating praxis. She notes that the novel emphasizes "Tiger's need to reconcile himself with his peasant roots in the cane community, as a vital and necessary grounding, if the process of creolization is not to lead to a crisis of disconnection and directionlessness" (p. vii). Indeed, it is important for Tiger to test his new knowledge against the power of tradition; his discourse even holds the possibility that tradition itself might be reformed through literacy and better management. The narrative itself, however, seems to counter any suggestion that the past may, in the end, prove to have any redemptive value. On the contrary, the image of the cane revives a communal history of total reification (p. 47).

But Tiger's bitter memories of the canefields begin to lose their resonance in view of the modernizing process taking place in the sugar estates, a process that promises recompense for past suffering; indeed, he sometimes wavers between his historical knowledge of the cane as a force that represses identities and his dream that cane might indeed become a source of pleasure (p. 143). And in the end, because he realizes he cannot escape from the plantation system, Tiger will "modernize" the colonized space in his imagination, representing it as an agrarian landscape with a teleological value that is definitely utopian: "Urmilla was bearing another child, perhaps the greatest thing of all. And the very earth had done a job, bearing the cane that made the harvest possible" (p. 181). In reality, however, the subject is caught in the mythical narrative of modernity—the belief that suffering in the past and present will lead to a better life in the future. As we have already seen, in Caribbean nationalist discourse, political independence is supposed to signify the utopian moment in which the errors of the past will be rectified.

But Selvon, like Lamming before him, realizes that the apotheosis of nationalism does not necessarily erase the errors that initiated the "beginning of our history, when Columbus thought he was going to India, and call these islands the Westindies."[40] In the neocolonial Caribbean, where modernization sometimes functions as a mask for the continued domination of the decolonized landscape by old colonial interests, narrative becomes a means of interrogating the drama of independence and its claims to provide a decisive break with the colonial past. The cultural space of postcolonialism is, of course, much more complex than the colonial situation because with the coming of independence the binary opposition between blacks and whites has been partly collapsed, and multiple identities based on color, class, and caste have emerged to make their mark on the new nation. Nevertheless, the Caribbean subject must still negotiate a thin line between the "white mythology" and the claims of indigenous culture.

Indeed, Selvon opens *The Plains of Caroni* by playing the two forces against one another as he seeks a space in which the emerging language of the nation can be represented. At the beginning of the novel, the colonial past evoked by the mythology of Sir Walter Raleigh going up the Caroni River is challenged by the postcolonial idiom signified by calypso, carnival, and a new *parole* (of Trinidadian neologisms), all of which suggest a new discourse.[41] In writing after colonialism, Selvon recenters the culture and language of the subaltern (even when fetishized as "tourist art") as the essence of a national culture. However, what is intriguing in *The Plains of Caroni* (which can be read as a prelude to the texts of Cliff, Hodge, and Edgell discussed in my final two chapters) is the way a new national identity is sought through the revision and reversal of the principles and explanatory concepts of colonial modernism. Thus sugar, which in Selvon's previous novels was associated with the forces of destruction and displacement, now acquires a double image, indeed functions as both a metaphor and a metonymy.

In the first instance, characters identify with sugar as metaphor (and

40. Selvon, "Three into One," p. 20.
41. Samuel Selvon, *The Plains of Caroni* (Toronto: Williams-Wallace, 1985), p. 2. Further references are in the text.

source) of a new wealth that has led to the modernization of social life: the village in the sugar plantation exhibits "all the signs of independence and progress which were bound to come with self-government," creating prosperity for former peasants like Harrilal (p. 3). We could hence argue that independence has legitimized colonial modernity by according new respect to plantation labor, whose economic motives and dehumanizing aspects remain unchanged. On the other hand, by reconfiguring, though not necessarily changing, the relationship between colonizer and colonized, independence justifies the metonymic function of the plantation system. In other words, by celebrating modernity—even when invalidating the common function of tradition as an instrument against colonial modernism—independence initiates a radical dislocation in social and class relationships.

Thus, although her Hindu culture does not accord much authority to women, Harrilal's wife, Seeta, can—through her mastery of new modes of sugar production—transform her arranged marriage into a source of authority: "It was she who was in charge of the household. This was so unlike the traditional image of the obedient and servile Indian wife that Harrilal did not dare to let anybody know the true state of affairs in his house" (p. 3). Because independence is the source of both his new wealth and the denigration of his authority, Harrilal has developed a schizophrenic relationship with independent Trinidad: he benefits from the new economy, but he is resentful of the changes it has brought to the social scene, especially to gender relationships. Indeed, very early in the novel Selvon emphasizes the precariousness of reading the postcolonial situation in binaries such as tradition/modernity, new/old, or even colonialism/independence, and of attaching any definitive value to either entity. For if sugar has become the source of the new wealth, it is also shown to still retain its power to destroy human beings.

This ambiguity—no doubt a synecdoche of the independent situation itself—is clearly represented in the relationship between Balgobin and his cutlass. Initially, the cutlass is represented as a figure of analogy and similitude: "He clutched the comfort of his cutlass now, as it leaned against his side. His fingers curled and fitted the piece of wood, flesh and bone and wood blending as if the cutlass was an extension of his arm" (p. 10). But this identification between subject and object is shown to be based on a nullification of the difference that traditionally gives the subject dominance over the object. In fact, "the marks of time" on the cutlass are shown to be signs of violent denigration rather than symbols of progress, as is the texture of Balgobin's skin and the odor of his body—"by smell alone, he was part of a sugar plantation" (p. 10). The irony, of course, is that when mechanization is introduced as a way of rescuing Balgobin from the labor that has destroyed his self-worth, he sees it as a threat to his identity as a laborer. And to the extent that mechanization denies people like him even the right to work, we could argue that it accentuates their degradation. The point, though, is that neither in manual labor nor in mechanization can we find a center of real positive value.

Even in temporal terms, the past and the future are apprehended solely in terms of their disjunctive and ironic relationships, not in any positive causal connections they may have. More important, the human subject is now erased from the discourse on modernization. It is interesting to note that in that dramatic scene in which Balgobin and his cutlass challenge the tractor to a duel, the narrator underscores not the difference between Balgobin and the machine, but their similarity: "He was like a machine himself, performing automatically without pause, incorporating the action of wiping beads of sweat off his face as part of the general movement" (p. 75). The actor in this drama is man turned into not one but two objects—the cutlass and the tractor (the "eighty eight"): "The moonlight cast the shadows of the man and the cane and the cutlass in a mingled confusion: it doubled him and his cutlass but it also doubled the remainder of the eighty eight, and in his frenzy he attacked both shadow and reality" (p. 75).

If we recall the teleological suspense in the two previous novels—the belief that the meaning of the subject's life and its fulfillment will be revealed by the future—then we can appreciate why Selvon seems to collapse those distinctions that suggest that change and movement are desirable. Take the theme of modernization itself: it is adopted in the postcolonial situation as the sign that the colonized have acquired the authority to fashion themselves even in the image of the colonizer, proof that the problematic other is no longer the mediator of social values. But in this novel, modernity stands out because of its excess: metal chairs have "invaded Trinidad" (p. 6); the "industrial revolution" is threatening group identities and collective memories; worse still, the neologisms that have been fashioned to explain the new state of things ("Trinfashion," "Trinhabit") are often hyphenated as if to draw attention to the incompleteness of the "modern" language. In effect, we are left in a real interpretative quandary: modernization and technological innovation threaten peoples and their traditions (p. 56), but is there any value in preserving a tradition founded on commodification? Modernization opens up new spaces of expression, but will it make things better? The value of temporality itself is put into question when the postcolonial subject is like that man in the novel who wins a lottery and walks backwards all the time "as if he hoped to get back into the past, or keep away from the future" (p. 5).

This problematic nature of temporality is a common feature of New World culture in which, as Octavio Paz once observed, modernity is "cut off from the past and continually hurtling forward at such a dizzy pace that it cannot take root, that it merely survives from one day to the next: it is unable to return to its beginnings and thus recover its powers of renewal."[42] But the question still remains: is there any value in the past, in beginnings that reflect the power and desire of the other? And if the past must be transcended in its totality, on which foundations are we to engender new beginnings? These are the questions Selvon tries to negotiate in *The Plains of Caroni*, especially in his representation of Seeta, a woman who embraces modernity as liberating her from repressive gender traditions but still finds it difficult to create an authentic image for herself.

Clearly, for Seeta there is no value to be recuperated from the past or from old traditions. As a young woman she was forced to abandon the man she loved (and the father of her son) to satisfy her parents' desires; since then her activities have been motivated by a pressing need to escape from that past. She has made a libido investment in the future, in the form of her son Romesh, as if she can recover and sustain the forbidden marriage in the imaginary realm. What is interesting about Seeta's quest for ways of breaking with the past is that what she desires is an already existing image—that of the "liberated" European woman—which forces her deeper still into that mimicry which is the unfortunate fate of colonized peoples even after independence. We are told, for example, that when Seeta is with Romesh, she tries "to be as correct as she could in her speech, using as much proper English as she could command" (p. 18); it is only when she gets emotional that she "lost control of her words and was speaking more dialect" (p. 25). For this reason, we are never sure where the old Seeta ends and the new one begins.

But one thing is clear about Seeta's strategies of negotiating the

42. Octavio Paz, *Alternating Current*, trans. Helen Lane (New York: Viking, 1973), pp. 161–62.

landscape of independent Trinidad—she does not seek to subvert the old colonial structures or values or even to transgress against the old order of things; on the contrary, her ruthless drive to make Romesh succeed is a calculated appropriation of such structures and values. She shares a belief, common in postcolonial society, that independence has opened the gates for the ex-colonials to be equal, if not similar, to the colonizer. Thus she knows that cane has brutalized her old lover, Balgobin, but she now sees it as the right thing to use to get her son "on the right road": "Sugarcane had been their burden, she could turn it into the means of success" (p. 28). A schizophrenic identity has become Seeta's way of mastering the present: "It was possible for some individuals like Seeta to have a village face and a city face, or exhibit certain manners and behavior which fooled people into believing they had her typed, when at will she was able to transform herself into somebody else" (p. 47). In temporal terms, this self-division foregrounds the present and, at the same time, brackets the past and the future. In effect, Seeta is able to initiate her Machiavellian maneuvers because she has invested no value in the past or future: having been forced to marry a man she didn't love, she erases the past by refusing to reflect on it or even to acknowledge her lover, Balgobin (her husband's brother), who lives in the same estate; she suppresses the future by seeing herself as living solely for Romesh. It is not by accident that it is Balgobin and Romesh who have to bear the pain and burden of Seeta's genealogy and modernity. Although Balgobin is sick and dying, "his thoughts wandered over the past, and he thought of the future, too" (p. 100); and Romesh has to struggle to make sense of Seeta's secret past—to discover the identity of his real father—while struggling to come to terms with the future his mother has invented for him.

But like Tiger in the other novels, Romesh discovers that a concrete knowledge of the past does not make the future clearer, nor does it resolve the subject's crisis of selfhood; he concludes that if the future is to have any meaning and truly belong to him, then it must be detached from the past and the present. He perceives the death of his father as a moment when all notions of time—as a continuum in which past, present, and future are joined by a common thread of identity and experience—can actually be foreclosed from his consciousness. The funeral of his real father hence creates a historical tabula rasa: "It might be the funeral of a stranger for all he knew about his father. He had no desire to speculate, to wonder what life might have been had he known, if things could have been much different" (p. 138). Here, Selvon might not be asserting that the past has no value for Caribbean peoples, but in trying to develop a hermeneutics of Caribbean modernity, he seems to suggest that the future cannot be built on what has already been because we would then be repeating the original errors of "discovery" and "conquest." Selvon's novels hence foreground and sustain the problematic of the Caribbean's compromised beginnings and the islands' struggle to emerge from European doctrines of history and the modern.

4

The Deformation of Modernism: The Allegory of History in Carpentier's *El siglo de las luces*

> The American novelist, whatever the cultural zone he belongs to, is not at all in search of a lost time, but finds himself struggling in the confusion of time. And, from Faulkner to Carpentier, we are faced with apparent snatches of time that have been sucked into banked up or swirling forces.
>
> —Edouard Glissant, *Caribbean Discourse*

> There is nothing absolutely primary to interpret because at bottom all is already interpretation, each sign is in itself not the thing which offers itself to interpretation, but the interpretation of other signs.
>
> —Michel Foucault, "Nietzsche, Freud, Marx"

The agonizing about selfhood, language, and identity which dominates the texts discussed in the previous pages has deeper roots than the issues of exile and displacement I have chosen to foreground—it originates from a larger Caribbean concern with historiography and the problem of what I have called the narrative of history. As Glissant has observed in his limpid discussion of temporality in the novel of the Americas, New World writers, irrespective of the cultural spaces they occupy, have been compelled to deal with the anxiety of time, the meaning of spatial reality, and the implications of memory as it affects narration; thus in the works of American novelists "we must struggle against time in order to reconstitute the past."[1] While the relationship between narration and the temporal process is a generic characteristic of the novel, New World writers, especially those in the colonized sectors, have often confronted Eurocentric notions of time as a way of questioning or subverting the European episteme. For Glissant and his contemporaries, this confrontation with time, and the rejection of the temporal process as it has been defined in European historiography, is a precondition for the Caribbean irruption into modernity.

Indeed, according to Glissant, the temporal anxiety that characterizes most Caribbean texts is a reaction to the Eurocentric and colonial notion of a "single History," a notion imposed on the Caribbean as a condition of the Western will to power in the conquered space.[2] To reject the singularity of history and the configuration of power embedded in it, Caribbean writers have also had to struggle to evolve narrative forms that assert a decolonized temporality and evolve a decolonized version of history. In seeking to narrate a modern Caribbean culture, one liberated from both the European conquerors and their allies, the planter class, Caribbean writers such as Alejo Carpentier and Paule Marshall have selected historiography and the drama of history as the terrain of cultural resistance; these writers seek to regenerate memory and to make it generate meanings for the present. For both Carpentier and Marshall, what is at stake in the Caribbean narrative of history and its corollary issues of experience and representation is the form and design of the chronicle of the Americas and the character of its subject. As Carpentier observed in the 1949 prologue to *The Kingdom of This World*, written after a visit to Haiti, because of the formation of its landscape, its ontology, "the presence of Indian and Black," and "because of the fecund mestizajes that it propagated," the American landscape has yet to exhaust its "mythological mine"; what is the history of all America "if not a chronicle of magic realism?"[3]

At the heart of Carpentier's notion of magic realism, as in the aesthetic of the Haitian novelist Jacques Stephen Alexis who evokes a similar figure to characterize Caribbean writing, is the belief that the West Indian landscape proffers literary forms that deform the rationality and chronology embedded in colonial doctrines of modern-

---

1. Edouard Glissant, *Caribbean Discourse: Selected Essays*, trans. J. Michael Dash (Charlottesville: University Press of Virginia, 1989), p. 145.
2. Glissant, p. 93.
3. Alejo Carpentier, "Preface," *El reino de este mundo* (Mexico City: E.D.I.A.P.S.A., 1949), p. 5.

ism. In fact, to comprehend the longing for a literary style that might challenge rationalized discourse, we need to recall that for writers like Carpentier and Alexis, colonial modernism was defined by an authoritarian grip on the historical process and the subjection of culture and temporality to the political economy of the plantation. Time and culture, in the world of the "sugarocracy," were overdetermined by the technology of sugar production and its demands on slave labor. As Manuel Moreno Fraginals has observed in *The Sugarmill*, his historical study of the Cuban sugarocracy, the Caribbean planter class held up technological advances and the maximization of profits as marks of its modernity. Thus Arango y Parreno, a leading member of the Cuban planter class, would be confident enough to posit the future as "the time when the wealth of the island will multiply and it will have five or six hundred thousand Africans within its shores."[4] The unprecedented merger of slave labor and new technology, reports Moreno Fraginals, was "the sugarocracy's proof to the metropolis and to themselves that the future held unsuspected possibilities and that they belonged to that future—and the proof was in solid cash."[5]

In their drive to claim and surpass European modernity, especially as it was defined by the Enlightenment, the planter class would seek to control the past as a way of mastering the future, a future in which everything was subservient to sugar production. As Roberto Gonzalez Echevarria points out, in order to increase sugar production—the source of the cash that guaranteed them the future—Cuban planters could even claim the power to measure time: "There was a day of rest every tenth day instead of every seventh. The sugar industry altered, therefore, the perception of time, the liturgical way of encompassing it, and the rhythm of life for entire groups of individuals, both black and white."[6] And when it came to the writing of history, the planter class had no use for memories that predated the rationalization of sugar production; for them, Moreno Fraginals says, everything important in Cuba happened "with sugar and sugarmen; with them, history began. Erasing the past was also a spiritual revolution against the pattern set by the old noble families."[7]

What the planters did not allow for, and this is the central subject of

4. Quoted by Manuel Moreno Fraginals, *The Sugar Mill: The Socioeconomic Complex of Sugar in Cuba* (New York: Monthly Review Press, 1976), p. 13.
5. Moreno Fraginals, p. 59.
6. Roberto Gonzalez Echevarria, "Literature of the Hispanic Caribbean," *Latin American Literary Review* 8 (Spring–Summer 1980), 2.
7. Moreno Fraginals, p. 59.

Carpentier's novel as a critique of "the age of the Enlightenment," is that such commodified and Eurocentric notions of modernism were being challenged by African slaves even as they were being instituted by the planters. If the planters sought to elevate the commodity above culture, the Africans would adopt and consolidate their cultural practices as a weapon of resistance, "a weapon to save their bodies from destruction and their souls from extinction," says Gonzalez Echevarria.[8] If the planter class operated on the basic premise that their culture was an extension of Europe, the slaves functioned within a subtext whose language and desires echoed Africa. The resulting contending views of culture and history would become evident in the Caribbean during the revolutionary period marking the transition from the eighteenth to the nineteenth century. During this period, as C. L. R. James dramatizes so vividly in *The Black Jacobins*, his classic history of the Haitian Revolution, even history itself was contradictory and contested, subject to suffixes that were going to shape the future of the Caribbean.[9] The sugarocracy would embrace the French Revolution because it would liberate them from the tyranny of the old nobility, but they could not espouse the extension of the ideals of liberty and equality to the slaves who produced their wealth. In temporal terms, as the Cuban novelist Miguel Barnet has observed, the planter "had one foot in the bourgeois future and the other in the slave past. In this vacillating position he aspired, on the one hand, to the highest bourgeois conquests, all the superstructure made possible by free production; and on the other hand, he wanted to retain the protective shield of the slavemaster."[10]

For the African slaves, in contrast, the French Revolution simultaneously promoted the rhetoric of freedom and the reality of historical stasis; therefore, this European event had to be subjected to a black reversal that would deny its claim to be a universal movement toward a perfect society. In Carpentier's novels, notes Gonzalez Echevarria, the blacks "upset history; they question its central tenets or, better yet, the myths about its centrality."[11] Pursuing this argument, my thesis in

8. Gonzalez Echevarria, "Literature of the Hispanic Caribbean," p. 2.
9. C. L. R. James, *The Black Jacobins: Toussaint L'Ouverture and the San Domingo Revolution* (New York: Vintage, 1963).
10. Miguel Barnet, "The Culture That Sugar Created," *Latin American Literary Review* 8 (Spring–Summer 1980), 40.
11. Gonzalez Echevarria, "Socrates among the Weeds: Blacks and History in Carpentier's *Explosion in a Cathedral*," in *Voices from Under: Black Narrative in Latin America and the Caribbean*, ed. William Luis (Westport, Conn.: Greenwood, 1984), p. 42.

this chapter is that in *El siglo de las luces*, the dominant European discourse is drawn into the Caribbean archipelago, but its central doctrine (in this case the Enlightenment) is systematically denigrated. The Caribbean intellectual (Esteban) is placed in the European "circus of civilization" (the French Revolution) to test its modernist claim to have ushered society into a previously unknown period of freedom and happiness, but he returns home disillusioned with European notions of temporality and the project of modernity itself. As a result, the Caribbean subject is forced to turn inward, to seek what Bell Gale Chevigny calls an American hermeneutics—"a means of interpreting America and an American way of interpreting."[12]

Significantly, in re-presenting the European intellectual adventure as it plays itself out in the Caribbean, Carpentier does not aim to enhance the official doctrines of historical continuity and renewal which were favored by the Cuban planter class as it sought to show how Caribbean colonial societies could regenerate the European tradition in the islands. Rather, Carpentier's text foregrounds the discontinuity and retardation of European history in the Caribbean and its eventual collapse in the Antillean landscape. The degeneration of European history (and historiography) in the West Indies is here proposed as a precondition for a new Caribbean episteme: at the moment when European forms collapse, the colonized writer rewrites American realities anew. At this juncture, says Carpentier, Latin American and Caribbean novelists "have to name everything—everything that defines, involves and surrounds us; everything that operates with a contextual power."[13]

Gonzalez Echevarria has rightly noted that history is the main topic of Carpentier's fiction, "and the history he deals with—the history of the Caribbean—is one of beginnings or foundations."[14] But it is important to remember that Carpentier is not concerned with beginnings and foundations because he begins with a "primary vision of History," as J. Labanyi has argued, nor does he start with a basic conception of

12. Bell Gale Chevigny, "Unsatiable Unease: Melville and Carpentier and the Search for an American Hermeneutics," in *Reinventing the Americas: Comparative Studies of Literature of the United States and Spanish America*, ed. Bell Gale Chevigny and Gari Laguardia (New York: Cambridge University Press, 1985), p. 36.

13. Alejo Carpentier, "Problematica de la actual novela latinoamericano," in *Tientos y diferencias* (Montevideo: Editorial Arca, 1967), p. 37.

14. Roberto Gonzalez Echevarria, *Alejo Carpentier: The Pilgrim at Home* (Ithaca: Cornell University Press, 1977), p. 25. My reading of Carpentier and his place in Caribbean (and American) modernity is heavily indebted to Gonzalez Echevarria's works.

reality.[15] Rather, his discourse on history is informed by a keen awareness that Caribbean history in the post-discovery period is already a
pre-interpreted sign. In other words, American reality is never conceived as a natural experience—although nature does play an important role in the novel—but as what Gonzalez Echevarria calls the
"actualization of a fiction; the founding of a world that had its origins
in books before it became a concrete and tangible *terra firma*."[16] Thus
the "aura of ambiguity which pervades the work" sustains a doubleness that is implicit in Caribbean historicity: Carpentier writes about
European modernity to debunk it; he adopts the language of Western
modernism to expose its theoretical estrangement in the Caribbean
landscape.[17] More significant, ambiguity and allegory are forms of
dispersal which, by presenting the reader with a double structure,
create doubts about the European drive toward rationalization and
systematic representation. In this novel, asserts Gonzalez Echevarria
in a keen turn of phrase, Carpentier "problematizes the idea of modernity by its own apparently anachronistic form."[18]

Furthermore, Carpentier's novel does not merely seek to reverse the
European drive toward systematization, but also to represent what
Frederico de Onis calls the two "spiritually contradictory worlds" of
the Caribbean at the turn of the eighteenth century.[19] By confronting
European historiography and theories on human nature with a Caribbean archeology and archive, Carpentier triggers a narrative process
that subverts the premise that rationality liberates the individual and
enriches everyday social life; what the Enlightenment casts as a totality
of culture is exposed as a fragment suspended in a temporal void
somewhere between Europe and the Caribbean. This temporal suspension between Europe and its other generates Carpentier's text and
also conditions our reading of the novel.

15. J. Labanyi, "Nature and the Historical Process in Carpentier's *El siglo de las luces*,"
Bulletin of Hispanic Studies 57 (October 1980), 56.

16. Gonzalez Echevarria, *Alejo Carpentier*, p. 28.

17. See Mary A. Kilmer-Tchalekian, "Ambiguity in *El siglo de las luces*," *Latin American
Literary Review* 4 (Spring–Summer 1976), 48.

18. Gonzalez Echevarria, *Alejo Carpentier*, p. 226. The anachronistic forms of modernism are
discussed by Manfredo Tafuri, *Architecture and Utopia: Design and Capitalist Development*, trans.
Barbara Luigia La Penta (Cambridge: MIT Press, 1976), pp. 7, 10, and 14; and Jürgen Habermas, "Modernity—An Incomplete Project," in *The Anti-Aesthetic: Essays on Postmodern Culture*,
ed. Hal Foster (Port Townsend, Wash.: Bay Press, 1983), p. 9.

19. Frederico de Onis, "Introduction," in *Latin America and the Enlightenment*, ed. Arthur P.
Whitaker (Ithaca: Cornell University Press, 1969), p. xii.

The Architecture of the Future

Nowhere is this temporal suspense—which is manifest on both the ideological and narrative levels—as vividly illustrated as in the enigmatic prologue to *El siglo*, which defies both the European Enlightenment's desire for totality and all established notions about closure and beginnings as privileged moments of interpretation in the novel.[20] The opening of the novel—"I saw them erect the guillotine again tonight"—already calls attention to Carpentier's use of repetition and doubleness. The use of the first person pronoun foregrounds a clearly defined narrator and subject; but even after reading this introductory fragment several times, the reader will not discover who the speaker is or his or her position in the text. Furthermore, while the authority of homodiegetic narrators derives from a certain appeal to the authority of personal experience and position, the "I" here displaces his or her own knowledge not only by appealing to shifting figures of speech, to which no determinate meanings can be affixed, but also by stressing contradictions.

This sense of indeterminacy is further exemplified in the initial portrait of the guillotine. In revolutionary France, the guillotine is generally considered to be a very transparent symbol of death and revolutionary violence; in the prologue to Carpentier's text, however, this symbol generates contradictory meanings. The guillotine is first compared to "a doorway opening on to the immense sky" and to the "scents of the land"; it reads like an object whose meanings are fixed in time and space (p. 7). But almost immediately the narrator questions this meaning, asserting that although the time in which the guillotine stands is fixed ("Time stood"), it is a time unknown; temporality is fixed in constellations that "I do not know, for it is not my job to know." This situation of undecidability is further underscored by the narrator's assertion that the objects she or he observes shuffle "the allegories they symbolize" (p. 7).

This combination of symbol and allegory is important because, in their traditional definition, the two figures posit two distinct modes of

20. I use the English edition retitled *Explosion in a Cathedral*, trans. John Sturrock (New York: Harper, 1963), and refer to the original text of *El siglo de las luces* (Barcelona: Biblioteca de Bolsillo, 1983). I use the Spanish title (which can be translated as "the century of light") because of its ironic implication. Further references, which are in the text, are from the English translation.

representation. The structure of the symbol is synecdochical because it is, in Paul de Man's famous definition, "a part of the totality that it represents," whereas allegory is a figure of difference in the sense that it points to the disjunctive relationship between subject and object.[21] In Carpentier's prologue, linguistic figures seem to symbolize because they denote a certain kind of unity between signs and signifiers and hence present the possibility of being known. But as we will see later in this chapter, the subject's decision to allegorize such objects casts doubts on the values we would like to attach to them. As a symbol, the guillotine is a "doorway" to something else—it appears as a "solitary skeleton" rising above the crew "like a presence, a warning, which concerned us all equally" (p. 7). Indeed, in its European connotation, in which it is associated with the French Revolution and the Modern Age, the meaning of the guillotine, in de Man's words," is founded on an intimate unity between the image that rises up before the senses and the supersensory totality that the image suggests."[22]

But once it has been cast in the Caribbean context, the guillotine has already become a sinister abstraction, a sign with no Caribbean signified; it appears to the viewer as a "guide," as "some gigantic instrument of navigation" defined by its absences, by its deviation from the European norm—"no banners, drums and crowds attended it here; it was not the object of the emotions, fury, weeping, drunkenness, of those who had surrounded it like the chorus in a Greek tragedy" (p. 7). In this second sense, the guillotine is an allegorical sign because, to borrow de Man's theoretical formulation, it does not postulate "the possibility of an identity or identification" but designates "a distance in relation to its own origin, and renouncing the nostalgia and the desire to coincide, it establishes its language in the void of this temporal difference."[23]

This allegorization of events and objects, as we discover later in the novel, manifests Esteban's rejection of the revolutionary rhetoric that had attracted him to Europe in his youthful innocence; it is a projection of his desire to renounce the Enlightenment ideals of reason and progress which had drawn him to Europe. Thus, the privileged moment of reading and entry into *El siglo*—and, by implication, an important instance of Caribbean modernism—is the ironic and allegorical

21. Paul de Man, "The Rhetoric of Temporality," in *Blindness and Insight* (Minneapolis: University of Minnesota Press, 1983), pp. 191, 207.
22. De Man, p. 189.
23. De Man, p. 207.

moment when the subject discovers the gap between a European sign and a Caribbean signifier and thus finds it impossible to identify with his previous constitutive categories. The moment of writing, and thus also of reading, is neither the beginning nor the end of a historical period in the Caribbean, but a hiatus, a moment of silence—"that silence which a man thinks of as a silence because he can hear no other voice like his own. A vital silence, full of a steady throbbing, and not, as yet, the silence of the lifeless corpse" (p. 8). History has evacuated the spaces previously occupied by European discourse, and silence has replaced the already uttered.

Still, a more fundamental question is raised by Carpentier's decision to open his novel with a middle rather than a beginning or ending: Does time have any constitutive value here? Can we make any fundamental distinctions between past, present, and future? In his influential reading of this novel, Gonzalez Echevarria has established a common tendency to see Carpentier's decision to open with Esteban's monologue as a way of reclaiming the future for the past, so that "temporality, in the guise of an ever present future, dissolves any possibility of fixed meanings," and the historical narrative is "always in the future: at the moment when history and its outcome are one."[24] While I share Gonzalez Echevarria's first assertion—there is no doubt Carpentier devalorizes temporal moments to dissolve meanings that are imposed on the Caribbean from outside—his valorization of a future "when history and its outcome are one" is based on a questionable association of the beginning of the novel with a future in which suspended meanings are achieved. In contrast, what I find fascinating about Carpentier's treatment of Esteban's desire for meanings is precisely his emphasis on temporal discontinuity and the total collapse or reversal of the terms that usually demarcate time, namely *past, present,* and *future.*

The end result is the negation of chronology, teleology, and historical closure. While most of the monumental changes affecting the Caribbean in the eighteenth century—the French Revolution, the Haitian Revolution, and the Counter-Revolution—are dramatized in the novel, on a deeper level things remain the same. What is important in this context is that both past and future are cast "in a new light."[25] Indeed, although Esteban rewrites the Caribbean experience from the

24. Gonzalez Echevarria, *Alejo Carpentier,* pp. 235–36.
25. See de Onis, p. xi.

vantage point of his (post)European experiences—from a perspective of disillusionment and dystopia—there is a sense in which his basic strategies of representation have not changed. True, the Esteban who returns from Europe in the prologue seems to be a radical skeptic who allegorizes experiences to deny them their authority; as the example of the guillotine shows, he specializes in showing how each phenomenon contains the possibility of another, opposed meaning. And yet, the same will to allegorization is evident in his childhood. Indeed, even a cursory glance at chapter 1 shows Esteban's inclination to represent things in a disjunctive manner: he sees the city as "a gigantic baroque chandelier" defined by a jumble of colors, architectural styles and incompleteness (p. 11). So the very crisis of meaning that will haunt Esteban in later life is also apparent in his youth. What needs to be stressed here, though, is that this crisis of meaning is clearly tied to the colonial Cuban bourgeoisie's ideology of progress, which has not been able to harmonize the desire for modernity with feudal modes of production.

In many instances, Carpentier uses architectural dissonance to underscore, or even signalize, the gap between the sugarocracy's desire for European forms and the persistent hold of the old Caribbean political economy. Indeed, at every stage in the novel, an adoption of European modes of existence or representation—of which the architecture is a synecdoche—is often threatened by the "other" fragment, the form the dominant ideology seeks to exclude. Thus in Havana "the palaces proudly displayed their splendid columns and coats of arms carved in stone; during the rainy months they rose out of the mud which clung like an incurable disease to their masonry"; and "those manorial houses could not escape the primeval slime" (p. 12). The collision between the palaces built to imitate European forms and the rain and slime that are native to Cuba is an appropriate image of the temporal division that defines Caribbean colonial culture.

The architecture—and the social schizophrenia it signifies—have their linguistic counterpart in what Chevigny calls the "divided mother tongue"; American writing has to negotiate a split between the grammar of the New World and the lexicon of the European mother tongue, and thus "the problematic negotiation of the relationship between originality and imitation may be seen as a synecdoche for the negotiation of independence from Europe."[26] This issue is evident in Carlos's

26. Chevigny, p. 36.

148

ideology: as the heir apparent to the plantation system, he strives both to be loyal to the family tradition and to experiment with new forms. Thus he is able to indulge in his music—and hence sustain "an illusion of independence" from the plantation system, which frowns on such leisure—while he is economically sustained by his father's "uncultured" mercantile system. With the death of the father, however, the son must redefine his own relationship with both the past and the future.

Moreover, if we assume that the authority of tradition—and hence the power of fixed and inherited meanings—is derived from the father, then it is appropriate that Carpentier initiates his discourse on Caribbean modernism with the death of the family patriarch, a gesture that foregrounds the crisis of foundations and beginnings which, as I have argued in previous chapters, is a central issue of Caribbean writing. In this novel, the death of the father exposes the anachronism and limits of planter modernity in the Caribbean. This crisis is notable for the way the father's death disrupts the son's superstructure and the illusion that sustains it: "His father's death was going to deprive him of everything he enjoyed, side-tracking his plans, cutting him off from his dreams. He would be condemned to look after the business" (p. 13). In a sense, Carlos is forced to confront the dehumanizing commodities (tobacco, sugar, and slavery) that make bourgeois culture, and its ideology, delectable.

The need to confront the material sources of culture and leisure is important to the redefinition of colonial society because before the revolutionary period it was possible for members of the plantocracy to foreground elements of European "high culture" (such as the opera) as marks of "civilization," while the real source of power for this class (the commodity) was veiled and masked. Forced by the death of his father to face reality, Carlos realizes that it is indeed the commodity that defines Cuban culture and that his music is out of place here (p. 14). Moreover, the death of the father exposes the great mythology of colonial modernism—the belief, propagated by the sugarocracy, that advance in technology and exchange relations constitute the advent of a new age. On the contrary, Carlos sees himself not at the dawn of a new age, but "wrapped prematurely in a shroud fashioned by the stench of beef, onions and brine, the victim of a father who he reproached . . . for the crime of having died too soon" (p. 14).

But if Carpentier is here rejecting the Cuban bourgeoisie's notion of its own modernity, it is not because he wants to define the events that

149

dominate his text (the Enlightenment and the French Revolution) as the doorway to the modern age. On the contrary, the first sections of the book are structured to underscore the doubleness of temporality and its representative figures, and to question modernity's investment in a future beyond the constrains of contemporary history. Thus, as we have already seen, the guillotine is both a doorway, an opening to a new epoch, and a figure of death. Similarly, the legal "Executor" is introduced as a surrogate father, but he also prefigures Victor Hugues and the real "executioners" who carry out death sentences in the name of revolution. The same kind of semantic doubleness surrounds the family patriarch: he is eulogized as "a dearly beloved father, a mirror of goodness and an exemplary man" (p. 16) even as his death grants his children a "sensual feeling of freedom" (p. 17); he is perceived as the man who kept the house in order, but on his death, the house is shown to be a place in decay. Later, of course, the father's piety will also be discredited when his sexual exploits are disclosed (p. 45).

In addition, Carpentier's text systematically deconstructs any doctrine of temporal progression, particularly any notion that value is invested in the future. Indeed, as Gonzalez Echevarria aptly states, the future evoked in the novel is characterized by "its quality of being simultaneously a past."[27] European modernity, formulated by the philosophers of the Enlightenment as the drive toward "objective science, universal morality and law" demands a clear demarcation between past and future; according to Habermas, the term *modern* "again and again expresses the consciousness of an epoch that relates itself to the past of antiquity, in order to view itself as the result of a transition from the old to the new."[28] *El siglo* treats modernity's "rhetoric of temporality" ironically, especially its claim to break from the past and hence transcend previous historical categories; but for this irony to be effective, an illusion of temporal transition must initially be set up and sustained.

Indeed, before Victor comes knocking on the door, ushering in the modern period, the three heirs—now released from the authority of the dead patriarch—have rejected temporality and returned to an earlier phase of history (pp. 24–25). Now they live in a hermetic pre-Enlightenment world which still invests value in Archimedean science, natural history, and mythology: "Everything was transformed

27. Gonzalez Echevarria, *Alejo Carpentier*, p. 234.
28. Habermas, p. 3.

into a perpetual game which established them at one more remove from the outside world, within the arbitrary counterpoint afforded by lives led on three different planes" (p. 27). The crucial phrase here is "arbitrary counterpoint" ("arbitrario contrapunto"), for it suggests that the heirs have adopted a mode of life which does not merely reflect their desire for sensual freedom, but is also built against reason or the law, two central tenets in the world that is soon going to overtake them. *Arbitrario* suggests liberation from tradition and institutions, while *contrapunto* denotes that which has been added to the already existing, contrasting the original force, but also balancing it. Thus the first term connotes rebellion, but the second places this rebellion squarely in the world that is being rejected.

It is this arbitrariness of transformation which Gonzalez Echevarria seems to have in mind when he argues that *El siglo* is situated in "a counterpoint between self-conscious modernities: the Enlightenment's and our own."[29] Indeed, this counter-point could also be read as what de Man has called "the curiously contradictory way" in which modernity and history relate to each other, a relationship that goes well beyond "antithesis or opposition": "If history is not to become sheer regression or paralysis, it depends on modernity for its duration or renewal; but modernity cannot assert itself without being at once swallowed up and integrated into a regressive historical process."[30]

Modernity, History, and Repression

Once it has been drawn into the swirling forces of the Caribbean landscape and the domain of the colonial repressed, European history cannot escape from the regression embedded in its structures, despite its constant evocation of modernity. Moreover, rather than renewing temporal progression, the French Revolution will be shown to be a moment of repression and paralysis. As one character in the novel aptly notes, "We live in an illogical world. Before the Revolution a slave-trader sailed these seas, owned by a *philosophie* and a friend of Jean-Jacques. And do you know what she was called? The *Contract Social*" (p. 189). Interestingly enough, it is in the middle of a text with an indeterminate beginning and ending that the ironic dimensions of

29. Gonzalez Echevarria, *Alejo Carpentier*, p. 226.
30. De Man, "Literary History and Literary Modernity," in *Blindness and Insight*, p. 151.

the new age ushered in by the Enlightenment and the French Revolution become apparent. Functionaries of the revolution such as Victor Hugues might be deceived into believing that the ideal of modernity moves history into a utopian future in which authority will be restored to the individual and the rights given to people by nature will be recuperated; the philosophers of the age might even be deluded into believing that modern history follows a logical temporal arc. But once this history is transferred to the Caribbean, the tension between history and modernity is so obvious that the reader cannot be deceived by the claims of a logic that sustains its coherence through omission. Even at that moment in the novel when Victor comes knocking at the door of the dead patriarch in Havana and announces the arrival of the new age, the rhetoric that the text promotes questions historicity and makes it ironic, debunks the central tenets of the Enlightenment, and appeals to a new Caribbean economy of representation built around difference and dispersal.

In effect, modern history enters the text as a process of displacement and duplicity, rupture and discontinuity. Just before Victor enters the house, Sofia has comfortably developed her own peculiar relationship to things; but Victor, who conceives himself as the agent of history and modernity, disturbs this relationship and thus functions as a *contrapunto*. And yet it is this disturbance that makes her aware of her historicity; she becomes conscious of the arbitrariness of history and what Michel Foucault would call its "duplicated representation"—the consciousness that "the relation of the sign to its content is not guaranteed by the order of things in themselves."[31] In addition, while the heirs had appealed to an order of nature, experience, or exchange to define their position in the world of things, either for or against such things, with the entrance of Victor, we are told, "words were divorced from things. Each of them spoke out of a mouth which did not belong to him, even though it might be opening above his own chin" (p. 47). What we see developing in the narrative of history at this juncture is an arbitrary space in which the value of things is not sanctioned by a resemblance to words, or signs, or thoughts, but by the relation of signs to signs, or the dissociation of characters from the things that define them.

For example, after the servant Remegio discloses the patriarch's

---

31. Michel Foucault, *The Order of Things: An Archeology of the Human Sciences* (New York: Vintage, 1973), p. 63.

sexual "sins," Sofia is forced to admit that she has never loved her father anyway; having dissociated herself from the patriarchal regimen of meaning she "felt alienated, estranged from herself, as if she were standing on a new epoch of change" (p. 47). Indeed, she stands at the threshold of a new century, one in which things will not really change—as the bulk of the text confirms—but also one in which the characters' modes of mediation and signification are radically altered. For both Sofia and Esteban, then, things acquire value through the figures and signs that mediate them: schooners take shape on chest drawers (p. 47) and pictures seem to speak "another language" (p. 48), a language of figuration rather than the language of calculation which rules Victor's life. What guarantees the value and relationship of such signs which are now dissociated from the real world of historical change and progress? Indeed, what guarantees the value and validity of temporality and history?

In truth, Esteban's "maturation" already draws our attention to the mixed terms that denote temporality in the novel: "By re-ascending the ladder of time Esteban had given back their true meaning to the hours that had been reversed by the habits of the household" (p. 49). This assertion is, however, enigmatic: how does an ascendance recover original meanings, especially when such meanings have already been reversed? Clearly, in this narrative, what side is up, what is natural or normal, have become questionable terms, surrounded by a linguistic playfulness that questions any notions of sequential temporality or ordered referentiality. For example, after a cyclone that leaves the city in ruins, Sofia walks about the family warehouse "dazed" by "the unusualness of a situation which had disorganised the normal order of things and established a chaos in the rooms reminiscent of the past" (p. 60). But if we recall that what Sofia bemoans as "the normal order of things" is already the disorganization of an organization imposed on her by Victor (the situation is referred to as "desorganizado lo organizado" in the Spanish text), then we become skeptical of any claims to a normal order of things. What is normal or abnormal is determined by a relationship of ideas in the subject's mind.

Carpentier's text has brought us to the kind of representative situation formulated by Foucault in *The Order of Things*: "The relation of the sign to the signified now resides in a space in which there is no longer any intermediary figure to connect them: what connects them is a bond established, inside knowledge, between the *idea of one thing* and

153

the *idea of another.*"[32] The revolutionary age strives to make a connection between the ideas of renewal, youth, and historical transformation; but the text, by pointing to the gap between the "idea" and the "thing," underscores the "atmosphere of unreality" in which the colonial modernist project is predicated. The novel also takes up time and space, two important categories of European modernism, and exposes them not as agents of freedom but as commodified forms. In this respect, the novel raises the question of what the social theorist Anthony Giddens calls "commodified time-space" as a central problem in the modernist economy of representation. In this situation modernism is shown as "neither only a protest against lost traditions, nor an endorsement of their dissolution, but in some degree an accurate expression of the 'emptying' of time-space."[33]

Carpentier's thematic concern with the commodification and colonization of geographical and temporal spaces is brilliantly illustrated through the figure of Victor, who functions in the novel as the modern hero, what Walter Benjamin once called "the true subject of modernism."[34] For in whatever guise we encounter him (as liberator, revolutionary, or reactionary), Victor constantly reminds us that the central problem of Caribbean culture is the imposition of meanings by the European other. We are told that he is memorable for "his dominant anxiety to impose his own opinion and convictions" (p. 31), or for the power he has "to transform reality"; in fact, he is often described as an ideological conjurer (p. 76). The contradictions that define Victor's relationship with his age are both a reflection of the consciousness of the planter bourgeoisie as it enters the new age and an indication of the epistemology of the eighteenth century. Described as a man of "indeterminate age," Victor is, nonetheless, deterministic—his ideological drive is to rationalize nature and to impose a new system of representation in which the discordant figures and thoughts of the age are formalized into a rational system.

Victor's political economy draws on the modern world system as if to affirm his commitment to doctrines of progress: "He talked of the coral forests of the Bermudas; of the wealth of Baltimore; of Mardi gras in New Orleans, just like that in Paris" (p. 32). The universalism Victor

---

32. Foucault, p. 63.

33. Anthony Giddens, "Modernism and Post-Modernism," *New German Critique* 22 (Winter 1981), 16.

34. Walter Benjamin, *Charles Baudelaire: A Lyrical Poet in the Era of High Capitalism*, trans. Harry Zohn (London: NLB, 1973), p. 74.

exhibits throughout the novel is matched only by his desire to manage time and manipulate space to secure his power over others and to legitimize his image as the new rational man. But Victor is also a contradiction in terms: although he owns slaves in Guadeloupe, it is he who introduces the notion of the equality of races into the Cuban merchant's house (p. 43); he bestows "the stature of a woman" on Sofia (p. 57) and gives her words new meaning (p. 58), but he also sets out to usurp the position of the dead family patriarch. So, as the narrative unfolds, we realize that Victor's claim to originality is suspect: his blind revolutionary zeal is exposed as a form of mimicry and his integrity is questioned by his acts (pp. 126, 190, 322).

Victor is crucial to Carpentier's deconstruction and deformation of colonial modernism in the Caribbean for another reason—he draws the reader's attention to the problem European systems of meaning encounter as soon as they have been transferred into the margins of the New World economic system. As a representative of the planter modernists, Victor encounters the European epistemology at that temporal juncture at which, according to Foucault, it begins to question its own prehistory, when the "space of old" is shattered. An ambiguous configuration is established between "organic structures" and "representation" as a temporal process in which things address themselves "to a subjectivity, a consciousness, a singular effort of cognition, to the 'psychological' individual who from the depth of his own history, or on the basis of tradition handed on to him, is trying to know."[35] The tension between the shattered "space of old" and the new "man" who needs to order things to "know" is poignant in El siglo.

Throughout Carpentier's novel, the shattering of the old spaces is dramatized by the French Revolution, which masquerades as an unprecedented historical event; but this shattering gesture has already been prefigured by the painting—"Explosion in a Cathedral"—which dominates the text. The painting is variously described as "the apocalyptic immobilisation of a catastrophe," as "a great colonnade shattering into fragments in mid-air," and as "this illustration of the End of Time" (pp. 18, 19). And yet, against this ambivalent code—a constant reminder that temporality itself has been broken up—the people who constitute themselves at the beginning of the nineteenth century strive to rationalize, to reorder things, so that they can establish their uniqueness in the precariousness of things. Here the central question posed

35. Foucault, p. 240.

by Carpentier's text is whether the "modern" Caribbean subject is produced by a new historical context, functions in a tabula rasa, or is simply a consequence of the reworking of the already-written and already-begun world of "labour, life and language."[36]

Victor begins with the second option: by using trade to challenge the existing system of exchange, the self fights the tyranny of the old system of domination and thereby engenders itself. "One had to begin somewhere, because people here seemed to be asleep, inert, living in a timeless marginal world, suspended between tobacco and sugar," Victor tells Sofia (p. 69). But if Victor seeks to establish a new master version of history, one that draws its authority and contents from the doctrines of the French Revolution and the Enlightenment, the text valorizes the conflicting meanings of history by immediately promoting an alternative version of the American experience. In this instance, Victor returns to his base in Haiti to discover that the black slaves have risen in revolt, destroyed his property, and begun to reorder history: "His life was reduced to a cypher, without promises to fulfill, without debts to pay, suspended between a past which had been destroyed and a future it was impossible to foresee" (p. 87). Now released from the tyranny of property, Victor believes he can use his own labor, rather than inherited wealth, to "reconstruct" himself from nothing; and in keeping with the doctrine of the Enlightenment, he equates engenderment with self-knowledge and posits both as the keys to individual and autonomous action.

As a disciple of the Enlightenment, Victor promotes self-knowledge because it is supposed to draw on the practical experience of the individual rather than on inherited meanings; in the thinking of this period, Lucien Goldmann once wrote, self-knowledge is not regarded "as something whose content is determined by the collective action of mankind in history."[37] True, Victor will always represent his dubious revolutionary fervor as the triumph of the collective will, but he will also cast himself as the hero fulfilling a mission against the claims of history. Ultimately, Victor's belief that the revolution restores authority to the individual is questioned rigorously by a narratorial voice that constantly contests the hero's rhetoric of revolution and foregrounds its precarious representative authority. Thus, while Victor and Ogé

36. Foucault, p. 330.
37. Lucien Goldmann, *The Philosophy of the Enlightenment* (London: Routledge, 1973), p. 2. For Enlightenment theories of history and reason, see Goldmann, p. 35, and Frank E. Manuel, *The Age of Reason* (Ithaca: Cornell University Press, 1951).

introduce the revolution as a natural and universal phenomenon that follows a temporal sequence—"The Revolution is on the march and no one can stop it" (p. 69)—the "majesty of tone" in which this claim is represented creates suspicion in the reader's mind. Even young Esteban can already tell that a gap exists between "authoritative" statements about the revolution and the thing they are supposed to signify: "And this Revolution, thought Esteban, had been reduced to four lines of news about France, published in the local paper between a theatre programme and an advertisement for a sale of guitars" (p. 70).

Indeed, the more Victor and Ogé expostulate about the revolution, the more precarious their representative authority becomes: their exposition is "muddled" and "reckless," painted in colors that are lurid and yet so detached from their referent that utterances about the revolution end up being forms of projection. As a result, the revolution is reduced to a spectacle in which the self can project its own needs and desires: "To talk revolutions, to imagine revolutions, to place oneself mentally in the midst of a revolution, is in some small degree to become master of the world" (p. 71).

Given the central place of revolutionary rhetoric in the novel, many commentators have written about the fundamental link between temporality and the French Revolution: Labanyi sees the revolution as "the mainspring of the historical process," while Mary Kilmer-Tchalekian sees it as both a European "historical enterprise" and a more universal "cyclical renewal of the quest for perfection."[38] Disputes however, continue, as to Carpentier's conception of the temporal process: does the corruption of the revolution in the Caribbean represent the author's rejection of the modernist desire for temporal transcendence and thus a return to a circular and repetitive world in which there is no escape from the past? Raymond Souza argues that Carpentier's works are informed "by the conviction that there is a progression of meaning and order in history," while Donald Shaw detects in El siglo what he terms Carpentier's rejection of "the inevitable and unstoppable progression of humanity."[39] It is difficult to side with one view of time in the novel or the other because Carpentier's text seems to sustain both arguments: the modernist present is shown to be corrupt because it has not attained the perfect time it promised; but the corrup-

38. See Labanyi, p. 57, and Kilmer-Tchalekian, p. 48.
39. Raymond D. Souza, *Major Cuban Novelists: Innovation and Tradition* (Columbia: University of Missouri Press, 1976), p. 50; Donald L. Shaw, *Alejo Carpentier* (Boston: Twayne, 1985), p. 79.

tion of the French Revolution enables the Haitian Revolution, which recenters the Caribbean in history.

Commenting on the reversed movement of time in Carpentier's novel, Gonzalez Echevarria concludes that history in *El siglo* "turns out to be an error, the errancy inherent in all action, as opposed to theory or intention. Just as gnosticism is knowledge twisted by the force of desire, so history is intention bent by reality."[40] The errancy of history is evident when Esteban returns to the Caribbean after his disillusionment with the French Revolution and decides to anchor his quest for an American hermeneutics on the past. Victor has dismissed Esteban's views as unscientific, taking an agonistic view of history which is in turn questioned by the revolt of the slaves, predicated on what Octavio Paz has called "retrilinear time" in which the temporal process engenders itself by consuming itself and the present "does not repeat the past and each instance is unique, different, and self-sustaining."[41] At this point the European and African notions of modernism are brought into contestation.

Carpentier's problem with the French Revolution—as a modernist project—is its claim to have broken with its history and prehistory even as it draws its legitimacy and authority from both. The rhetoric of the revolution, as Esteban discovers during his European adventure, is essentially ironic—"Everything here has come to mean its opposite" (p. 111)—but for ideological reasons the revolutionaries have no sense of the ironic and can thus justify literal meanings simply by appealing to a utopian future. As time progresses, however, "the Revolution began to simplify itself in people's minds; freed from the uproar and rhetoric of street meanings, the Event was reduced to its basic elements and pared of contradictions" (p. 117). Back home in Havana, Esteban will treat the revolution as an event rather than an experience; for whereas an experience derives its authority from its claim to be original, an event is shown to be a rhetorical device, an effect of language and narration. Esteban joins the revolution to become part of what is deemed to be a natural and inevitable experience; but he returns "laden with history and stories, to somewhere where they would listen to him in amazement, as if he had been a pilgrim returning from the Holy Land" (p. 127).

Thus a revolution that started as a unique historical event has now been reduced to a story; when "Historia" becomes "de historias" (in

40. Gonzalez Echevarria, "Socrates among the Weeds," p. 41.
41. Octavio Paz, *Alternating Current*, trans. Helen Lane (New York: Viking, 1973), p. 2.

the Spanish text) an equivalence is established between the two narrative forms and the monological and factual claims of history are diminished. My contention is that the idea of revolution is denigrated because it is part of a European history whose utopian desire to systematize and co-opt the margins of empire into the empirical system is problematic and questionable; this denigration opens a gap in which the African version of history can be brought into play. This reversal is generated by a basic irony: the revolution is not transferred to the Caribbean—its rhetoric notwithstanding—to restore freedom to the slaves, but to establish a new system of regulation and exchange. To rewrite the Caribbean in European terms, as Victor so often tries to do is to continue the project of European conquest initiated by the "discovery."

Once more—in the crucial center of the text—we can see how what were revolutionary symbols in Europe are brought to the Caribbean as figures intended to transform and colonize the space of the other, and how, in reaction, the islands rewrite such signs into a new system of meanings. For example, once it has arrived in Haiti, the guillotine is algebraized and turned into "the centre of the life of the town" and a center of exchange: "The scaffold had become the hub of an exchange, of a forum, of a perpetual auction sale. The executions no longer even interrupted the haggling, importuning and arguing. The guillotine had begun to form part of normal everyday life" (pp. 151–52). In the meantime, we are brought face to face with the peculiar dilemma of language and representation in the Caribbean text: the absence of a determinate relationship between European words and American things, and the existence of duplicity of representation, which creates an ironical relationship between signs and signifiers—"there were certain events for which the chronology of the Revolutionary calendar was not adequate" (p. 204). As a Caribbean writer, Carpentier must invent signs for things to account for the manifold forms of the Antillean landscape; he turns to the allegory of history to expose the failure of European modernism to institute an adequate language for Caribbean things.

The Allegory of History

Having rejected the totalizing drive of European history and a notion of representation predicated on the primacy of the natural experience, Esteban returns to the Caribbean to face the question of modernity from the other end of the geographical spectrum. His challenge now is to reconfigure European forms, to expose their limits, and to critique the inability of such forms to account for those aspects of the Caribbean which resist linguistic domestication. To account for Antillean things for which the colonial language has yet to develop names, Esteban sets out to evolve a mode of representation which takes into consideration the ruptures and contradictions of the European experience as they are played out in the Caribbean theater; the islands are shown to possess Byzantine powers (p. 33) which distort the order of things. And thus, as Gonzalez Echevarria says, the theme of the Caribbean landscape as a "generator of strange, odd shapes and forms is quite germane to the issue of the unfolding of history in the novel."[42]

By allegorizing history, the text also discredits and eventually rejects the Enlightenment's logocentric faith in natural experience and the transcendental dimension of temporality. Esteban's previous desire for European forms was logocentric in the sense that he sought the representation of that mode of experience which, to use Derrida's terms, "has always designated the relationship with a presence, whether that relationship had the form of consciousness or not."[43] In fact, when he left the Caribbean to participate in the French Revolution, Esteban was seeking a historical presence related to a higher form of consciousness, one that made it possible for him to be centered in "world" history. By his own reckoning, to witness the revolution would allow him to "start his life as a man in a new world" (p. 70); he could stop living like a blind man "on the fringe of the most exciting realities" (p. 71). In the end, however, the revolution does not affirm experience in the logocentric sense: it is no longer a presence or an object of knowledge, nor is it the origin of temporalization; rather, it is an obtrusive and dangerous figure, described as a "Great Delirium" (p. 261) whose claim to transcendence is not founded on facts but on fine talk "of Better Worlds created by words" (p. 261).

What makes the "Great Delirium" so incomprehensible to Esteban is that it broke out "in the very country where civilisation seemed to have achieved a perfect equilibrium, a country of serene architecture and incomparable craftsmanship, a country where Nature had been tamed, and where the language itself seemed to have been made to fit the measures of classical poetry" (p. 260). In comparison to the Carib-

---

42. Gonzalez Echevarria, "Socrates," p. 44.
43. Jacques Derrida, *Of Grammatology*, trans. Gayatri Chakravarty Spivak (Baltimore: Johns Hopkins University Press, 1976), p. 60.

bean—a place of erratic figures and indeterminate tropes—France's previous claim to cultural superiority lay in its coherence of cultural forms and the mastery of nature. The revolution, however, has exposed the linguistic delirium underlying the illusion of symmetry. Once this illusion has been exposed, the Caribbean artist can no longer claim that the islands can only be represented or apprehended through European forms. As a writer, Esteban faces the most pressing question confronting those who seek an American hermeneutics: what form will the "marvelous reality" of the Americas take?

In *El siglo*, as in his previous works, especially *El reino de este mundo*, Carpentier adopts allegory, itself a modernist form of expression, to deal with this representative problem. He is attracted to the figure of allegory for the same reasons it appealed to Walter Benjamin and his generation of European modernists: allegory allows the author to represent a fragmentary and enigmatic world while accounting for "the inner experience" of life itself. Our view of the "extraordinary" American continent, says Carpentier, "must be ecumenic."[44] Allegory, in this context, is not an artifice cut off from experience or its referents; rather, though denying experience its traditional authority—its claim to be an original presence—allegory also points to the inner essence, and hence power, of things contained in the fleeting signs that signify them. And so, as Bainard Cowan has shown in a theoretical exposition of this figure, allegory both affirms the existence of truth, especially where ideological duplicity has put historical and natural phenomena into question, and recognizes the absence of such truth: "Allegory could not exist if truth were accessible: as a mode of expression it arises in perpetual response to the human condition of being exiled from the truth that it would embrace."[45] As a narrator of Caribbean modernity, Esteban must discover in allegory a detour around the condition of being exiled from the truths of the Americas.

Carpentier draws the reader's attention to the essential nature of the Caribbean as allegorical throughout the text. This effort is apparent in the numerous strategies he adopts to foreground the baroque, an essential form of fragmentation and incompleteness. If young Esteban is attracted to France as the country of symmetrical architecture, it is because he lives in a world in which both natural and architectural

44. See *Into the Mainstream: Conversations with Latin American Writers*, ed. Luis Harss and Barbara Dohmann (New York: Harper, 1967), p. 44.
45. Bainard Cowan, "Walter Benjamin's Theory of Allegory," *New German Critique* 22 (Winter 1981), 114.

forms are marked by excess, discontinuity, and difference. For example, early in the novel the city of Havana is compared to "a gigantic baroque chandelier" (p. 11), and its most remarkable characteristic is the way modern forms conceal almost Neanderthal creations, as if to emphasize the fact that Caribbean temporalizing does not entail a decisive break between history and prehistory. In a city that prides itself on its technological achievements, the ships under construction in the harbor "looked like giant fossils with the soaring ribs of their hulls" (p. 40). After a hurricane, this modern city is left "a mere skeleton of bare rafters" (p. 58), and the resulting inundations are "like shafts of ancient columns torn down by earthquake" (p. 59). This allegorization of things has a double purpose: First, the emphasis on the baroque calls attention to the power of the other, of the repressed which claims its identity against the mainstream's drive for systematization. As Gonzalez Echevarria has noted in another context, the baroque appealed to Carpentier and his generation because it provided an avenue for expressing "the different, the strange, that is to say, the American."[46] Second, allegorizing the "modern" form questions history's claim to be a natural phenomenon by exposing it (as Esteban later describes the revolution) as a "performance," not an experience.

In his classic discussion of the relationship between allegory and the baroque in *The Origin of German Tragic Drama*, Walter Benjamin observes that the baroque "conceives of history as created events": where the history of the modern period strives to valorize itself by claiming a break with its prehistory, the allegory points to sinister connections with the past; thus allegories become "in the realm of thoughts, what ruins are in the realm of things."[47] If we pursue this line of thought, we can conclude that the Caribbean invests heavily in the meaning of erratic figures and signs—the ingredients of "magical realism"—as compared with the European drive for rationalization. In other words, for the Caribbean subject to allegorize history or experience—to transform things and events into figures and signs—is also to vitiate their meaning and to turn them into something else.

46. Gonzalez Echevarria, "Guillen as Baroque: Meaning in Motivos de Son," *Callaloo* 10 (Spring 1987), 305. In his classic study of the baroque, Jose Antonio Maravall defines the style as a technique of cultural crisis and incompleteness; the baroque leads "human beings to be other than themselves, to go out of the beaten path." See *Culture of the Baroque: Analysis of a Historical Structure*, trans. Terry Cochran (Minneapolis: University of Minnesota Press, 1986), p. 213.

47. Walter Benjamin, *The Origin of German Tragic Drama*, trans. John Osborne (London: NLB, 1977), p. 175.

In this regard, Carpentier's most radical form of transformation is his use of unexpected analogies, a process by which one sign is transferred into another and their value is equated, against conventions of meaning. Thus, the guillotine recalls a cross which in turn recalls the image of Esteban's "crucifixion" (p. 15), which is then compared to a painting (p. 16). The guillotine is clearly the central code of reversal and transformation in the novel. As we have already seen, it is introduced into the Caribbean as a thing with a very specific meaning: it signifies "revolutionary morality" (p. 122) and the dawn of the new age. On closer examination, however, the guillotine serves as an ambiguous figure defined by both its difference and its identity: it is described as "a geometrical projection from the vertical, a false perspective, a configuration in two dimensions of what would soon take on height, breadth and a terrible depth" (p. 124). The guillotine is an appropriate example of what Gonzalez Echevarria formulates as the figure of *retruécano* in Carpentier's text; it is "a rhetorical inversion, a baroque figure that . . . resembles a specular movement in which it is impossible to tell what takes precedence over what, what is the reflection of what. The *retruécano* is an equivalency in the process of displaying itself both in its inherent repetition and difference, in its reiteration and desired simultaneity."[48] The power and value of the guillotine, as a figure, lie in its ability to point to something else, something abstract and more sinister than the world of fleeting appearances which we read on the surface of the text.

Curiously enough, Victor Hugues resists any allegorical reading of the guillotine; he prefers to read the object of terror either in its pure literalness, or to represent it as a symbol rather than an allegory. To underscore the value of the guillotine as the "insignia of his authority," Victor will transform the "machine" into "a symbolic figure" (p. 131). Why does Victor prefer the symbolic to the allegorical mode? Possibly because a symbol, as Hans-Georg Gadamer argues in his discussion of the hermeneutical implications of the two figures, is not a sign pointing to another sign, but has meaning in itself, a meaning that derives from "its own sensuous nature": "The meaning of the symbolon depends on its physical presence and acquires its representative function only through the fact of its being shown or spoken."[49] Thus borne erect in the bows of a ship, the first guillotine in the New World derives its power from its physical presence—"shining like new, and completely

48. Gonzalez Echevarria, "Socrates among the Weeds," p. 43.
49. Hans-Georg Gadamer, *Truth and Method* (New York: Crossroads, 1985), p. 65.

unveiled so that all should see it clearly and recognize it" (p. 133).
Victor resists an allegorical reading of the guillotine because allegorization would pluralize the meaning of this instrument of power and thus disperse its authority.

Against Victor's desire for symbolic or even scientific meanings, the Caribbean landscape—"where words and phrases multiplied with surprising fertility" (p. 38)—is shown to evoke its own (allegorical) version of history and reality. Although the Enlightenment pretends to be the triumph of Western reason and knowledge over nature and magic, it does not have effective remedies for the Caribbean landscape and its realities. The limitation of Western knowledge is illustrated vividly by the presence of Ogé, the black doctor and magician from Haiti. When Victor introduces Ogé into the household as the only hope for curing Esteban's multiple maladies, Sofia resists the doctor because of his color: "She could not bring herself to accept that a negro would become the family doctor, or that one could surrender the body of a relation to a coloured person. Nobody could entrust a negro with the building of a palace, the defence of a criminal, the direction of a theological controversy or the government of a country" (p. 43). Despite the cries of liberty and equality ringing in the Caribbean, blacks are excluded from modes of knowledge as defined by the church, the law, and the government. Yet it is Ogé's "proper knowledge of nature" which enables him to cure Esteban's asthma, for according to the Haitian, "certain illnesses were mysteriously connected with the growth of a grass, a plant or a tree somewhere nearby. Every human being had a 'double' in the vegetable kingdom, and there were cases where this 'double,' to further its own growth, stole strength from the man with whom it was linked, condemning him to illness while it flowered or germinated" (p. 44). The excluded black subject and its modes of knowledge reintroduce nature as a key component of culture and society.

Years later, Esteban's crisis of consciousness, which is triggered by his disillusionment with European history and culture, is "cured" when he discovers a vegetation similar to that in Cuba (p. 161). In the world of nature, the "proper" meaning of experience is established; the subject can now identify with natural symbols at a time when he could not reconcile himself to historical ones; nature is shown to be the originating source of a holistic temporal process that reconciles Esteban to "real experience" (p. 163). Thus, if the European historical process denotes a world in which Esteban "felt a stranger to the times he lived," an absurd world in which "a Revolutionary Catechism . . . no longer corresponded with reality" (p. 164), the allegory of nature, the "economy of zoological forms," preserves the "Baroque of creation" (p. 176). In other words, the allegorical emblems of the baroque have stripped things down to their generic existence, stripped them of their linguistic contrivance, and lifted the veil of ideology off the objects of knowledge.

This ostensible distinction between history and nature does not mean, however, that the two forms exist in a relationship of radical disjunction in either a figurative or a temporal sense. Even Walter Benjamin, to whom I am indebted for my reading here, recognizes that nature and history exist in a state of mutual interdependence. It is fallen nature, says Benjamin, which "bears the imprint of the progression of history."[50] Does this mean that a reflection on nature and the process of decay which recuperates essential and complete meanings is already an illusion, a projection of the self onto a spectacle it mistakes for nature? In his excellent treatment of this problem, Labanyi has argued that for Carpentier, "history is judged implicitly in terms of its adherence to, or deviation from, natural norms. . . . History is not . . . a return to Nature, but its successes and failures depend on its capacity to maintain contact with Nature as an original point of departure. A point of departure that must be superseded but never lost from view."[51] Now, if we accept Benjamin's notion—as it has been reformulated by Cowan—that nature bears the imprint of historical "attrition, wearing away, destruction," then Esteban's ideal of autonomous and ahistorical nature is nothing more than a fantasy.[52] The value of nature does not lie in its inherent meanings but in its capacity to force the subject to recognize history, in Cowan's phrase, as "a highly paradoxical and deeply troubling concept, for it is both the source of all suffering and misunderstanding, and the medium through which significance and, indeed, salvation are attained."[53]

Such a gesture of recognition is already obvious in Esteban's increasing tendency to allegorize history to account for its "double, self-opposed movement."[54] Allegorization makes the historical referent problematic by making it remote from its source of origin, thus forcing

50. Benjamin, The Origin, p. 181.
51. Labanyi, p. 56.
52. Cowan, p. 117.
53. Cowan, p. 116.
54. Cowan, p. 116.

it to appear "unreal and strange" (p. 93); plunged into this figurative "history," Esteban feels a sense of temporal release—"Everything was strange, unforeseen, amusing" (p. 94)—as if he had been dropped "into a huge carnival" (p. 93). Even in the midst of the revolution, allegory displaces the literal version of history and forecloses the referent from the subject:

> One seemed to be in the midst of a gigantic allegory of a revolution rather than a revolution itself, a metaphorical revolution, a revolution which had been made elsewhere, which revolved on a hidden axis, which had been elaborated in subterranean councils, invisible to those who wanted to know all about it. Esteban was unfamiliar with these new names, unknown yesterday and changing every day, and he could not discover who was responsible for the Revolution. [P. 95]

Here, allegorized history foregrounds its two conditions of possibility: its utopian and apocalyptic impulses. "Enlightened" about his temporal condition and its possibilities, Esteban conceives history as utopia: his journey to Europe is like that of Percival in search of himself, a journey "to the Future City which, for once, had not been situated in America like those of Thomas More and Campanella, but in the cradle of philosophy itself" (p. 99). But even as he thinks about utopia, the boy's dreams are "about the Wormwood Star of the Apocalypse" (p. 100).

Finally, we need to consider the allegorization of history in another sense—as *arch-écriture*. This is the sense in which the allegorical perspective conceives of "the world as a kind of writing"; the allegorical view now, as Cowan says, is a deconstructive process by which experience "is chastened and shriven of its hubristic dream of self-sufficiency."[55] In *El siglo*, allegorized history is shown to be an "impromptu piece of rhetoric" (p. 101); deprived of its claim to universality (especially now that its difference and alienness are so apparent to Esteban), European history can be rewritten and even managed. Esteban used to be troubled by the avalanche of regulations and decrees that destabilized his historical referent and displaced his modes of knowledge (p. 108), but once he discovers that the value of history is determined not by its events but by its rhetorical figures, then he can bear to live with history. Thus, his escape into holistic nature, and even his rejection of contemporary history and political economy (because

55. Cowan, p. 112.

he prefers esoteric fictions), are not real detours around the problem of temporality; they are just new ways of self-representation within the fragmented discourse of history. Indeed, Esteban rejects time on one level, but this rejection is just a temporal deferral of history; as a colonized Caribbean subject, he must eventually define his own relationship with history. He will thus perish in another revolution, confronting history—but on his own terms.

Esteban's earlier failure to come to terms with his Caribbean history could hence be attributed to his inability to give greater credence to the subversive African forms that surround him. For example, at the height of what one may call his revolutionary fervor, Esteban—"after living a life given over to repetition and recollection for so long" (p. 93)—feels as if he has been dropped into a giant carnival. But for him carnival denotes escape from the reality of things and the materiality of events, not their affirmation. In contrast, the black slaves adopt the latest importation from Europe (the revolution) as just another event in a carnival; they conceive the carnivalesque as a form of inversion which generates an alternative history, what Gonzalez Echevarria calls "a ritual in which the previous ones have not been erased, but new shapes have been superimposed on them to create a sense of motion, of dynamic transformation."[56] As we see in the next chapter, the confrontation between the carnivalesque Caribbean version of history and colonial and neocolonial modernism is the key to understanding the novels of Paule Marshall.

56. Gonzalez Echevarria, "Socrates," p. 51.

5

Modernism and the Masks of History:
The Novels of Paule Marshall

> History can be apprehended only through its effects, and
> never directly as some reified force. This is indeed the ulti-
> mate sense in which History as ground and as transcendable
> horizon needs no particular theoretical justification: we may
> be sure that its alienating necessities will not forget us,
> however much we might prefer to ignore them.
> —Fredric Jameson, *The Political Unconscious*

> After struggling for some time, I was finally able . . . to bring
> together what I consider to be the two themes most central
> to my work: the importance of truly confronting the past,
> both in personal and historical terms, and the necessity of
> reversing the present order.
> —Paule Marshall, "Shaping the World of My Art"

Against the grain of colonial modernism, which has sought to impose a single notion of history (one subordinated to European power)
on the colonized space, Caribbean writers have often reverted to the
culture of the subaltern to institute an alternative narrative of history,
even an ideal history of the West Indian landscape. The result has been
not only the kind of redefinition of history which I have discussed in
previous chapters, but an attempt to establish—through the dynamics
of deformation apparent in popular culture, minor characters, and
black slaves—a distinctly Afro-Caribbean notion of modernism. Here,
the act of narration acquires a political resonance akin to what Hous-

ton Baker calls the "deformation of mastery": the subaltern subjects comprehend their social and cultural spaces "within their own vale/ veil more fully than any intruder" as they evolve a diasporic, indigenous language. Forms of popular culture, such as carnival and calypso, are enlisted to deform the rational discourse of European modernity; and, at the same time, the folk are introduced into the domain of cultural production "to refigure the very notion of 'culture' for the modern world."[1]

In almost every text discussed in the previous chapters, the colonial narrative of history is haunted by the popular folk version which it tries to repress. For example, in Lamming's *Pleasures of Exile*, vodun is the form in which the repressed returns to represent the unspeakable; in *In the Castle of My Skin*, the officially censored version of history breaks through the dream of the village elder Pa, and the ancestral spirit, "speaking through the voice of an old man on the eve of his death, provides the kind of history which the village could not have learned from its official school."[2] Similarly, the poor and unrepresented in works as divergent as James's *Beyond a Boundary* and Carpentier's *El siglo de las luces* appropriate figures and artifacts of colonial culture, such as cricket and Catholic rituals, and turn them around through strategies of reversal and improvisation (amid instruments of Western culture), Baker says, "as a way of transforming such artifacts . . . into resources for a world where mastery has been deformed."[3]

For Paule Marshall the transformation of the instruments of Western culture under the power and influence of the folk is a primary condition for the production of black culture in the New World. In her principal works, the folk return not only to disturb the dominant version of history and culture, but also to promote an Afro-American modernism that, by sustaining the tension between the persistent ancestral voice in black cultures and imposed European forms, seeks to affirm an indigenous language of history and self in the space of the other while unraveling the ideological and political necessity that justifies a Caribbean narrative. In Marshall's novels, as Edward Brathwaite succinctly observes, "we find a West Indies facing the metro-

1. Houston A. Baker, Jr., *Modernism and the Harlem Renaissance* (Chicago: University of Chicago Press, 1987), pp. 51 and 66.
2. George Lamming, "Introduction," *In the Castle of My Skin* (New York: Schocken, 1983), p. xvii.
3. Baker, p. 66.

politan west on the one hand, and clinging to a memorial past on the other. Within this matrix, she formulates her enquiry into identity and change."[4]

Moreover, the question of how to represent and understand colonial modernism and its narrative of history is of the utmost importance to Marshall; it provides the ideological and theoretical underpinning for most of her major works. If her texts seem to keep on returning to the terms by which the colonized can articulate the past, it is because she believes that the present order of oppression and reification can only be reversed if its material conditions—and what she might consider to be the necessity of history—are fully comprehended. But Marshall's novels are unique in another sense: they probe the rules by which the black experience in the New World can be interpreted and represented. These novels struggle with the linguistic and psychological blockage that hampers the hermeneutical act, the rules of overdetermination that often make it impossible for the reader to gain access to those original meanings that have been repressed in the middle passage of the black experience. Marshall's major works thus strive to provide a metacommentary on the painful coexistence of European modernist institutions and the dynamic survivals of the African experience in the islands. In addition, Marshall's subjects often make narrative turns toward the Caribbean landscape in an attempt to capture what she aptly calls "thoughts and feelings about the Middle passage," and to elaborate "the psychological damage brought on by history."[5]

Although Marshall perceives history in terms of its effects rather than as what Fredric Jameson, in the epigraph above, calls "a reified force," her novels—like those of her contemporary George Lamming—also strive to unmask the necessity of alienating history and even to provide a theoretical justification for an alternative episteme. Indeed, underlying Marshall's well-known concern with the nightmare of history and its alienating necessities is the desire for an ideal (and hence modern) version of the black experience which both transforms African culture and transcends the colonial tradition. History causes pain and suffering for Marshall's subjects, but as I argue in this

4. Edward Brathwaite, "West Indian History and Society in the Art of Paule Marshall's Novel," *Journal of Black Studies* 1 (December 1970), 227. According to Brathwaite, Marshall's incisive understanding of Caribbean modernism is probably due to her "partial" relation to the West Indian culture of her ancestors: "Had Paule Marshall been a West Indian, she probably would not have written [*The Chosen People*]. Had she not been an Afro-American of West Indian parentage, she probably could not have written it either" (p. 227).

5. Paule Marshall, "Shaping the World of My Art," *New Letters* 40 (October 1973), 110.

chapter, the alienation occasioned by this history is a necessity because it triggers the cultural response that, in the words of Sylvia Wynter, "had transformed the New World Negro into the indigenous inhabitant of his new land."[6] The roots of Caribbean modernism can actually be traced to the paradoxes and contradictions Wynter recognizes in the Africans' attempts to adapt themselves to the Caribbean landscape while transforming its nature:

> Out of this relation, in which the land was always the *earth*, the centre of a core of beliefs and attitudes, would come the central pattern which held together the social order. In this aspect of the relation, the African slave represented an opposing process to that of the European, who achieved great technical progress based on the primary accumulation of capital which came from the dehumanization of Man and Nature. . . . The African presence, on the other hand, '*rehumanized Nature*,' and helped to save his own humanity against the constant onslaught of the plantation system by the creation of a folklore and folk-culture.[7]

In effect, folklore and popular culture played a central role in the transplanted Africans' quest for an indigenous language that could help them transcend reified history. According to Wynter, "Folklore was the cultural guerrilla resistance against the Market economy."[8] This resistance constitutes a key subtext in Marshall's novels: it is represented by the stories told by Barbadian emigrants in *Brown Girl, Brownstones*, the indigenous carnival sustained by the peasants of Bournehill in *The Chosen Place, the Timeless People*, and the national dances of Carriacou replayed by the displaced descendants of African slaves in *Praisesong for the Widow*. Whereas colonial history is represented as painful and alienating, a servant of the plantation system and the market economy, the voices of the subaltern affirm the history of the Africans, and the forms that history takes, as the "absent cause" that is shaping a Caribbean national culture.

The Political Unconscious

Simple issues of meaning—in particular the process by which individual subjects develop a material understanding of their conditions of

6. Sylvia Wynter, "Jonkonnu in Jamaica: Towards the Interpretation of Folk Dance as a Cultural Process," *Jamaica Journal* 4 (1970), 35.
7. Wynter, p. 36.
8. Wynter, p. 36.

existence—constitute an important prelude to the larger historical questions that mark Marshall's novels. For example, the central motifs in *Brown Girl, Brownstones*—the mirror and the body—are intended to raise phenomenological questions about vision and representation. Confused and threatened by the harsh logic of Western materialism, Selina often struggles to define the meaning of her body, to even understand her own subjectivity. Her disjunctive relationship with the acquisitive world of her mother is often manifested in the division she feels between herself and her family. The ethic that drives her mother has no reality for Selina—indeed, her growth is stifled by the mother's insistence that the acquisition of material things is a manifestation of one's subjectivity. On the contrary, Selina's existence is defined by exclusion and an acute sense of the unreal.

A significant representation of the resulting repression of selfhood comes early in the novel when Selina reflects on the family photograph "which did not include her": "She wanted suddenly to send up a loud cry to declare herself."[9] Because this family icon does not include Selina, she believes that it has no reality for her; it is "the picture of a neat, young family and she did not believe it" (p. 7). Selina's world is one of illusionary and shifting figures without a center of significance: the family photograph signifies connections with an ancestral home in Barbados, but she does not belong there any more than she belongs to her mother's brave new world in New York. Since her father is the only person who appears real in the family portrait, Selina expects him to provide a link to the ethics and impulses of the ancestral past: "For her, he was the one constant in the flux and unreality of life" (p. 8). But for the father, like all the other Barbadian immigrants who populate Marshall's novel, connections to the past are at best tenuous; instead of functioning as a source of certainty and true understanding, the past often generates fear and shame. For example, Selina's father fears that Suggies's codfish will "insinuate itself into his clothes and he would carry it with him all night as the undisputable sign that he was Barbadian and a foreigner" (p. 22). And while her mother celebrates the Caribbean past in her stories and language, she also believes that in New York the success of her family can only be secured if the past and its ethics are rejected or modified.

When the past is celebrated in its pastness but rejected as anach-

9. Paule Marshall, *Brown Girl, Brownstones* (New York: Feminist Press, 1981), p. 6. Further references are in the text.

ronistic in the drive for modernity, as my discussion of *The Chosen Place, the Timeless People* indicates, selfhood continues to be a contentious issue for the black subject even in a postcolonial situation. Moreover, the uncertainty of self which often haunts Marshall's characters functions as a metaphor of a larger crisis of historiography in her novels. Her characters are driven by a double, and often contradictory, movement: on one hand, they want to write themselves into the scheme of things and to be recognized by the dominant other as subjects with a culture and history; but, on the other hand, they believe that their mastery of the codes of the dominant culture—especially wealth, property, and status—will guarantee their autonomy and integrity in a hostile world. The end result, however, is a process of repression, disguise, and self-division.

In *Brown Girl, Brownstones*, self-division is apparent in Selina's painful quest for subjectivity, her struggle to walk the tightrope between her mother's desire to be assimilated into the materialist ethic and her father's dream of returning to Barbados. When the mother forces Selina to wear "throw-offs," which the little girl perceives as symbols of her own alienation in her mother's mortgaged world, it is the father's "voice" which restores her to her own sense of self (p. 11). But as we saw in previous chapters, the repressed or marginalized Caribbean self can never find wholeness and deep meanings in the world of the other; because this self cannot belong wholly to the other's scheme of things, it must live as a fragment of both its culture and the value system of the dominant. For this reason, there is often a disjunction between the soul and the body in Marshall's text. In moments of despair, anger, and an acute sense of betrayal, Selina realizes that all her efforts to secure the integrity of her inner self have come to naught because "she was not free but still trapped within a hard flat body" (p. 62). The body belongs to the other—the dominant culture, her mother, the Barbadian community—and thus her attempts at transgression and self-engenderment are bound to fail.

The problem of self-identity in situations of displacement is further accentuated by the fact that one cannot develop a synthesis between the real (black) self and an assimilated self which might mask and protect the former. Self-division does not restore authority to one part of the self; on the contrary, it nullifies all the different entities that struggle within the divided self, and there is confusion about which self is authentic and which is merely figurative. The struggle for an authentic self, amid the travail of double consciousness, characterizes the quest of Jay Johnson in *Praisesong for the Widow*. Frustrated in his previous attempts to master the rules of the dominant white culture (even after a painful process of self-education he will not get a job as an accountant because of his race), Jay sets out to destroy his spontaneous and natural self and to adopt the hard, cold logic of "progress" as a tactic for survival. But what is the meaning of this new self? What are its values and how is it to be interpreted? For his wife, Avey, who was responsible for nudging him toward this change in the first place, the new Jay is "like the vague, pale outline of another face superimposed on his, as in a double-exposure."[10]

Now, a doubly exposed image has no clear outline; it exists as a fragment of two things without the representative value of either. So, in the end, Jay is defined by distance and difference from the things that were supposed to mark his new selfhood, including a suburban home. Significantly, in striving to be the equal of the other, Jay has repressed his individual utterance: "The voice was clearly his, but the tone and, more important, the things he said were so unlike him they might have come from someone . . . who had slipped in when he wasn't looking and taken up residence behind his dark skin; someone who from remarks he made viewed the world and his fellow men according to a harsh and joyless ethic" (p. 131). Throughout the text, we could always identify the old Jay because of the similarity among his self, voice, and tone; in the new Jay, on the other hand, there is marked tension between voice and tone. Indeed, Jay's voice has now become a mask of his self rather than its signifier.

The persistent image of the veil or mask in Marshall's works denotes the impossibility of developing an essentialist sense of self and of truly knowing the colonized subject. The inaccessibility of the black subject is not always a negative condition, however, for as Baker has noted, the mastery of the mask "constitutes a primary move in Afro-American discursive modernism."[11] Moreover, the African mask signifies the deep meanings that the colonial economy of representation relegates to the margins and contains within it what Henry Louis Gates has called "a coded, secret, hermetic world, a world discovered only by the initiate."[12] For instance, in *The Chosen Place, the Timeless People*,

---

10. Paule Marshall, *Praisesong for the Widow* (New York: Dutton, 1984), p. 131. Further references are in the text.

11. Baker, p. 17.

12. Henry Louis Gates, Jr., *Figures in Black: Words, Signs, and the "Racial" Self* (New York: Oxford University Press, 1987), p. 167. Many studies of masks have explored the correlation between masking, identity, and selfhood. Theodore Thass-Thienemann has, in fact, defined

the mask idiom reflects the most complex hermeneutical codes and rules for understanding the world of the black peasantry. Trying to understand a character such as Ferguson is like trying to read a mask; first we must question our preconceived rules of interpretation: "Everything about him was overstated, exaggerated. His face, his neck, his clean-shaven skull, had the elongated, intentionally distorted look of a Benin mask or a sculpted thirteenth-century Ife head. With his long, stretched limbs he could have been a Haitian Houngon man. Or Damballa."[13] The masked figure merges forms from Africa with those invented in the diaspora; in the process, new meanings about self, history, and culture are created. Such meanings are further enhanced, through paradox, by a neat balance between disguise and intelligibility. On the surface, Ferguson is presented as a deformed figure, but through this deformation he is connected to African masks and hence to a tangible black referent. And so Marshall invites us to read history as distorted and disguising, but at the same time fixed and deep.

Indeed, in *The Chosen Place*, which is one of the monumental texts on modernization and colonial historiography in the Caribbean, the central questions all subjects have to confront sooner or later have to do with representation and interpretation—how do we penetrate the disguise to tap the deep meanings of an alienated history and culture? Most of the characters in the book have to struggle to develop new modes of knowledge in a world in which the old relationship between master and slave, the colonizer and the colonized, has been reconfigured in the period of decolonization. More important, the middle passage of black culture is represented as a modern discursive space in which historical and other meanings cannot be taken for granted. In effect, the text postulates the problems, and possibilities, of recovering the most hidden meanings of a culture that has always used duplicity and self-masking as weapons of survival.

Nothing illustrates this interpretative problem as vividly as Saul's travail as he tries to understand the island of Bourneville. As a scholar,

---

masking as the quest for an objective way of looking at selfhood; see *The Interpretation of Language*, vol. 2 (New York: Jason Aronson, 1973), p. 55. See also Andreas Lommel, *Masks: Their Meaning and Function* (New York: McGraw-Hill, 1972), and Walter Sorell, *The Other Face: The Mask in the Arts* (London: Thames and Hudson, 1973). African masks and their poetics are discussed in Franco Monti, *African Masks* (London: Paul Hamlyn, 1969), especially pp. 15–23; Leon Underwood, *Masks of West Africa* (London: Alec Tiranti, 1964); Dennis Duerden, *The Invisible Present: African Art and Literature* (New York: Harper, 1975), p. 131.

13. Paule Marshall, *The Chosen Place, the Timeless People* (New York: Vantage, 1984), p. 121. Further references are in the text.

Saul is a fervent believer in the Weberian doctrine of modernization as a rational process that liberates the self from restrictive traditions, but nothing in the American anthropologist's previous education or experience has trained him to understand the Caribbean subaltern's modes of representation and cultural production.[14] Saul heads a research study of Bourneville, which is predicated on the belief that rational knowledge is the key to historical and social transformation, but for most of the text he is forced to spend time reflecting on the inadequacy of his own modes of interpretation which seek to rewrite the Caribbean landscape in terms of the Western metanarrative on progress and material wealth. Witness how the proposed anthropological study of Bourneville is represented in the methodical and dead language of economic and social modernization:

> The proposed plan for Bourneville, as outlined during the talks at the Center prior to their departure, was to be done in three stages. There would be a preliminary study of six months to a year to obtain a general picture of life in the district as well as to discover why a number of other projects previously attempted there had failed. Once this was completed, the second or action phase of the work would begin with an expanded research team and one or more demonstration projects. [P. 51]

Once he encounters the island, however, Saul discovers that rational knowledge cannot measure up to the fleeting nature of reality in Bourneville; here the traditional and predictable oppositions (tradition/modernity, past/present) which sanction social analysis are quickly invalidated because the unconscious side of history determines the lives of the islanders more than Saul had expected. Thus in his attempt to "read" the island, Saul is confronted by realities he cannot fix in a temporal or historical scheme: "He could be struck by the feeling, too fleeting to grasp, that he had stumbled upon a world that was real, inescapably real, yet at the same time somehow unreal; of the present but even more so of the past" (p. 216).

It is clear that the signs and figures that denote this "illogical" mode of representation—the motionless figures of the cane cutters and the "ancient windmills"—negate all the key assumptions in the Center's modernist discourse. Indeed, if we accept Jean-François Lyotard's

---

14. See David Kolb, *The Critique of Pure Modernity* (Chicago: University of Chicago Press, 1986), pp. 3–10.

famous definition of the modernist imperative as the drive "to seize and systematize the world and so liberate human possibilities by mastering the conditions of life in a cognitive and manipulative system,"[15] then the admixture of the real and unreal which Saul encounters in the island undermines all notions of systematization embedded in his education and ideology. In other words, the binary oppositions—reality/illusions, past/present, and tradition/modernity—which the researchers hoped to establish conclusively to master the conditions of life in the island, are nullified by the "marvelous" reality of Bourneville, which does not allow for such oppositions.

There is an even more important consequence to this collapse of binaries—the rational authority of the analyst is put into question when the analysand refuses to fit into the former's preconceived models, which are then shown to be inadequate because they were fashioned elsewhere. Saul's frustration grows when he begins to realize that the "real" meaning of the island is actually inaccessible to him and that the unconscious (or irrational) side of knowledge has more authority than his rational scheme. Although his research is going well and he and his assistant Allen are collecting impressive data about Bourneville, "he could not rid himself of the feeling that something about the place was eluding him, some meaning it held which could not be gotten at through the usual methods of analysis" (p. 215). Furthermore, not even his rational mind is immune from the power of the imaginary: "He was letting his imagination get the better of him, he told himself, seeking more in things than was there . . . and he couldn't help feeling as the weeks came and went vaguely surrounded by a mystery, and he became increasingly puzzled, even annoyed. Something, goddamn it, he swore to himself, about the place was being withheld, hidden from him" (p. 216).

Saul's interpretative quest—his modernist desire for a master narrative for Bourneville—mirrors Marshall's textual and cultural desire for a metadiscourse that will "bring together all the various strands (the word is synthesis) and thus make of the diverse heritage a whole."[16] Wholeness and synthesis, however, do not come easily to Marshall or her characters. Despite the authoritative narrative voice that promises a coherent narrative in The Chosen Place, the text is marked by an inner anxiety about meanings; the authority of characters, as interpreters of

15. Quoted by Kolb, p. 257.
16. Marshall, "Shaping the World," p. 106.

culture and history, is either compromised and questioned by their personal doubts and crises of selfhood, or is unsettled by the tension between their desire for solid and complete meanings and the historical discontinuity that surrounds them. Thus Merle Kinbona has struggled for eight years to make sense of the history of the island, to resurrect the hidden and unofficial history of her people—which is built around the myth of Cuffee Ned and his slave revolt—only to discover that such a discordant and subversive history is not easily written into the master text of colonial history: "Saul could see how the lonely eight-year search for coherence and vision had exhausted her" (p. 229). Rather than seeking a coherent set of meanings—a historical and even linguistic deep structure—beneath the fragmentary reality, Marshall's text eventually returns to history itself not to provide solutions to the problem of interpretation and representation in a colonial world, but to provide a metacode of Caribbean history itself, to provide what Jameson calls (in another context) "a commentary on the very conditions of existence of the problem itself."[17]

The Nightmare of Colonial History

What is the reality of the colonized (black) self? What are the original and forgotten meanings of its experience and how can they be recovered? Within the context of modernist discourse, people like Saul begin their Caribbean experience with the belief that the subject does not create its meanings, but uses its interpretative powers to recover preexisting meanings. For such Weberian modernists, to use David Kolb's formulation, "modern identity is not just another in a sequence of historical constructs; it is the unveiling of what has been at the root of those constructs."[18] To his horror—but eventual satisfaction—Saul finds that during his research in Bourneville he has not been unveiling preexisting meanings but basically rewriting the island to reflect his own "personal meanings" (p. 217). He soon discovers, as does the reader, that the narrative of history can be established not by a general appeal to an original experience but through an act of projection in which the subject rewrites the past to reflect its own desires. In the

17. Fredric Jameson, "Metacommentary," in *The Ideologies of Theory: Essays 1971–1986*, vol. 1 (Minneapolis: University of Minnesota Press, 1988), p. 5.
18. Kolb, p. 10.

process of narration, the subject realizes that history, instead of being the crucible of fixed meanings, is a source of disorder and neurosis. As Merle Kinbona concludes after eight years of trying to decipher its meanings, Caribbean history is so displaced and so disturbing that we should avoid its study altogether; only then can we insulate ourselves from its pain: "Ah, well, ah, history. . . . Any of you ever studied it. . . . Well, don't if you haven't. I did it for a time—West Indian history it was and I tell you, it nearly, as we say in Bourneville, set out my head. I had to leave it off. It is a nightmare, as that Irishman said, and we haven't awakened from it yet" (p. 130).

Merle's passionate invocation of James Joyce's notion of history as a nightmare is not uncharacteristic of other characters in Marshall's novels: in her major works subjects are often haunted by their sense or knowledge of history; an encounter with the past creates a sense of betrayal and often ends in bitterness because this is a past of pain and loss. But if these characters see history as a nightmare, it is because they often start from a false premise—the belief that a "return" to the past, to ancestral sources, is an encounter with the heroic and monumental side of the black experience and that knowledge of this positive polarity, the better side of an often rapacious and dehumanizing existence, will become an antithesis to the reification that characterizes the present moment. In the end, however, Marshall's texts represent history as the object that blocks desire and fixes subjects and communities in reified positions. In other words, history is a ruse: it promises one thing but delivers another. Yes: history appears in Marshall's texts as deceptive, divergent, and full of contradictory meanings; it also comes loaded with predetermined images that tell us more about those who read and write it than about its actual "original" meaning.

The allegory of history often begins as an architectural process, complete with monuments that supposedly represent the "timeless place and the chosen people," but the effects of this process are ironic and fragmented. Consider the meaning of the brownstones in *Brown Girl*: for many of the Barbadian immigrants in New York, these buildings have become the very embodiment of the American dream, the objects of desire at the end of an eschatological process in which hard work leads to wealth and happiness. However, a closer reading of these monuments of social uplift and desire shows how Marshall has loaded the brownstones with meanings that reverse their overt intentions.

If the ownership of a brownstone is the mark of self-engenderment, the notion that the owners of the brownstones have subjectified themselves by acquiring property is undermined by the buildings' uniformity: "They all shared the same brown monotony. All seemed doomed by the confusion of their design" (p. 3). Each of the brownstones is supposed to be distinctive to emphasize the individuality of their owners, but this individuality in style is already suspect: "Looking close, you saw under the thick ivy each house had something distinctively its own. Some touch of Gothic, Romanesque, baroque or Greek triumphed amid the Victorian clutter" (p. 3). And this is precisely the problem of the modernity project in relation to the identity and heritage of the Caribbean subject: it draws fragments from different European styles, but it does not fuse them into a new, redesigned form; hence the confusion that has doomed the social meaning of the brownstones even before their owners have paid for them. Furthermore, if the right to property has now been posited as signifying self-engenderment—and is hence conceived as a source of pleasure and fulfillment—the ivy that covers the buildings (all were "draped in ivy as though in mourning") is a symbol of death and decay. The buildings, like history itself, are hence fated to cause disappointment and hurt.[19]

Similarly, for many subjects in The Chosen Place, history hurts not only because the experience of the middle passage is painful, but also because the values and cultures submerged during the crossing from Africa to the Americas cannot be recovered holistically. Therefore, those characters such as Merle Kinbona who desire wholeness from this history are condemned to live with the yawning gap between their desire and the temporal situation; history, like modernism, is an incomplete project. Indeed, very early in the novel, history and the temporal experience are represented to us solely as fragments, ruins, or remnants of something buried so deep in time that its true value and form can never be established. More specifically, the history of the postcolonial state which, as I have argued in earlier chapters, was supposed to mark a break with the colonial past, is shown to be nothing but a shoddy, old-fashioned replica of the old order of things.

19. For a study of history as an "absent cause" that causes suffering and disappointment see Fredric Jameson, The Political Unconscious: Narrative as a Socially Symbolic Act (Ithaca: Cornell University Press, 1981), p. 102. See also Deborah Schneider, "A Feminine Search for Selfhood: Paule Marshall's Brown Girl, Brownstones," in The Afro-American Novel since 1960, ed. Peter Bruck and Wolfgang Karrer (Amsterdam: Gruner, 1982), pp. 53–74; Kimberly Benston, "Architectural Imagery and Unity in Paule Marshall's Brown Girl, Brownstones," Negro American Literature Forum 9 (Fall 1975), 67–70.

In the first part of the book (appropriately titled "Heirs and Descendants" because it is concerned with the genealogy of modernity in
the Caribbean), the ruins of history appear in various guises: Merle's
Bentley is the former state car of the colonial governor, "but the car had
been badly used since then, and was now little more than a wreck";
her body, too, "had begun the slow, irreversible decline toward middle
age" (p. 4). A succession of motifs reinforces this image of decay,
decline, and incompleteness: Merle's dress and decorations are fragments from diverse cultures; their beauty is obvious, but their meaning is indeterminate:

> All this: the dress with its startling print, the strange but beautiful
> earrings that had been given to her years ago in England by the woman
> who had been, some said, her benefactress; others, her lover; the noisy
> bracelets, the shoes—all this could be easily taken as an attempt on her
> part to make herself out to be younger than she was. But there was more
> to it than one sensed. She had donned this somewhat bizarre outfit,
> each item of which stood opposed to, at war even, with the other, to
> express rather a diversity and disunity within herself, and her attempt,
> unconscious probably, to reconcile these opposing parts, to make of
> them a whole. Moreover in dressing in this manner, she appeared to be
> trying (and this was suggested by those unabashedly feminine shoes) to
> recover something in herself that had been lost: the sense and certainty
> of herself as a woman perhaps. There was no telling. But her face, as she
> stood breathing angrily down at the muddy swill at her feet, attested to
> some profound and frightening loss. [P. 5]

Several points in this description need to be underscored: First, the
representation of the subject is cast in a rhetoric of doubt, exemplified
by the divided opinion over Merle's relationship with the English
woman (was she her benefactress or her lover?). The narrative gives us
perspectives (or voices) which are not sanctioned by the narrator and
hence have no authority at all. Second, a set of important qualifiers
("all this could be easily taken . . ."; "somewhat bizarre . . .") leave the
reader in a state of doubt about the meaning and value of Merle's
actions: why does she dress the way she does? We are not sure.
Finally, by foregrounding Merle's sense of uncertainty—both about
"herself as a woman" and as a character in history—the narrative
ensures that we can never accept her as Marshall's "center of consciousness."

In the paragraph that follows, Merle's face is refigured as a mask
that has been despoiled "much the same way as the worn hills to be

seen piled around her on all sides had been despoiled"; this face is a sign of historical denial—"something of great value had been taken from her" (p. 5). However, there is an important duality in this temporal loss: worn out by time, the mask has acquired the status of an antique and its "vital center remained intact": "This sense of life persisting amid that nameless and irrevocable loss made her face terribly affecting, even beautiful" (p. 5). When we eventually try to make sense of the history of Bourneville, we will have to learn how to describe not only the worn-out surface, but also the inner core, for the meaning of the past seems to lie in a strange conjunction of loss and survival. And there is a prior question, too: do the ruins that confront us on the surface of Bourneville have any value as historical signs?

In his famous discussion of the allegory of history, Walter Benjamin asserts that ruins provide the guise for history, "and in this guise history does not assume the form of the process of an eternal life so much as that of irresistible decay." More important, the ruin appears "as the last heritage of an antiquity which in the modern world is only seen in its material form, as a picturesque field of ruins."[20] The ruin or remnant in *The Chosen Place* is intractable and conceals a sinister past. Take, for example, the room that houses the nightclub in Bourneville: it is described as a "long, high nave, whole areas of which were lost to the shadows dwelling beyond the reach of the touring lights" (p. 81). But the room is just the visible part of something more important. "It occupied the second story of a former sugar warehouse" and if you dug beneath the warehouse, you would possibly discover the slave barracoons: "The rusted remains of the iron manacles that had been fitted around the ankles and wrists, around the dark throats, could still be seen, some said, in the walls of the cellar. It had all begun here" (pp. 81–82). With this kind of antiquity, the island appears as a picturesque jumble: "All the discards of the nations, all the things that had become worn out over the centuries or fallen into disuse might have been brought and piled in a great charnel heap here" (p. 82). Elsewhere, Bourneville is often compared to "a ruined amphitheater whose other half had crumbled away and fallen into the sea," and to "some half-ruined coliseum" (p. 99).

Ultimately, history in *The Chosen Place* is shown to be a dialogical process that takes many forms, operates on diverse levels, and is often

20. Walter Benjamin, *The Origin of German Tragic Drama*, trans. John Osborne (London: NLB, 1977), p. 178.

the source of contention. Merle is fired from her teaching job because she insists on teaching the history of the repressed: "She was telling the children about Cuffee Ned and things that happened on the island in olden times, when the headmaster wanted her to teach the history that was down in the books, that told all about the English" (p. 32). There are differing philosophies of history, too: Vere is entrapped in a history that takes the form of repetition; he returns to the islands from the United States expecting things to have changed, only to discover that "nothing had changed. He had been foolish to imagine that it ever could, this being Bourneville" (p. 35). In contrast, Allen Fuso's research is propelled by an Aristotelian confidence in the rational doctrine that allows "everything, including people" to be put in "their proper categories" (p. 15); on the opposite end of the spectrum are the poor people of Bourneville who believe in the performative power of history. Merle, too, shares this faith in the performative function of history: when she retells the history of Cuffee Ned, we are told, "her voice held the awe of someone viewing it for the first time" (p. 101). At one point, the narrative contrasts performed history (retold by Merle) with Allen's "scrupulously objective" rendering of the same history according "to the historical records" (p. 102).

In all cases, Marshall's subjects are involved in a quest for a meta-discourse to justify their actions or rationalize their place within the scheme of things established by colonialism or the postcolonial state.[21] This appeal takes different forms, but it is often crystallized in a binary opposition between, on one hand, an appeal to wealth and material progress and, on the other hand, an evocation of the spirit of history. Thus, in *Brown Girl*, Selina's life is influenced and shaped by the tragic opposition between Deighton Boyce's yearning for deep historical meanings and his wife's rejection of the Bajan past in favor of the success ethic. Similarly, the drive to create wealth becomes the most important source of legitimacy for Jay Johnson in *Praisesong*, and is contrasted to the final quest for the meaning of the spirit of black history which engages Avey Johnson at the end of the novel.

In *The Chosen Place*, Marshall confronts both the limits and possibilities of colonial modernity and eventually proffers a dramatic contrast between the rational discourse of modernism and the claims of an-

---

21. On the relationship between modernity and metadiscourse see Jean-François Lyotard, *The Postmodern Condition: A Report on Knowledge*, trans. Geoff Bennington and Brian Massumi (Minneapolis: University of Minnesota Press, 1984), p. xxiii.

cestral meaning. As we have already seen, the rational discourse of modernism in this novel is associated with Weberian scientists such as Saul and Allen; their empirical study of Bourneville is intended to systematize knowledge so that the individual subject can be liberated from the "tyranny" of the past. Although these investigators scrutinize and analyze the objects of the past and the present, their temporal investment is in the future. If a unified knowledge of Bourneville as a whole can be established, they reason, then the island can be transformed as a whole.

The important point to stress here is that both analysts and their objects are uneasy about the past; they live in fear of the unknown history of the island and their own individual histories which they have carefully repressed or masked. Indeed, the researchers' sponsoring organization, the Center for Applied Social Research (CASR), uses its modernizing mission as a mask for some shameful economic activities by its financial backers, including active involvement in the slave trade (p. 37). So, in many ways, what the modernizing project proposes as a movement away from the past has deep roots in a history it would like to, but cannot, deny. For Marshall, then, the benevolent phase of late capitalism is just another face of the Caribbean mercantile and plantation system, which created most of the problems the modernizers are trying to solve. Although it has posited itself as the agency for historical transformation, CASR is, at the same time, shown to be linked to the very foundations of Caribbean slave society. Thus the new modernism promoted by this agency is exposed as a repetition of an equally dubious modernist movement in Caribbean history—the institution of the culture of sugar and slavery.

Implicit in such historical instances of repetition and reversal is a discursive irony that is crucial to Marshall's deconstruction of the modernists' claim to represent a new relationship with time. The manners and world view of the new ruling class in the island suggest that they are the agents of change and transformation, but their utterances to this effect are always undermined by a subtle subtext reminding the reader that these individuals have already been fixed by the old, colonial economy of meanings. The "surface ease and charm" of the new Caribbean elite cannot entirely mask the fact that "in spite of their secure air, they were not altogether sure that the relatively new affluence and position they had come into were truly theirs" (p. 53). In spite of the nationalism that veils it, modernity is just a continuation of the European vision of history imposed on the island during the

colonial period. Lyle Hurston's "imposing white house" is a synec-
dochal representation of the uneasy and duplicitous nature of Caribbean modernity: the house appears to be modern, but it is really built
on the remains of an old Georgian house; it retains the ugly elements
of the latter though it tries to conceal them under a "profusion of
modern touches that were suspect." The house, concludes the narrator, "was a failure, although this was not immediately apparent, and
most people thought it handsome, progressive and new. But the de-
signer, in trying to blend the old and the new, had failed to select the
best from each—those features from the past and present which
would have best served his end" (p. 54). And so the present bears the
baggage of the past even against its will.

Here Marshall is posing important questions hinted at variously in
the other texts I have examined: Why does independent Caribbean
society try to sustain the affirmative character of European culture
even as it rejects colonial domination? Why is the mask of modernity
so valuable to the maintenance of power and domination in the independent state? Indeed, why does Hurston, as a representative of the
native ruling class, promote a discourse of resistance against colonial
ideologies even as he helps reinforce and rebuild the institutions of
colonialism? The theoretical response to these questions has been
provided by Louis Hartz, who argues that members of the "creole"
ruling classes in the New World require their European origins or
modes of knowledge "to rationalize their class position."[22] In Marshall's text, this class inscribes its difference from the ordinary people
of Bourneville by insisting on the ways in which their mastery of
European forms has legitimized their position as agents of modernity
and modernization. The assumption here is that the general populace
cannot effect change; Bourneville's people "don't take easy to anything new, even when it might be to their good" (p. 158). In contrast,
the "creole" elite can effect change by "breaking the old pattern of
depending on the outside for everything. . . . Once we industrialize on
a large enough scale we will then have means to finance the changes
needed in agriculture" (p. 206). This is how an old colonial modernity
comes to wear a nationalist mask.[23]

22. Louis Hartz, *The Founding of New Societies* (New York: Harcourt, 1964), p. 11.
23. According to Jean Franco the magic of modernity is an attempt to control the past to
show postcolonial peoples "how much better off they are in the present"; in this sense, "the
modern state is a kind of illusionist which needs the past only as a lament and whose miracle is
the economic miracle of dependency." See "The Nation as Imagined Community," in *The New
Historicism*, ed. H. Aram Veeser (New York: Routledge, 1989), p. 206.

Both the foreign and native modernists in the novel privilege their ideology by appealing to three theoretical positions: the mastery of the discourse of modernism and the belief that they are the only ones amenable to historical change; the assertion of a vision of history which is supposed to be "true" and "right" because it is contained in documents and is invested with the idea of progress; and the representation of island society as a unified whole, one that does not allow for social, class, and race differences or for different political articulations. Both Saul and Allen invest in empiricism because they hope to established a logical explanation for social change. This logic is predicated on the suppression of the irrational and the unconscious, the magical and the romantic. Ironically, it is not Saul and Allen who master Bourneville; on the contrary, the island brings out the repressed in both characters—Allen's homosexuality and Saul's empty love life.

And if the reader is looking for a dramatic confrontation between the ideal of progress and repressed histories, Vere's life and death provide the example. For like many other characters in Marshall's novels—those who subscribe to what I have been calling modernity—Vere is always in search of techniques of *dédoublement*. He feels anachronistic within the island culture, finds it difficult to reconcile himself to its immobility, and yearns to engender himself differently: his restoration of the old Opel is nothing less than a test of his capacity for subjectivity. But the young man's belief that he can express his character and identity through the technical mastery of the machine is contrasted to his aunt's rejection of the rational notion that human beings have power over the instruments they use: "It was as though she believed beyond question that all such things as cars, all machines, had human properties, minds and wills of their own, and those were constantly plotting against those whom they served" (p. 185). Ultimately, Vere's death in the car (pp. 366–67) seems to be enough proof that there are important Caribbean meanings that are closed to Western knowledge and technology.

The Longing for the Ideal of History

In his influential discussion of the relationship between history and literature, Glissant makes the following comment on the Caribbean writer's desire for the "ideal of history":

> The passion for or the preoccupation with history does not manifest itself in the writer as a need for a reserve of information to which he has easy access, not as a reassuring framework, but rather as the obsession with finding the *primordial source* toward which one struggles through revelations that have the peculiarity (like myth in the past) of obscuring as well as disclosing.[24]

Carnival and the carnivalesque function in *The Chosen People* as a "primordial source" that obscures as well as discloses: they suspend time and mask the drudgery of everyday life while also functioning as expressions of the peasants' desire for an alternative means of organizing history and language. For outside observers, the carnivalesque is obscure; for the peasants of Bourneville, it discloses a collective genealogy and perpetuates their "national" spirit. Through their subversive interpretation of the official carnival masque, these peasants adopt the carnivalesque as an alternative narrative of history, one in which ancestral memories can be retained and the ideology of colonial modernism can be contested. Carnival, as Hortense Spillers has argued in her superb reading of the novel, is Marshall's "master sign and controlling figure."[25] Indeed, the poor people of Bourneville establish their mastery of language by adopting the minstrel mask, the weapon of the trickster and of black modernism.[26] These peasants are hence compared to Anancy, the trickster in Afro-Caribbean folklore, who "though small and weak, always managed to outwit the larger and stronger creatures in his world, including man, by his wit and cunning" (p. 224). The subterranean and subversive space provided by the carnivalesque is introduced in the text to challenge the dominance and ideology of colonial modernism by dispersing the authority of meanings imposed from above.

Because carnival has become ossified into a commodity—it is a major tourist attraction in the island—the peasants must also strive to maintain its original meanings to secure their own subjectivity. In the

---

24. Edouard Glissant, *Caribbean Discourse: Selected Essays*, trans. J. Michael Dash (Charlottesville: University Press of Virginia, 1989), p. 79.

25. Hortense J. Spillers, "*Chosen Place, Timeless People*: Some Figurations on the New World," in *Conjuring: Black Women, Fiction, and Literary Tradition*, ed. Marjorie Pryse and Hortense J. Spillers (Bloomington: Indiana University Press, 1985), p. 165. See also Peter Nazareth, "Paule Marshall's Timeless People," *New Letters* 40 (October 1973), 113–31; and two articles in *CLA Journal* 16 (September 1972): Leela Kapai, "Dominant Themes and Technique in Paule Marshall's Fiction" (49–59) and Winifred L. Stoelting, "Time Past and Time Present: The Search for Viable Links in *The Chosen Place, The Timeless People* by Paule Marshall" (60–71).

26. Baker, p. 17.

end, however, the carnival functions as a space where conflicting versions of history meet. The upper classes and the tourists see the carnival as a meaningless spectacle that creates a temporal suspense that is useful because it represses class, racial, and caste differences. Lyle Hurston describes it as "a marvelous sight, and a much needed one . . . in a world where all of us manage to be so ugly to each other, especially over this whole stupid question of race and color" (p. 200). But Hurston's interpretation of the carnival is overdetermined by his equivocal position within the culture: as the representative of Bourneville in the legislature, he has one foot in the "native" culture; but as a privileged member of the neocolonial elite, he has his other foot in the colonizer's Anglo-Saxon culture. In the latter position, he views the carnival from without, as a spectacle that mirrors his own desire to master and control his people, or to mediate the relationship between the margin and the center.

The real spirit of carnival as a mode of social expression, as Mikhail Bakhtin argues eloquently in his famous study of Rabelais, derives from the fact that the people don't view it as a spectacle, but "live in it, and everyone participates because its very idea embraces all the people."[27] In fact, the peasants of Bourneville position themselves within the carnival and subject themselves to the gaze of others and even the contempt of the rest of the community because they view the masque as an expression of their world view and sense of self and hence insist on representation in their own terms.[28] As Harriet puts it aptly in a letter to her friend Chessie, "For some reason people in Bourneville insist on enacting the same masque or story every carnival, which is against the rules. But they say it's cheaper, because then they don't have to buy new costumes" (p. 233). Unable to grasp the importance of this adherence to old meanings, and exasperated by the peasants' failure to modernize their masque, the rest of the island tries to bar the poor people of Bourneville from the carnival altogether. Furthermore, the reason the people of Bourneville give for their failure to change their routine is obscuring. In reality they have made the conscious decision to challenge the carnival as a depository of official truths and to inscribe their own narrative of history within the dominant culture.

27. Mikhail Bakhtin, *Rabelais and His World*, trans. Helene Iswolsky (Cambridge: MIT Press, 1965), p. 7.
28. According to Rex Nettleford, the festival is "a positive expression of people's worldviews and sense of self." See "Implications for Caribbean Development," in *Caribbean Festival Arts*, ed. John Nunley and Judith Bettelheim (Seattle: University of Washington Press, 1988), p. 196.

Against the grain of modernity—which values the future more than the past, change and transformation more than myth and ritual—the peasants promote a narrative built on repetition and changelessness. They feel that the new carnival, as an official spectacle, has become institutionalized in the capitalist system of exchange; by insisting on changelessness, these people have defied the logic of neocolonialism and its investment in the future.

Moreover, if the official carnival gestures toward the colonial notion of a single history, the peasants' masque foregrounds the ambiguity of historicism. Although their obsession with the past is seen by other members of the community as a form of escapism, by marching against "the rules" the people of Bourneville are in keeping with the true spirit of the original carnival, which celebrated the revolt of the slaves. Thus the people of Bourneville insist not only on repeating the masque of the previous year, but also on replicating the worn-out history of the Cuffee slave rebellion; to the embarrassment of the rest of the island, they come "dragging into town every year in the same old rags, looking s' bad and embarrassing decent people with some old-time business everybody's done forgot" (p. 283). In contrast, the new island elite, by using the carnival to celebrate their notions of modernization, are seeking relief from the past and its responsibilities. Furthermore, instead of becoming commodities in the carnival, the peasants use the carnivalesque as a subversive force that, to borrow Bakhtin's terms, celebrates "temporal liberation from the prevailing truth and from the established order."[29]

But this investment in the past—and hence in the notion of history as a form of repetition—runs counter to Bakhtin's description of carnival as "the true feast of time, the feast of becoming, change and renewal."[30] In temporal terms, the question Marshall poses here is not whether carnival celebrates change or affirms old values; rather, she is concerned with probing the value of a history that repeats itself. In the process, she seems to suggest that a recovery of the past contradicts the neocolonialists' claim to have restored the spirit of the modern nation through the mastery of imperial discourses. In contrast, the repetition of unofficial and incomplete histories, such as the Cuffee Ned revolt, is a reminder that we have not yet been reconnected to the past, that our modernity and our modern "national culture" are

29. Bakhtin, p. 10.
30. Bakhtin, p. 10.

achieved through the repression of the slave tradition of resistance. Thus the masque that the peasants of Bourneville repeat over and over again is not simply the Freudian repressed that returns to haunt us, nor merely the unconscious of history; rather, it is also an attempt to capture and articulate the voice of the black subject in the categories of its own modernity.

Consequently, the voice plays a prominent part in the Bourneville masque. At the end of the march, we are informed, the voices of the peasants rise as if from the depths of time, breaking through the ragged costumes that had masked the power of sound. "And the effect of that sudden uprush of sound, coming as it did after the numbed silence, was of a massive shock wave upon the air, and once again, New Bristol seemed to reel at its base" (p. 286). The voices resurrect the past and return us to the fixed scene of Caribbean beginnings, a scene determined by what Spillers calls "origins that must be appeased, at least recognized and named out loud."[31] Moreover, the value of re-peated history is shown to lie in its deep play: those who seek the mere spectacle in the Bourneville masque will only see old and worn-out costumes and hear tired and sour words; but those who listen care-fully will sense a "deeper level of consciousness . . . moving beneath its static surface" (p. 410).

At the end of the carnival, even the modernizers are forced to revise both their modes of interpretation and their conception of temporality. For example, Saul, who had earlier advocated modernization as a decisive break with tradition, now realizes that the past cannot be disavowed; ignored by generations of conquerors and rulers, the peas-ants of Bourneville perform the past to keep it alive, and in the process strive "to come into their own, start using their history to their own advantage" (p. 315). Repetition is hence a form of reterritorialization; the past is shown to be alive while time is momentarily stopped so that the lessons of history may not be lost. The carnival masque has re-jected the Anglo-American desire to move the colonial subjects into the future without first addressing the past. In this respect, the carni-valesque is a way of turning temporality inside out, thereby "telescop-ing whole centuries so that events which had taken place long ago and should have passed into history and had been forgotten seemed to have occurred only yesterday—time had had a stop" (p. 414). In Marshall's own words, the people of Bourneville have refigured the

31. Spillers, p. 158.

concept of time itself—"they seem apart from the Western notion of time altogether and as much a part of the past as the present. They might have been the rebel slaves who had refused to die. They might have been the original Africans who survived the crossing."[32]

Marshall's notion of temporal continuity is only possible, however, because of a painful paradox embedded in the idea of the carnival-esque: the carnival masque suspends time so that the participants can celebrate their tradition of resistance; but once the festival is over, the characters have to return to a fragmented and disjunctive world that represses the very freedoms articulated in the feast. There is no doubt that Marshall and her characters seek an essentialist African voice in the New World and that her texts are concerned with the forms and conditions in which the black diaspora has carried on the sounds and words of ancient African traditions and "the oral mode by which the culture and history, the wisdom of the race had been transmitted." Yet the quest for an African voice has to confront the larger imperial discourses established by European modernism.[33] The anxiety of Ca-ribbean history and the West Indian longing for the ideal of history are most explicit in the conflict between the African voice and European colonial discourse.

Like other Afro-Caribbean writers—most notably Glissant and Brathwaite—Marshall often posits the voice as a paradigm for the repressed African past in Caribbean and Afro-American cultures.[34] For example, in *Brown Girl*, Silla Boyce may strive to master the culture of capitalism and its celebration of property rights, but she cannot escape from the tradition of the voice that relives the past at every opportunity. For this reason, she has become "the collective voice of all the Bajan women, the vehicle through which their former suffering found utterance" (p. 45). This emphasis on the collective utterance would seem to suggest that the voice functions as a metaphor of the communal self or the allegory of its historical experiences. Indeed, when Mary Helen Washington asserts—in an excellent afterword to the novel—that Silla is "the avatar of the community's deepest values and needs" (p. 313), she assumes that the woman's voice and that of her community are identical, that there is a deep correspondence between voice, self, and community. And yet most of the novel is

32. Marshall, "Shaping the World," p. 111.
33. "Shaping the World," p. 103.
34. Edward Kamau Brathwaite, *History of the Voice: The Development of National Language in Anglophone Caribbean Poetry* (London: New Beacon Books, 1984), and Glissant, pp. 120–33.

about the disjunction between Silla and her community. While Silla's voice often echoes many of her people's fears and hopes, it is also marked by its *différance* from what could be considered the traditional Bajan ethos. Indeed, one of the central questions raised by the book is this: to what extent does the Bajan culture retain its integrity once it has become caught up in the ethics of North American capitalism?

It is more accurate to argue that Silla's voice signifies the metonymic displacement of the Bajan culture in New York: she retains traces of the original voice, but as her disdain for her husband indicates, the original must be transcended for the sake of "progress." Indeed, Silla is placed in a paradoxical situation: her voice echoes the past while her actions question the ethics inherent in that past and its traditions. No wonder Selina hears her mother's voice as the figuration of the paradoxes of Caribbean cultures dispersed from their source—"the mother's voice was a net flung wide, ensnaring all within its reach. She swayed helpless now with its hold, loving its rich color, loving and hating the mother for the pain of her childhood" (p. 46). The voice from the past contains both joy and pain; it ensnares and liberates at the same time.[35] Within the larger context of the African experience in the New World, the voice signalizes the slaves' history of loss and repression and, in many instances, the impossibility of recovering the African ideal or its idiom. For although such an ideal is desirable because it promises an alternative mode of representation, African culture in the Americas is already invested with the pain of Western history.

Marshall foregrounds this problem in the epigraph to *The Chosen Place*, a Tiv proverb that posits words as masks of historical hurt. And in the self-division in Merle Kinbona's voice, and the haunted echoes of the past in "the chosen place" itself, we have examples of how the voice represents the struggle between the utopian ideal of African synchronism and synthesis in the New World and the nightmare of Western history which places innumerable obstacles between the self and its desires. As a result Merle's voice is marked by an interesting duality: on one hand, this voice appears as the thing that represents her subjectivity (her personality is often identified by the way she talks); but, on the other hand, the narrative often stresses the extent to which this voice also masks a hidden and enigmatic self. In fact, Merle's voice appears to have acquired a life of its own, glancing off the

35. Marshall, "Shaping the World," pp. 98–101.

surface, out of control, refracting from its origins and drawing our attention away from the speaker. Very early in the novel, Merle's voice is shown caught up in "what seemed a desperate downhill race with itself" (p. 11). Her words flow unchecked, "the voice rushing pell-mell down the precipitous slope toward its own destruction" (p. 66); this voice is variously described as "desperate" (p. 67) or "anguished" (p. 92). As the novel progresses, however, we begin to realize that the voice masks an inner pain; Merle's surface talk ("it was the talk, you sensed, which alone sustained her") is a form of temporal suspense, almost akin to the carnival masque. By talking, Merle postpones confronting the past; as she admits, "if I was to ever stop talking that'd be the end of me" (p. 96).

The quest for the ideal of history also foregrounds a crisis of interpretation and self-understanding in the black tradition as it tries to adjust to the demands of the dominant culture. For example, in *Praisesong for the Widow*, Avey Johnson's crisis of identity is closely related to her uneasy relationship to the "black voice" and her past. Her material success and co-option into the modern system of exchange have ostensibly liberated her from her past, but even as she begins to enjoy this success—this Weberian liberation from tradition, as it were—the past seems to become more difficult to deal with. The past returns to haunt her with the power of an "eternal recurrence" that threatens the very foundation of her success—the belief that she has transcended her complex ancestral past. The notion of "eternal recurrence" in Marshall's text is connected to the larger question that concerns us here, namely, the notion of an American, or more specifically an Afro-American, hermeneutics, anchored not on the traditional modernist belief in the future as a moment of closure in which meanings are revealed, but on the past as the site where such meanings are initiated. Two concepts—the "ring shout" and the "circle of meaning"—are important to Marshall's revision of Western temporality in *Praisesong*.

In writing about the ring shout and the circle of culture in his monumental study of slave society, Sterling Stuckey has argued that African slaves in the plantations of the Americas posited the circle and the ring shout as an allegory of "African autonomy," marking the set of values and symbols which could condition the interpretation of the black experience as distinct from the system that sought to annihilate it:

The South Carolina storytellers, like those elsewhere, told tales in which the dominant spiritual configuration provided the means by which Africans, whatever their ethnic differences, found values proper to them when the slave trade and slavery divorced them from their homeland. Consequently, listeners in the slave community who had previously been unexposed to those tales immediately understood what was being related, irrespective of where their parents came from.[36]

Avey Johnson is born into this circle of black culture: her first memorable utterances are about the ring shout, and her initiatory memories are centered on the Ibos who had foreseen the tragedies of slavery and had decided to return home by walking across the ocean. As far as her grandmother is concerned, Avey's mission is to carry into the future memories of the past: "In instilling the story of the Ibos in her child's mind, the old woman had entrusted her with a mission she couldn't even name yet had felt duty-bound to fulfill" (p. 42). Avey's crisis of consciousness develops because in espousing the notion of temporality as a form of progression from the past to the future, she has forgotten her ancestral duties; now her repressed past has returned to haunt her and "her memory seemed to be playing the same frightening tricks as her eyes" (p. 57). In the moment of narration, Avey faces an interpretative problem: how can she recover the value of a past that now appears more remote from her than it was when she began pursuing the American dream?

The idea of a historical return is an important trope in *Praisesong* and is often proposed as a possible resolution of the crisis of temporality which grips characters like Avey Johnson. When subliminal echoes from the past force Avey to abandon her cruise ship and return to her home, she is unconsciously drawn to a Caribbean island in which the themes of return and historical continuity are inscribed into the collective memories of the people. Waking up in a Caribbean where the past still seems to be alive, Avey finds her mind cleared of the memories that repressed her Afrocentricity, "so that she had awakened . . . like a slate that has been wiped clean, a *tabula rasa* upon which a whole new history could be written" (p. 151). But how is this history written? Or rather, how is the subject inscribed into its founding mythology?

Again, we must remember that the so-called Carriacou excursion is, like the carnival in Bourneville, a performative act that has ensured the

36. Sterling Stuckey, *Slave Culture: Nationalist Theory and the Foundations of Black America* (New York: Oxford University Press, 1987), p. 10.

survival of the past in the present by annually repeating the African circle of meanings: in the great shout and dance, family and nation are recalled and connection with the past is reestablished. Every islander identifies with a nation or with a creole culture (p. 175), and hence there are no nationless people outside this circle. In a sense, by recognizing her own place within this circle, Avey has reconnected herself with her ancestral past and covered the "hole the size of a crater where her life of the past three decades had been" (p. 196). However, a final question still remains: what is the value of this form of self-recognition? The answer is contained in a passage in which Avey tries to endow the dance of the nations with a set of determinate meanings, but discovers that the quest for an African ideal is highly paradoxical:

> It was the essence of something rather than the thing itself she was witnessing. . . . All that was left were a few names of what they called nations which they could no longer even pronounce properly, the fragments of a dozen or so songs, the shadowy forms of long-ago dances and rum kegs for drums. The bare bones. The burnt-out ends. And they clung to them with a tenacity she suddenly loved in them and longed for in herself. Thoughts—new thoughts—vague and half-formed slowly beginning to fill the emptiness. [P. 240]

Historical continuity may be a desired ideal, but the dominant theme now is one of "separation and loss" (p. 244); what remains of Africa is merely the fragment of (an ideal) memory.

In the circumstances, it would be futile for the exiled Africans to recover "natural" African meanings; it is impossible to recuperate African objects of knowledge in a continuous and holistic way. However, the fragments of Africa which we see in the national dances of Carriacou are valuable because they are the only basis on which a new, black discourse can be initiated within a discursive formation bent on denying the value of black cultures. At the end of *Praisesong*, Avey Johnson realizes that the power of the cultural circle in Carriacou does not lie in the object it projects, but in "the unacknowledged longing it conveyed" which "summed up feelings that were beyond words, feelings and a host of subliminal memories that over the years had proven more durable and trustworthy than the history with its trauma and pain out of which they had come" (p. 245). The African fragment has value precisely because it is the central focus of the rules—both conscious and unconscious—that govern black discourse. The limit of the Western version of history is shown to be its enslavement to linear development, the emphasis it places on the continuity of that history initiated by Columbus, a history of repression and pain, which always seems to insist that the destiny of the Caribbean is to become European. And thus, as the women novelists discussed in the next two chapters constantly aver, the primal scene of the West Indian object is marked by the paradoxes of a society caught between colonial history and the longing for a national culture.

6

Writing after Colonialism:
Crick Crack, Monkey and *Beka Lamb*

> In national allegories, women became the territory over which the quest for (male) national identity passed, or, at best . . . the space of loss and of all that lies outside the male games of rivalry and revenge. . . . Under those circumstances, a national identity could not but be a problematic terrain for women novelists, although it was not something they could avoid.
>
> —Jean Franco, *Plotting Women*

> When yuh succumb to certain tings in silence yuh build up di power of di oppressor to exploit a next person.
>
> —Sistren, *Lionheart Gal*

To consider the question of gender and subjectivity in modernist discourse is also to confront the ambiguous role women play in the construction of national identity. I have already hinted at this ambiguity in the previous chapters: in the central (male) texts of Caribbean modernism women either signify the social space over which the colonizer and the colonized struggle or function as what Franco, in the epigraph above, calls a space of loss. In many of the novels discussed earlier, women are often confined to private spaces, largely excluded—like Sophia in Carpentier's *El siglo*—from the historical events that obsess and overdetermine the men's lives and experiences. Alternatively, as in the case of Lamming's *In the Castle of My Skin*, while the figure of the mother represents the utopian space of the nation, of home and belonging, the mother is still notable for her prolonged silence and subordination to the son's quest for identity. Where women embrace modernity and modernization as a way out of the dominant patriarchal structures, often defined as tradition (Selvon's Seeta is an apt example here), they are seen not as agents of social change, but as destabilizers of the family and the cultural body. Ultimately, as Merle Kinbona discovers in *The Chosen Place*, the end of colonialism does not rescue women from their historical confinement—they still remain modernism's "other," excluded or marginalized from the signifying systems of the new nation.[1]

In writing about gender and representation in colonial and postcolonial Mexican society, Jean Franco observes that the relationship between women and the discourse of national identity and modernity was different from that of men and hence demanded a reconsideration of the diverse configuration of colonial subjects and the articulation of gender and subjectivity in the terrain of the nation. If nationalism and modernization constituted the master narratives, and hence the symbolic systems that cemented colonial and postcolonial societies, argues Franco, these narratives also "plotted women differently into the social text."[2] In the circumstances, women writers—unable to find a detour around the issue of the new nation and determined to tell their own stories within the national signified—have provided inevitable revisionings of the Caribbean narrative.

It is true that Caribbean male writers such as Earl Lovelace and Michael Thelwell have written trenchant critiques of what Fanon once called "the pitfalls of national consciousness," but it is the emergence of the Caribbean woman writer in the post-independence period which forces us to reconsider the very definition of modernity and its concordant discourse on national identity.[3] For if the colonized body has been equated with the mother who has to be rescued from the conqueror and restored to her true identity and her real cultural norms, it is pertinent to question how women writers perceive this mother figure and how they locate her in the signifying systems of the colony and the new nation. As Olive Senior has succinctly noted, the emergence of the Caribbean woman writer has opened a completely

1. Jean Franco, *Plotting Women: Gender and Representation in Mexico* (London: Verso, 1989), p. xii.
2. Franco, p. xii.
3. Frantz Fanon, *The Wretched of the Earth*, trans. Constance Farrington (New York: Grove Press, 1968), pp. 148–205.

new approach to the topic of the Caribbean mother and the cultural forms with which she is associated.[4] Caribbean women writers compel us to examine the relationship between national identity, gender, and subjectivity in Caribbean discourse.

Moreover, in challenging male definitions of the nation, its past history, present crisis, and future destiny, and by underscoring the crucial relationship between gender and identity, Caribbean women writers are redefining Caribbean literary history. According to Carole Boyce Davies, "A substantial number of women writers, living both at home and abroad, have emerged, giving different shape and voice to this literature and challenging the preeminence of the largely male writers whom we used to think of as 'Caribbean literature.' The reality of gender presents, perhaps, the crucial difference between this group of writers and the preceding generation."[5] Apart from forcing us to question the meaning of the central terms in colonial and postcolonial discourse—terms such as *culture, nation,* and *selfhood*—Caribbean women's writing has also raised the question of silence and the absence of Caliban's woman—"an absence which is functional to the new secularizing schema by which the peoples of Western Europe legitimized their global expansion," according to Sylvia Wynter.[6] In other words, whereas male discourse in the Caribbean was previously obsessed with the Prospero/Caliban dialectic and the slave's inheritance of his master's language, women writers strive to underscore the converse process—the absence of the female subject and its silencing in the master/slave dialectic.

Carole Davies and Elaine Fido have provided us with a limpid definition of absence and voicelessness as preconditions for a revisionist female discourse in the Caribbean:

> The concept of voicelessness necessarily informs any discussion of Caribbean women and literature. It is a crucial consideration because it is out of this voicelessness and consequent absence that an understanding of our creativity in written expression emerges. By voicelessness, we mean the historical absence of the woman writer's text: the absence of a specifically female position on major issues such as slavery, colonialism, decolonization, women's rights and more direct social and cultural is-

4. Charles H. Rowell, "An Interview with Olive Senior," *Callaloo* 11 (Summer 1988), 485.
5. Carole Boyce Davies, "Writing Home: Gender and Heritage in the Works of Afro-Caribbean/American Women Writers," in *Out of the Kumbla: Caribbean Women and Literature,* ed. Carole Boyce Davies and Elaine Savory Fido (Trenton, N.J.: Africa World Press, 1990), p. 59.
6. Sylvia Wynter, "Afterword," in Davies and Fido, *Out of the Kumbla,* pp. 361–62.

sues. By voicelessness we also mean silence: the inability to express a position in the language of the "master" as well as the textual construction of woman as silent. Voicelessness also denotes articulation that goes unheard.[7]

Paradoxically, the Caribbean women writers' consciousness and ultimate reversion of voicelessness into sound and words have led to the revision of Caribbean modernist discourse in two respects: First, silence arises from what we have called the confinement of women to the private space, which is denied the value and resonance of public discourse articulated in borrowed European forms such as the novel and the essay. But in the same private spaces that were supposed to denote silence, Caribbean women writers have nurtured a language that, in the words of Olive Senior, "personalizes the socio-political issues": now the individual life becomes the primary focus "so all experience tends to be filtered through a particular consciousness" struggling against the pull and push of history.[8] Second, amid the linguistic struggle between Prospero and Caliban, the language of the folk in particular and popular culture in general has been inserted as a third term that challenges and deconstructs the claims of both colonialism and male-centered nationalism.

A vivid example of how this third discourse functions can be found in one of the most memorable scenes in Merle Hodge's *Crick Crack, Monkey*. The author presents us with a symbolic confrontation between North American modernity (as articulated by Manhatt'n) and the Afro-Caribbean vernacular:

> Manhatt'n was an individual who at some obscure date had 'gone-away.' Some of the boys said he'd only been to Curacao where he'd got a job for a few months; one section of opinion had it that he merely worked down on the Base for a few weeks. Manhatt'n himself gave it out that he'd been up Stateside, fellers, up Amurraca-side—for he always spoke with his mouth screwed to one side and all the words coming out of his nose. When the fellows were in a tolerant mood they would let Manhatt'n tell of his encounter with the sheriff in Dodge City and how he outdrew him; or of the blonde chick in Manhattan who wouldn't leave him alone, kept coming to his apartment when there was this red-head thing he was working at (Martinis, yer know, and a lil'

7. Carole Boyce Davies and Elaine Savory Fido, "Introduction: Women and Literature in the Caribbean: An Overview," in *Out of the Kumbla*, p. 1.
8. Rowell, p. 485.

caviar on the side). And when the fellows screamed with laughter Manhatt'n looked imbecilically happy. But when one day someone maliciously murmured 'Crick-crack!' at the end of one of these accounts in perfect Western drawl, Manhatt'n in his rage forgot to screw his mouth to one side before starting to speak.[9]

Manhatt'n lives out the fantasy of colonial and neocolonial modernism—the desire to be European or American—but this fantasy is constricted by the realities of the folk culture of which the "Crick-crack" narrative formula is an important subversive agent. ("Crick-crack" is the opening formula or refrain for many folktales in the Afro-Caribbean tradition; it is intended to remind listeners, especially children, that the story is imaginary.) And although values in this "modern" world are primarily masculine and women are instruments of imaginary exchange and verbal degradation, women still manage to subjectify themselves in their stories and produce narratives that not only celebrate their lives and ancestry, but also deflate "the make-believe value system" of the colonizer.[10] As the women of the Sistren collective have asserted, the function of narrative in the patois, the displaced *parole*, is to lift the veil of silence surrounding the lives of Caribbean women and hence break the power of the oppressor; writing after colonialism demands a literary form and language that allow the narrators to confront, rather than escape, their material objectification in the language of the colonizer, as a precondition for subjectivity.[11]

The basic premise in the works I examine in this chapter—Merle Hodge's *Crick Crack, Monkey* and Zee Edgell's *Beka Lamb*—is that the unveiling of the lives of Caribbean women not only recenters them in history as custodians of an oral tradition, but also functions as an indicator of sources of domination that might have been lost or repressed in both the colonial text and male-dominated nationalist discourse. Indeed, according to Hodge, colonial education, by presenting the lived experiences of the Caribbean people as invalid, negated the very subjectivity of the colonized by taking them away from their "own reality": "We never saw ourselves in a book, so we didn't exist in

9. Merle Hodge, *Crick Crack, Monkey* (London: Heinemann, 1981), p. 7. Further references are in the text.
10. Kathleen M. Balutansky, "We Are All Activists: An Interview with Merle Hodge," *Callaloo* 12 (Fall 1989), 657.
11. See Sistren with Honor Ford-Smith, *Lionheart Gal: Life Stories of Jamaican Women* (Toronto: Sister Vision, 1987), pp. 1–19.

a kind of way and our culture and our environment, our climate, the plants around us did not seem real, did not seem to be of any importance—we overlooked them entirely. The real world was what was in books."[12] In a situation in which existence and significance are defined by the texts we write and read, as Hodge seems to suggest here, then the absence of female texts in the Caribbean canon meant that political independence had not restored speech to the Caribbean female subject, an important producer of West Indian culture. The culture of West Indian women, argues Hodge, hadn't "been given a name and it didn't get recognized as a culture."[13] Even in the period after independence, according to Honor Ford-Smith, there exists among the women of the Caribbean "a need for a naming of experience and a need for communal support in that process. In the past silence has surrounded this experience."[14]

Narratives like those of the Sistren collective are indeed some of the most important ways Caribbean women devise what Pat Ellis aptly calls "strategies to overcome the obstacles that threaten to curtail their freedom."[15] And if the doctrine of modernity transfers the authority of power and utterance in the Caribbean to the black male, then a feminist renaming of experience implies the revision of modernism, even the outright rejection of its totalizing tendencies; by positing gender differences as a site for representing and reconstructing new identities (in narrative and semiotic terms), Caribbean women writers are establishing what a leading feminist scholar of modernism has called "the conditions of existence of those subjects who are muted, elided, or unrepresentable in dominant discourse."[16]

The two texts I have selected to illustrate this point deal with the same colonial condition discussed in previous chapters, but they have a different formal and thematic emphasis; they also present a different structural relationship among subjects, dominant discourses, and their situations of production. These texts posit the linguistic terrain as one of multiple struggles rather than a Manichaean relationship between self and other. Instead of striving to establish a dialogue be-

12. Quoted in *A Handbook for Teaching Caribbean Literature*, ed. David Dabydeen (London: Heinemann, 1988), p. 78.
13. Balutansky, p. 653.
14. Ford-Smith, p. 7.
15. Pat Ellis, "Introduction—An Overview of Women in Caribbean Society," in *Women of the Caribbean*, ed. Pat Ellis (London: Zed, 1986), p. 1.
16. Teresa de Lauretis, "Feminist Studies/Critical Studies: Issues, Terms, and Contexts," in *Feminist Studies/Critical Studies*, ed. Teresa de Lauretis (Bloomington: Indiana University Press, 1986), p. 9.

tween the colonizer and the colonized as a means of revising the status of the colonial subject in the colonizing structure, the priority of these texts is the despoilment of what Michelle Cliff calls the master's "cultural soup"—"mixing in the forms taught us by the oppressor, undermining his language and co-opting his style, and turning it to our purpose."[17] Whereas earlier generations of Caribbean writers sought ways of appropriating and nationalizing European forms of representation—hence Césaire's indebtedness to surrealism or Lamming's affinity with high modernism—both Hodge and Edgell, writing after colonialism, are as much indebted to their Caribbean precursors as they are to the colonial text. They reverse and revise both the colonial and black male texts even as they try to validate the oral tradition. Rejecting the common notion of a subject whose identity is defined and fixed by the dominant patriarchal culture, Hodge and Edgell posit a self that is defined by ideological ambiguity and a self-contradictory identity.

Writing the Individual Life: *Crick Crack, Monkey*

Crick Crack, Monkey was the first major novel by a Caribbean woman—in the period after independence—in which the writer assumed the consciousness of her subject and gave it expression, hence using "autobiography" as a textual space for exploring the effects of colonialism on the budding Caribbean national culture.[18] Hodge's strategy in this book was not to concentrate on the evolution of a public consciousness in her main subject, Tee, but to foreground questions of difference and the quest for a voice in a social context that denied expression to the colonized self and hence cut it off from the liberating forms of popular culture and the oral tradition in the Caribbean. For Hodge, this emphasis on voice as a precondition for black subjectivity in a colonial situation was necessitated by both ideology and technique. First of all, in the plantation societies of the Caribbean, the voices of the oppressed and dominated slaves and indentured laborers survived against the modes of silence engendered by the master class. For these slaves and laborers, the preservation and inscription of a distinctive voice came to signify the site of their own

17. Michelle Cliff, "A Journey into Speech," in *The Land of Look Behind: Prose and Poetry* (Ithaca, N.Y.: Firebrand Books, 1985), p. 1.
18. Balutansky, p. 654.

cultural difference. Second, the voice was variously an instrument of struggle against domination and a repository of African values in a world in which the slaves' traditions were denigrated and their self-hood repressed.[19] In narrative terms, the recovery of voice would become one way through which unspoken and repressed experiences could be represented.

In Merle Hodge's novel, then, the voice is a synecdoche of the unwritten culture of the colonized, the culture of Aunt Tantie and Ma; and its privileging in the text signifies an epistemological shift from the hegemony of written forms (which, as we saw in previous chapters, have been a source of anxiety for colonized peoples) to an African-derived orality. At the same time, the negation of the spoken utterance through education and assimilation functions as a mark of deep aliena-tion. Within this tenuous relationship between the oral and the writ-ten, as Tee discovers when she opens her retrospective view of her childhood at the beginning of *Crick Crack*, the past cannot be narrated without a cognizance of the contradictory voices that defined it— repressive voices coexisting with liberating ones. The figure of the voice is shown to be both central to the narrator's conception of her childhood and a paradigm that defines the context in which her multi-ple selves were produced. Indeed, at the opening of the novel, an ambiguous moment in which the birth of a new baby is superseded by the death of its mother, the world appears to Tee merely as a relation-ship of voices: "a voice like high-heels and stocking," "an old voice . . wailing," "some quavery voices," "a grumble of men's voices" (p. 1). The girl's subsequent alienation in the colonial world of Aunt Beatrice and the school is already prefigured by her inability to identify with any of these fetishized voices.

In addition, Tee's alienation as a narrating subject is obvious in the way her authority of representation is propped up and denied at the same time. For example, at the opening of the narrative, the narrator is not placed in the position of innocence and the absence of conscious-ness which is common in the Caribbean *bildungsroman*. At the begin-ning of the novel, Tee, along with her brother, has placed herself on a physical and narrative pedestal ("We had posted ourselves at the front window, standing on a chair" [p. 1]) from which she can represent her

19. Edward Kamau Brathwaite, *History of the Voice: The Development of National Language in Anglophone Caribbean Poetry* (London: New Beacon Books, 1984), and Edouard Glissant, *Carib-bean Discourse: Selected Essays*, trans. J. Michael Dash (Charlottesville: University Press of Virginia, 1989), pp. 120–33.

own experience with ostensible authority, controlling the reader's response to her social context. On closer examination, however, the
reader discovers that what the girl represents is not her unique "reading" of phenomena, but her reproduction of the views and opinions of
adult figures. Even what appears to be the narrator's clear perception
of things is quickly proven to be hazy and ill-defined (pp. 2–3). Because the reader already knows that Tee's mother and the new baby
are dead, and that her father has left the country, the narrator's limited
knowledge is obvious in her conclusion that Papa "had gone to see
whether he could find Mammy and the baby" (p. 3).

Hodge's narrative thus develops along what appear to be contradictory lines: the subject is privileged in the discourse, but this privilege is
undercut by her function as the reporter of others' speech, or by her
limited knowledge and perspective. This is an important strategy for
showing how the subject develops in multiple and contradictory ways
and for indicating the extent to which a unique sense of self is often
produced by a painful struggle with the discourse of others. In this
novel, we have moved away from trying to invent a new language of
self to a recognition of Bakhtin's famous assertion that "language, for
the individual consciousness, lies on the borderline between oneself
and the other. The World in language is half someone else's."[20] Tee
tries to constitute herself by striving for the fragmented languages of
other people; but even as she reproduces other people's words and
views, she is frantically seeking to institute the integrity of her voice
and her privileged position as an observer and narrator. In other
words, against her limited authority and truncated mastery of language, she still struggles to express things "otherwise," to endow
received discourse with what Bakhtin would call the subject's "semantic and expressive intention."[21]

Thus while her mother lies dying, Tee, who is only aware of the
original reason for the mother's hospitalization (the birth of a baby),
sits watching at the window, "struggling to keep my eyes open," her
words expressing her now belated expressive intention and expectation: "There were fewer people going past now, so that I all but fell
asleep between each set of footsteps. But I always revived to see if it

20. M. M. Bakhtin, *The Dialogic Imagination: Four Essays*, ed. Michael Holquist, trans. Caryl
Emerson and Michael Holquist (Austin: University of Texas Press, 1981), p. 293.
21. Mikhail Bakhtin, "Discourse Typology in Prose," in *Readings in Russian Poetics: Formalist
and Structuralist Views*, ed. Ladislav Matejka and Krystyna Pomorska (Cambridge: MIT Press,
1971), p. 190.

was them, and if not to shout 'We gettin a baby!' to whoever it was" (p. 2). And yet her attempt to evoke a narrative authority built on her position as an observer—that is, an eyewitness account—is immediately shown to be seriously flawed because she is not privy to the knowledge of death and suffering which, at this point in the story, is shared by the adults. At this juncture Tee's voice and perspective are overwhelmed by a multiplicity of adult voices that are disconcerting because they are totally estranged from their speakers. Now her own semantic and expressive intentions become secondary.

The result is further ambiguity in Hodge's narrative strategies: to the extent that the adult Tee is the narrator of this story, her position in the narrative is one of authority and control; but because young Tee is also the subject of this narrative, the fear and confusion of her childhood experiences can only be apprehended if her voice is contrasted with other voices. More important, the author rejects the kind of objectified descriptions we saw in our discussion of Lamming's early novels which might mediate the worlds of the juvenile subject and the adult narrator. Instead of evoking a narrative detached from speakers and narrators, Hodge presents us with a self at odds with the language in which it hopes to subjectify itself; within the confines of the novel, Tee's confusion and ambivalent relationship to her hybrid culture are paramount to any enlightenment and resolutions which the narrator might have arrived at as an adult. As Tee's voice is overwhelmed by adult voices, her subjectivity is shown to be more than an effect of her reality; rather, experience here is shown to be an effect of the character's attempt to create an image for herself outside conflicting social codes. Alternatively, self-perception becomes a projection of her fears and desires.

An important example of this kind of projection is apparent quite early in the novel when Tee is brought forward to pay her final respects to her dead mother:

> The house was still full of people and there were flowers in thick bunches that didn't look like flowers at all but like a bristly covering for some sinister animal sleeping underneath; there was a shiny thing in a corner that I was afraid to look at and then an old woman took my hand and led me towards the corner and I grasped her hand tightly and shut my eyes and suddenly I was being lifted into the air and opening my eyes in alarm saw that I was passing over the shiny thing half-smothered by ugly still stuck-together flowers and then I landed into the shaky

arms of another old lady on the other side; and then they picked Toddan and he screamed and kicked, so that they nearly dropped him with fright. [P. 3]

This paragraph is an excellent example of the kind of ambivalence that characterizes *Crick Crack, Monkey*. A narrative strategy of reversal is at work here. As we well know, the long complex sentence is traditionally a mark of the narrator's sophistication and mastery of form and situation. In this context, however, the long sentence foregrounds the child's confusion, especially her inability to create significance and to make sense of the solemn occasion—her mother's wake—which appears to her as surreal. The narrative situation becomes more complicated when we try to identify the speaking voice—the narrator or the character? The impressions seem to be those of young Tee, but the semantic situation is that of the adult Tee who retrospectively narrates her childhood story.

The above narrative situation is an example of what Roy Narinesingh, in his introduction to the novel, calls a meeting point where the child's and adult's visions "are made to coalesce" (p. vii). But to understand Tee's struggle to inscribe herself using the language of others, or to overcome her odd relationship to the language(s) that constitute her, we must also be cognizant of the splitting of her voice into what Bakhtin, in his theoretical studies of discourse in fiction, calls "two speech acts . . . two entirely separate and autonomous voices."[22] We must be sensitive to the dual voices that determine the nature of narration in the text and Tee's self-representation—the voice of the child caught in conflicting linguistic situations, and the voice of the sophisticated narrator trying to establish her individual language after colonialism and exile.

There is still greater tension in the novel between what we may call "objective reality"—the unmediated, non-projected experience—and the subject's self-representation in images and spectacles, what Hodge would call the fantasies that define the colonial situation.[23] For Tee, the self has the power to put the primary claims of experience into question, for it is only when the self has recreated reality in its own image, or evoked that reality as a projection of its desires, that self-representation (and hence narration) become possible:

22. Bakhtin, "Discourse Typology," p. 190.
23. Balutansky, p. 657.

> At the shed there was usually a fringe of children hanging about, and they let us shake the chac chac; there were some little boys who were regular pan-men and who even got to beat a pan on the road at Carnival. The players felt about idly and aimlessly on their pans for a long spell until without one noticing the sounds had converged into order. So close to the band that the bass-pans thudded through your belly, and the iron-section with the sounds crashing out from the touch of the tiny stick on the anonymous piece of engine entrails was your teeth clashing together in time with the beat. [P. 6]

The passage begins with a general description of the steel band shed, but as it progresses, we notice how the dichotomy between subject and object is narrowed; the narrator/character internalizes the objects (the bass-pans thud in her belly) and eventually merges the external with the internal so that at the end of the quotation she cannot tell the difference between the sounds from the iron-section and the clashing of her teeth. In essence, experience has value insofar as it is projected as a spectacle that the self itself has created. External reality is populated with the speaker's intention.[24]

There is another sense in which the above shift from an "objective" to a "subjective" form of representation brings out the ambivalence that characterizes, indeed produces Tee, as a colonial subject: the author needs to maintain a disjunction between Tee's functions as a narrator and as a character, and this necessitates not only the doubling of the self in language but also its alienation in the very strategies it develops to represent its doubleness. For if Tee were just to tell her story from the (ostensibly) non-problematic perspective of a child (an interesting comparison is Michael Anthony's *The Year in San Fernando*), the author might succeed in maintaining the integrity of the narrating self, but this unity could lead to the negation of her primary thematic concern—the alienation of this subject through her induction in "a make-believe value system."[25] On the other hand, if she were to narrate this story from the vantage point of the adult, then the representation of the subject's alienation could only be achieved through the erasure of the important illusion of integrity and unity we associate with the childhood narrator. Thus, although Hodge's goal is to express the theme of alienation, she operates from the premise that childhood holds the utopian possibility that Tee can exist, to quote Marjorie

24. Bakhtin, "Discourse Typology," p. 190.
25. Balutansky, p. 657.

Thorpe, "in complete harmony with her environment."[26] Furthermore, to understand the conditions in which the character becomes alienated in her inherited language and value system, we must also be in a position to read the gap that separates childhood from adulthood: as a character, Tee becomes alienated almost without her knowledge and consent; as an adult narrator, she posits self-representation in dominant discourse as a form of alienation which she has mastered through narration.

In his introduction to the novel, Narinesingh argues that the reader of Hodge's text is "made to share in the diversity and richness of Tee's experience without being able to discern at times where the child's voice with a child's perception of things slides into the adult voice and vision of the omniscient author" (p. vii). Now, while it is true that there are instances when the juvenile and adult visions seem indistinguishable, a more attentive reading of the text will surely highlight the differences between these two voices or call attention to their paradoxical relationship. If Hodge's intention is to expose the illusionary nature of Tee's desire for assimilation by highlighting the gap between her innocent (childhood) belief in the efficacy of the colonial system and her later (adult) troubled relationship with this system, the narrative is attuned to the divisions and separations the child goes through in her struggle to become the "other." For the narrating subject self-representation often calls attention to the gap that separates experience (scenes of childhood) and the moment of narration (adult self-consciousness).

Nowhere is this process more apparent than in those instances where obviously juvenile acts are represented in complex language and elaborate syntactical structures. In the following example, young Tee and her brother are prancing around with "Uncle" Mickey, but the description of this scene seems to suggest a more involved act:

> The rest of the time we were strutting in his shadow, off to raid the Estate or down to the Savannah to fly our kites that he made us; or it was the long walk with the sun all around and stinging and blurryness rising from the road and the smell of asphalt, and the road soft under your toes and the grass at the sides no cooler and just when it was getting too

---

26. Marjorie Thorpe, "The Problem of Cultural Identification in *Crick Crack, Monkey*," *Savacou* 13 (1977), 32. See also Leota S. Lawrence, "Women in Caribbean Literature: The African Presence," *Phylon* 44 (March 1983), 1–11; and "Merle Hodge," in *Fifty Caribbean Writers: A Bio-Bibliographical Critical Sourcebook*, ed. Daryl Cumber Dance (Westport, Conn.: Greenwood Press, 1986), pp. 224–28.

much we'd turn off the road and plunge between the bushes and down
the precipitous path to the water. [P. 6]

Here, the narrated experiences belong to childhood, but the language
is that of the adult narrator. There is thus a clear disjunction between
experience and language which, in turn, signifies the temporal shift
from a world in which the child's life was aimless to a time when she
has acquired the language to turn such aimlessness into art. What this
shift adds up to, everything else aside, is that there is no authentic
subject before its representation in language; the pleasure of writing is
inherent in the search for a language that will recover the fragments of
a past life and turn it into a spectacle in which the narrator can "read"
herself. After all, before the writing of *Crick Crack, Monkey*, who was
Tee but the projection of other people's desires and intentions—Aunt
Tantie, Ma, Beatrice, the colonial school?

The value of the juvenile perspective lies precisely in its capacity to
show how Tee was colonized by the utterances of other subjects. The
word *monkey* in the title of the book—a title that comes from the
opening refrain in Caribbean folk narratives—has "all the associations
of aping and imitation," as Hodge says, and is intended to call attention to the inauthenticity of Tee's adopted colonial world.[27] As a result,
a return to childhood does not establish a metaphorical relationship
between the child and her landscape; what she hears, and often appropriates, is the "disembodied voice" of another. Consider this example: "Women going past walked a gauntlet of commentary on their
anatomy and deportment. And for Mrs Hinds in particular they had
no mercy. Like any proper lady (it seemed to me) she had a high, stiff,
bottom and spectacles and stockings" (p. 7). Here we have the narrator
not only representing the child's perspective on the boys' comments
on Mrs. Hinds, but also using a parenthesis to make a distinction
between how things seemed to Tee then and her superior knowledge
now. Given the boys' commentary, Tee's juvenile view, and the narrator's qualifier, can we ever identify an original experience? My contention is that the loss of an original (childhood) experience—a loss that
becomes more and more apparent as Tee moves away from the "organic" worlds of Tantie and Ma and enters Beatrice's colonial orbit—is
what generates Hodge's "autobiographical" text.[28]

27. Balutansky, p. 657.
28. See Françoise Lionnet, *Autobiographical Voices: Race, Gender, Self-Portraiture* (Ithaca: Cornell University Press, 1989), p. 6. I concur with Lionnet's important assertion that the "auto-

Moreover, Tee's creative power seems to derive from her knowledge of the gap that separates her past and present images. Because the division of the subject—its splitting into a character and narrator—and its lack of originality are results of the experience of childhood under colonialism, we cannot resort to this same experience as the source of an innocent, unalienated image of selfhood. As Michal Ginsburg observes in a study of Flaubert, who often resorted to this kind of divided self-representation, "From the moment there is memory, or desire, or language . . . from the very moment there is a self, the self is divided from itself, doubled and alienated from itself, and this division and difference are experienced as a loss, but as a loss that has already occurred and hence cannot be either avoided or made good."[29] In the circumstances, the question raised by the "autobiographical" narrative does not concern how alienation can be overcome, but how it comes about, and how it can be manipulated to create a new self in language and a new consciousness of self.

In an important study of subjectivity and language, Emile Benveniste has insisted that "consciousness of self is only possible if it is experienced by contrast."[30] For the colonized or marginalized self, this contrast is negative and oppositional: the self defines itself by being at odds with the given or imposed language, by struggling against the hegemonic voices that stifle its utterances. Similarly, the ideology of the self in Crick Crack is dependent on the presence or absence of Tee's utterances, measured against the utterances of others. At the beginning of the novel, when Tee tries to announce the inevitable birth of her mother's baby even as the mother lies dying, the contrary perspectives (those of adults, the messengers of death) are apprehended through voices that are unreal and dead; indeed, one voice (that of Aunt Beatrice, it turns out) has acquired a life of its own and is perceived as "the high-heels and stockings voice" (p. 2). Furthermore, each character in the novel, and each social class or caste, is defined by, and associated with, a particular speech community: Tantie speaks the

---

biographical theme" is connected to "diverse language systems" and culturally distinct frames of reference: "The space of writing in which these frames intersect positions the writing subject at the confluence of complex and sometimes conflicting creative impulses, which complicate both the writer's and the implied reader's relations in (and to) the text under scrutiny" (pp. 21–22).

29. Michal Peled Ginsburg, *Flaubert Writing: A Study in Narrative Strategies* (Stanford, Calif.: Stanford University Press, 1986), p. 32.

30. Emile Benveniste, *Problems in General Linguistics* (Coral Gables, Fla.: University of Miami Press, 1977), p. 224.

creole version of the English language (the patois that, by doing "violence" to established speech, has acquired autonomy and identity); Ma's language reflects her ancient African and slave roots; Aunt Beatrice's utterances reflect her middle class, colonial image. It is against, or in relation to, these language forms (*langue*) that the subject must institute its individual utterance (*parole*).

But before the subject can fashion its own language, it must deliberate on the already given language. Thus in the course of her narrative Tee moves from one speech community to another without adopting the language of any of them into her consciousness: with the boys at the bridge, she shares the pseudo-cowboy language of Manhatt'n and his gang (p. 6); with Ma, she immerses herself in the language of the folk (p. 13); and at Mrs. Hinds's school, she begins to speak the formal language of the "Big-school" (p. 39). It must be emphasized, however, that at no stage does she speak any of these languages solely or rebel against them completely; rather, her identity is constructed by and within these speech or language systems. She belongs to all of them, but to none; in reality, she is consumed and confused by all of them. For this reason, what appeared at the beginning of the novel to be her narrative vantage point, a position of mastery and insight, is an adult position that conceals the uncertainty of the little girl. Similarly, her apparent security in the world of Tantie and Ma conceals, as does her later involvement with Beatrice's middle class culture, the state of anxiety and unbelonging she lives in.

My argument here runs contrary to Thorpe's influential reading of *Crick Crack*, where she casts the novel in a structural opposition in which Tantie's creole world represents "belonging and security" while Beatrice's colonial world stands for "alienation and displacement."[31] Admittedly, these binary oppositions can be sustained if we approach the text from the perspective of Tee the narrator, who after her exile in Europe is presumably nostalgic and appreciative of the creole world from which she has been displaced by the colonial culture. But from the perspective of Tee the child, there is a strong ambivalence toward oppositions such as colonial/creole, Beatrice/Tantie; in neither of these worlds can she posit herself as a subject. In Tantie's world Tee echoes and repeats her aunt's language and views (p. 12); after she has lived with Beatrice for some time, her utterances now reflect the language and ideology of the colonized bourgeoisie (p. 85). In neither of these

31. Thorpe, p. 37.

cultural universes can the child appropriate a language to designate herself as a subject which is not the effect of the other's language system; she cannot choose one entity as a way of overcoming her alienation. Nor can she return to Ma's world, which may represent the Caribbean cultural base but is inaccessible to the girl, not only because of the old woman's amnesia (she cannot remember her original name) but also because this peasant culture is marginalized in the colonial political economy.

So the value of Hodge's text does not lie in any possible resolution to the cultural dichotomies we have discussed so far. As Hodge has observed, Tee's enlightenment does not happen within the confines of the novel; her experiences only foreground her state of ambivalence and "unsatisfactory imitation."[32] The value of the novel hence lies in the author's capacity to sustain both the creole and colonial cultures as opposed sites of cultural production which the "modern" Caribbean subject cannot reconcile or transcend entirely. This cultural and linguistic opposition is embedded in the economic systems of the island (the world of the creole is one of peasant production while that of the colonial middle class is professional); but it is also reflected in a semiological opposition between the spoken and the written, between carnival and the school.

The power of orality is apparent in Tantie's mastery of creole speech and Ma's enchanted world of African mythology. Tee certainly feels at home in this world—indeed she celebrates it—but she is also aware of its incompleteness, of its marginalization in the modern economy. Her desire is hence for the scriptural universe of the colonial school which promises power and authority:

> I looked forward to school. I looked forward to the day when I could pass my hands swiftly from side to side on a blank piece of paper leaving meaningful marks in its wake; to staring nonchalantly into a book until I turned over the page, a gesture pregnant with importance for it indicated that one had not merely been staring, but that that most esoteric of processes had been taking place whereby the paper had yielded up something or other as a result of having been stared at. [P. 20]

Thus the power of the school is clearly linked to writing; in turn, writing is posited as both a mythological practice (an "esoteric process") and a form of empowerment (the paper yields knowledge,

32. Balutansky, p. 654.

obviously a kind of power). In retrospect, however, literacy is a form of mastery achieved at the expense of the self which, as we have already seen, becomes alienated in the modes of representation which were supposed to empower it: "My reading career also began with A for Apple, the exotic fruit that made its brief appearance at Christmas time, and pursued through my Caribbean Reader Primer One the fortunes of two English children known as Jim and Jill, or it might have been Tim and Mary" (p. 25). When she was illiterate, Tee was mystified by the esoteric nature of written language; now an ironic narrator has developed knowledge about her previous mystification.[33] She now knows that mastery of the colonial text does not lead to what Vévé Clarke has aptly called "diaspora literacy"—"the ability to read and comprehend the discourses of Africa, Afro-America and the Caribbean from an informed, indigenous perspective."[34]

And yet alienation from the diasporic universe is a precondition for the character's ascendancy into the colonial situation. Indeed, when Tantie allows Beatrice to introduce Tee into this alienating world after the "exhibition exam," she seems to confirm the girl's suspicion that the creole world is one of collective economic and political marginality and that only accession into the language and discourse of colonialism empowers (pp. 61, 68). As a result, Tee's cultural alienation is built around a crucial chiasmic reversal: the tangible reality of the creole culture, a reality that pulsates in its myths, its speech patterns, and its carnival (what Beatrice contemptuously refers to as "ordinary") is dismissed as an unreal construct, while the fictions promoted by the colonial textbook are now adopted as the "real" Caribbean referent:

> Books transported you always into the familiar solidity of chimneys and apple trees, the enviable normality of real Girls and Boys who went a-sleighing and built snowmen, ate potatoes, not rice, went about in socks and shoes from morning until night and called things by their proper names. . . . Books transported you into Reality and Rightness, which were to be found abroad. [P. 61]

The colonial library, represented here by the book van (which Tee awaits every Saturday "with the greatest of impatience"), is a mirage

---

33. I have borrowed this formulation from Paul de Man. See "The Rhetoric of Temporality," in *Blindness and Insight: Essays in the Rhetoric of Contemporary Criticism* (Minneapolis: University of Minnesota Press, 1983), p. 214.

34. Vévé A. Clark, "Developing Diaspora Literary: Allusion in Maryse Condé's *Heremakhonon*," in Davies and Fido, *Out of the Kumbla*, p. 304.

that has become a tangible reality in the girl's imagination and desire. The world of the "ordinary" is denied referentiality because, as Thorpe notes, it is the exact opposite of, indeed contradicts, "the values of the former colonial masters" and hence undermines the realm of colonial desire.[35]

In this context, in an attempt to deal with her dualities and crisis of identity, Tee begins to apprehend herself as the colonial "other": she invents a double, a mirror image of herself who is, nevertheless, white and thoroughly colonial, a subject so ideal that she doesn't have to negotiate the dangerous chasm between the contradictory creole and colonial worlds:

> Thus it was that I fashioned Helen, my double. She was my age and height. She spent the summer holidays at the sea-side with her aunt and uncle who had a delightful orchard with apple trees and pear trees in which sang chaffinches and blue tits, and where one could wander on terms of the closest familiarity with cowslips and honeysuckle. . . . Helen entered and ousted all the other characters in the unending serial that I had been spinning for Toddan and Doolarie from time immemorial. [P. 62]

In a world where the real is reversed into its contrary and the unreal becomes the object of desire, Helen is more than a double; she has usurped Tee's self. The spectacle in the mirror is the real person, and the real person is the unreal image in the mirror: "She was the Proper Me. And me, I was her shadow hovering about in incompleteness" (p. 62).

If we adopt the Lacanian notion of the "mirror stage," we can argue that the colonial subject has recognized itself in an ideal *I*, but this form of identification is also a misrecognition because the externalized image is achieved only in return for self-alienation.[36] Moreover, the subject can never assimilate this idealized image because it has no existence except in the imaginary. Yet the mirror image is, nevertheless, the object in relation to which the subject defines herself. The radical dualities that identify this subject and its entrapment in the imaginary, argues Kaja Silverman in another context, are "a consequence of the irreducible distance which separates the subject from its ideal reflection, [and] it loves the coherent identity which the mirror

35. Thorpe, p. 34.
36. Jacques Lacan, *Ecrits: A Selection*, trans. Alan Sheridan (New York: Norton, 1977), p. 2.

provides. However, because the image remains external to it, it also hates that image."[37] Tee does not express any overt hate for Helen, but there is obvious recognition (from the narrator) that there were profound tensions between the two characters. This tension is clearly brought out in an important passage in the novel when the narrator explains the social and historical conditions that necessitated a double:

> For doubleness, or this particular kind of doubleness, was a thing to be taken for granted. Why, the whole of life was like a piece of cloth with a rightside and a wrongside. Just as there was a way you spoke and a way you wrote, so there was the daily existence which you led, which of course amounted only to marking time and makeshift, for there was the Proper daily round, not necessarily more agreeable, simply the valid one, the course of which encompassed things like warming yourself before a fire and having tea at four o'clock; there were the human types who were your neighbours and guardians and playmates—but you were all marginal together, for there were the beings whose validity loomed at you at every book, every picture. [P. 62]

Tee is structured by a set of oppositions, none of which offers her true identity: her creole world is makeshift and marginal; her desired colonial universe is artificial. When she recognizes the sources of marginality and the nature of artifice, then she will outgrow Helen "in the way that a baby ceases to be taken up with his fingers and toes" (p. 62). As the adult narrator of her own experiences and subjectivity, Tee will not need such mediators; she will represent herself through writing.

In any case, if we look at the images and symbols that identify the ideal image, this time from the perspective of the narrator rather than the subject, we can see how the writer has used modes of representation which call attention to the arbitrariness of the colonial double and her world. In an ironic way, the coveted colonial world is signified by fetishes, such as old pictures. For example, Aunt Beatrice's only connection to the colonizer and conqueror—the entity that dominates her imaginary realm and represents her mirror image—is an old picture, that of "The White Ancestress, Elizabeth Carter": "The photograph was as faded as a photograph could manage to be, but Aunt Beatrice said that the minute Carol came into the world everybody could see that she resembled her, and so Carol's middle name was Elizabeth, as

37. Kaja Silverman, *The Subject of Semiotics* (New York: Oxford University Press, 1983), p. 158.

my poor mother was named" (p. 81). And so a faded object becomes the justification for alienation, for distancing oneself from "those common raucous niggery people and all those coolies" (p. 86). But because these idealized images are unreal, they also highlight the failure of the colonial subject to expropriate the colonizer's discourse for a new national identity. This failure originates or is manifested in the question of language.

In his discussion of discourse in fiction, Bakhtin has noted the ways language is overdetermined by intentions exterior to the self that uses it: "Language is not a neutral medium that passes freely and easily into the private property of the speaker's intention; it is populated—over-populated—with the intentions of others. Expropriating it, forcing it to submit to one's intentions and accents, is a difficult and complicated process."[38] Tee's struggle to populate other people's languages with her own intentions functions within the larger, problematic realm of anticolonial discourse in the independent period: what is the current status of the earlier nationalist (and hence male) belief that certain tenets of colonial modernity could be appropriated for the development of the new nation and in the fashioning of a narrative of national identity? The crisis of identity facing the child protagonist in her novel, asserts Hodge, is symbolic of the nascent Caribbean nations' quest for an integrated national culture.[39]

Rewriting the National Allegory: *Beka Lamb*

Inevitably, the awakening of the colonial subject to self-consciousness in Caribbean literature is closely connected to questions of nationalism and national identity. As the self struggles with its crisis of identity, so does the nation; as the nation strives for forms and styles of expressing itself, and yearns for a language in which to articulate what Benedict Anderson has aptly called its modalities, so does the subject seek its unique utterance. Notions of self and nation are indeed "artifacts of a particular kind."[40] But in Caribbean women's writing—as generally seems to be the case in women's literature in most of the so-called Third World—the relationship between self and nation is more

38. Bakhtin, *The Dialogic Imagination*, p. 294.
39. Balutansky, p. 653.
40. Benedict Anderson, *Imagined Communities: Reflections on the Origin and Spread of Nationalism* (London: Verso, 1983), p. 13.

complicated than the above exposition may suggest. In the first instance, as Jean Franco has recognized, the problem of national identity has often been presented as one of male identity, and it is often male writers "who debated its defects and psychoanalyzed the nation." If the doctrine of modernization is intended to map and encode "home territories and genealogies," women are excluded from the sites in which national culture is produced.[41]

Still another issue is made more explicit in Zee Edgell's *Beka Lamb*: although the imagination of an autonomous Caribbean self demands the radical reconceptualization of its territorial and social spaces, these spaces are defined by linguistic ambivalence. Both the self and its community have to reinvent themselves using the language and cultural symbols borrowed from the colonizer, because only such a language and such symbols are seen as adequate for synthesizing the often antagonistic ethnic and class differences that define the new nation. Although individual and national identities need to harness such differences and ambivalences to subvert the colonial machine of domination and its neocolonial successor, the question of rewriting the allegory of the nation once the colonizer has departed still dominates Caribbean discourse. This problem is crucial in Caribbean literature written after independence because there is suspicion among many Caribbean writers and intellectuals that some of the nationalist discourse developed during the anticolonial struggle is populated by the intentions of others and hence carries within it those forces that retard the awakening of self-consciousness and hence national identity and "nationness." Moreover, there is the outstanding question of whether Caribbean cultural diversity hinders or promotes the development of national consciousness.

In Edgell's text, published shortly after Belize's independence, the devalorization of colonial modernism and its authority is achieved through an appeal to figures and tropes of difference and ambivalence. As they are represented in language and ideology, such figures express the kind of diversity which according to Glissant allows Caribbean peoples to repossess their historical spaces. In Glissant's words, "Diversity, which is neither chaos nor sterility, means the human spirit's striving for a cross-cultural relationship, without universalist transcendence. Diversity needs the presence of peoples, no longer as objects to be swallowed up, but with the intention of creating a new

---

41. Franco, p. 131.

relationship. Sameness requires fixed Being, Diversity establishes becoming."[42] The colonial power fixes the colonized as objects of labor and/or appendages of the colonizing culture. Rewriting the Caribbean national allegory thus demands a narrative strategy that confronts the objects and historical forces blocking the desire for that diversity that establishes becoming. As a strategy of individual and national identity, ambivalence disperses the fixed sites of colonial cultural production; in semiotic terms, as Julia Kristeva says, it "implies the insertion of history (society) into a text and of this text into history."[43]

Consider the function of ambivalence in the opening sentences of *Beka Lamb*: "On a warm November day Beka Lamb won an essay contest at St. Cecilia's Academy, situated not far from the front gate of His Majesty's Prison on Milpa Lane. It seemed to her family that overnight Beka changed from what her mother called a 'flat-rate Belize creole' into a person with 'high mind.'"[44] This introduction appears to be constructed around a series of binary oppositions: the beginning of the novel is its end, the colonial school and prison are placed in contrast, and Beka's creole "past" is opposed to her new "high mind" (middle class) identity. On closer examination, however, the opposition between these entities cannot be easily sustained. For one thing, a novel that begins with its ending often promotes a moment of interpretation which is definite and conclusive; the reader is supposed to follow the incidents related in the flashback from the vantage point and certain knowledge denoted by narrative closure. But this is not the case in *Beka Lamb*: we are not certain that Beka, by winning the coveted essay contest, has initiated the decisive transformation of moral character and social class which her family and community expect. On the contrary, Beka's ostensible transformation is presented by the narrator as if it were merely the subjective (and possibly erroneous) assumption of her family—"It seemed to her family . . ."—a mode of representation clearly intended to create doubts about the given significance of the essay contest and the colonial economy of meaning with which it is associated.

The very notion of a radical shift in Beka's character and position in the community is further undermined by the problematic expression

42. Glissant, p. 98.

43. Julia Kristeva, *Desire in Language: A Semiotic Approach to Literature and Art*, ed. Leon S. Roudiez, trans. Thomas Gora et al. (New York: Columbia University Press, 1980), p. 69.

44. Zee Edgell, *Beka Lamb* (London: Heinemann, 1982), p. 1. Further references are in the text.

of temporality in the novel. We are told, on one hand, that "before time" (that is, in the past), Beka had no hope of winning the essay contest because "the prizes would go to bakras [whites], panias [mestizos] or expatriates" (p. 1). A new consciousness is hence dawning on Belize, and the creole majority is now being recognized as a powerful force. On the other hand, however, this "new" consciousness cannot be apprehended except in relation to the past. In fact, as we read the novel and retrace Beka's struggle to establish her identity within the social order of colonialism (represented by the school) and the as yet unrealized dream of national culture (expressed by her grandmother and other nationalists), we begin to realize that the essay contest is loaded with ironic implications. Initially promoted as the sign of historical transition—from past to present, creole to bakra, colony to nation—the essay instead draws our attention to the difficulties of forging new identities and expropriating colonial modernism and its discourse. The essay marks the gap between an unrealized identity and the realities of colonial domination and repression; it becomes a synecdoche of what is referred to euphemistically as "these hard times" (p. 3).

Like many of the other characters discussed in the previous pages, Beka Lamb casts her quest for a "new time" in the familiar terms of modernity enumerated at the beginning of this book. Modernism— especially as it is promoted by the school—is seen as the ability of the subject to be liberated from tradition and to evolve her own unique vision of life. Indeed, Beka's fantasy is to escape from both the world of "before time" (represented by her grandmother) and the vision of the damnation that, according to her Catholic teachers, awaits her at the end of her life. In this connection, Beka's moral and social strivings don't represent any significant form of self-engenderment; on the contrary, in making a "shift" from "the washing bowl underneath the house bottom to books in a classroom overlooking the Caribbean sea" (p. 2), she has to choose between two different forms of socialization, to try and fit into, or repeat, predetermined visions and ideologies. This repetition, then, frustrates the very quest for individuality which Beka thought she was involved in once she had won the essay contest. The essay may have earned her recognition both at home and in the school, but it also accentuates the tensions she feels as she is forced to choose between the values of her community and the agencies of colonialism.

In a sense, Edgell places Beka in a state of limbo between an emerging national culture and the colonial situation. As the texts discussed in the previous chapters illustrate so well, this position in itself is not new or unique in Caribbean literature; what is unique about *Beka Lamb*, though, is Zee Edgell's ability to develop a tense dialectic between the subject on one hand, and her community and colonial society on the other hand, without falling back on the old and worn-out polarities of tradition and modernity. In this kind of dialectic of subject and community, as John Brenkman has noted in his study of the self-constituting power of the speaking subject in language, "the experience of the subject, who is constituted by and constituting through language, is lived within the struggle between the unrealized community and those social institutions which, deriving from the divisions of the community, shape the situations, interactions, and arrangements of everyday life."[45] Significantly, in Edgell's novel, the subject and her community mirror each other's anxieties.

These anxieties are expressed most vividly in Beka's dream at the beginning of chapter 2 of the novel. In the dream, "barefooted old men" have chained "off the bridge approaches, in front and behind" Beka, cutting her off:

> It was too late. The bridge, shuddering beneath her feet, began turning slowly away from the show. Back and forth along the narrow aisle she ran, stopping again and again to shout and beat on the high wall separating the main traffic line from the pedestrian aisle. But the rattle and creak of machinery, and the noise from both sides of the creek, prevented the operators behind the wall from hearing her voice. [P. 6]

The dream, then, signifies Beka's anxiety at being displaced from her culture; she is cut off from her people by the bridge; a wall closes off alternative routes of escape; in the end, she is isolated and deformed: "She felt shrunken except for her head which had grown to the size of a large calabash" (p. 7). More important, this anxiety of selfhood is directly related to the community's fears about its own destiny as a nation, anxiety about Guatemala's long historical claims to Belize, and even about the country's capacity to survive as an independent economic entity because of its diminutive size. In effect, Beka's quest for a new image is subconsciously a collective undertaking, the kind of

45. John Brenkman, *Culture and Domination* (Ithaca: Cornell University Press, 1987), p. 174.

undertaking which, to borrow Brenkman's terms, "unfolds within the effects and the struggles of the social community's divisions."[46]

In many ways, nationalism and the national community are desired as the only sites in which the self can fully subjectify itself. At the same time, the unrealized—and hence desired—community is posited as an unknown terrain in which both the nation and the self might fail to find satisfaction or even survive. In *Beka Lamb*, the unrealized dream— the imagined, independent Belize community—is not only fenced on all sides, but is also structured by historical ambivalences. Indeed, the mahogany tree, which is supposed to be the national symbol of Belize, functions in the novel as a displaced signifier:

> In the brief sketch of the colony Beka had studied at school, there was a drawing of two black men, bare to the waist, standing on either side of the spreading branches of a mahogany tree. One held an axe, the other a saw. Beka had been told in history class, the year she failed first form, that the Latin words beneath the picture meant: "Under the shade we flourish." [P. 8]

The disjunctive relationship between Beka—and her community— and the symbol that is supposed to denote their communal desires is apparent here. First, the girl's knowledge of her national history is "sketchy," suggesting that the mahogany symbol is not sustained by a system of concrete knowledge; second, the national motto is in Latin, a dead language that is unintelligible to Beka. Later we are told that Beka had "never seen a mahogany tree in her life. . . . Moreover, Beka's dad was too impatient a man . . . to subject himself to the uncertainties of the mahogany tree scattered fewer than ten to an acre out in the bush" (p. 8). In addition, there is a crucial ironic reversal of the national symbol in the above passage: the mahogany is unreal for many of the people of Belize, as unreal as the European flora and fauna that Beka reads about in books, or the roses her mother attempts to cultivate year after year—"roses like those she saw in magazines which arrived in the colony three months late from England" (p. 9). Consequently, the self cannot invest in a symbol that, strictly speaking, represents the colonizer's fantasy about what Belize should be, rather than what it is.

The metonymic function of the mahogany is mirrored in other displaced images that represent Belize city and its creole culture. For

46. Brenkman, p. 174.

example, we are informed that "in three centuries, miscegenation, like logwood, had produced all shades of black and brown, not grey or purple or violet, but certainly there were a few people in the town known as red ibos" (p. 11). But what value does the word *miscegenation* have in this context? The blending of races does not lead to the end of differences because shades have come to denote racial categories, and "each race held varying degrees of prejudice concerning the others" (p. 12).

It is against this background of cultural ambivalence and shifting signifiers that Beka must constitute herself. She has three choices: she can develop a relationship with her country and its history and hence come to terms with her grandmother's vision of a new national community; she can adopt and reproduce the values of the colonizer and hence negate her communal identity; or she can reinvent herself and her own realities. In Edgell's narrative scheme, however, Beka cannot make any of these choices before she overcomes her fatal flaw—her habit of lying. This habit denotes more than a reluctance to tell the truth—it is part of Beka's drive to invent an alternative reality beyond the assimilative tendencies that repress selfhood. Thus Beka and her friend Toycie don't merely appropriate the legends of the country: "They never failed to make up stories about why the crippled British Baron had left his entire fortune to the country" (p. 13). Such "made-up" stories are strategies of subverting the truth of the already written, of conventionalized fashions of history. Beka's habit of lying is also part of the same process that leads her to construct her "world of fantasy" (p. 15); what her father would dismiss as "artificiality and sham" (p. 21) is her strategy of establishing her own position in the midst of conflicting social codes. In short, the dominant social field is subverted by the energies of the imagination.

Significantly, the imaginary allows Beka to hallow a space of self-constitution somewhere between the creole community and the colonial tradition. Although she cannot choose between the colonial past and the modernist future in which the hopes and aspirations of Belize and its people will be fulfilled (as we have seen, the symbols of the emerging nation are already overdetermined by the colonizer and are hence compromised), she has the power, in the present moment of transition, to create her own normativity out of the ambiguous codes provided by her hybrid cultures.[47] A remarkable example of how

47. I borrow the concept of normativity from Jürgen Habermas, *The Philosophical Discourse of Modernity* (Cambridge: MIT Press, 1987), p. 7.

ambiguity leads to normativity is the man who wears his mask to evoke not his inner essence and cohesion, but his alienation. The masked man, we are told, is a creole who "compromised the daughter of a Carib man who had befriended him. Maskman could not marry the girl, though he loved her, without losing face in the creole community, whose members seldom married among the Caribs, although these two groups shared, in varying degrees, a common African ancestry" (pp. 31–32). Difference and division having proven to be stronger than a common ancestral heritage, "so it was said," a group of Carib people "in painted masks" entered the man's room and touched his face and neck "obeahing him so that these parts of his body became dotted with white speckles, leaving the rest of his body black" (p. 32). The man would hence seem to wear a mask to hide the unusual convergence of white dots and a black skin.

Nevertheless, the meaning of the mask, like many of the stories told about the masked man, is very indeterminate. Indeed, if the normative value of the African mask lies in its containment of what Gates calls "a coded, secret, hermetic world," and in its symbolization of what we could consider to be the inner essences of a race or culture, the masked figure in *Beka Lamb* plays a reversed role: he is a figure of transformation and ambivalence, and his presence in the novel calls attention to cultural indeterminacy in Belize.[48] Moreover, the masked man foregrounds the paradoxical relationship between the plural cultures of Belize and their anxiety toward their ancestral African cultures. Rejected by both the creole and the Caribs, the masked man represents the pain of division, a pain Beka also shares as she is forced to reflect on the meaning of her given identities and her national "rights" (p. 37). In similar vein, Toycie finds it difficult to identify with her most valued possession—her guitar—which was made in Spain, an imperial power that is partly responsible for Belize's identity and political crisis: "Guatemala claims Belize from Britain through rights inherited from Spain, and Spain got rights from the Pope, and who are we going to get rights from?" (p. 36). In this historical record of treaties and rights, it appears that there is no place for Belize. But in trying to imagine a future autonomous community, the two girls feel they can harness their imagination to reclaim their national territory: thus, the

---

48. Henry Louis Gates, Jr., *Figures in Black: Words, Signs, and the "Racial" Self* (New York: Oxford University Press, 1987), p. 167.

sign "made in Spain" is erased from the guitar and Toycie scrawls "Belize" instead, thereby inventing a community with which she can identify (p. 37).

What we witness in the above examples is the transformation of an individual fantasy (the need to socially possess a significant object) into what Deleuze and Guattari, writing about desire and identity in general, call the "revolutionary pole of group fantasy"—"the power to experience institutions themselves as mortal, to destroy them or change them according to the articulations of desire and the social field."[49] Still, the kind of imaginary power which allows the two girls to erase Spain and replace it with Belize is cast in an ambivalent mode. For even as nationalism spreads in the colony and things British are questioned and even discarded by some, the act of erasing the past also deprives Beka of one of the few certainties she had—the knowledge that she was a "British subject" (pp. 53–54). At the same time, old people like Granny Stackler—those "that remember things from the time before" (p. 62)—are dying and with them memories of an ancestral past. Clearly the characters are shaped by their consciousness of a past that can no longer be recovered and a present that is fast being displaced by an unknown future; this rapid change causes much confusion in the colony, prompting the community to reread a past they would have preferred to ignore. For this reason Beka construes her great-grandmother's wake as both a rite of passage and "a small lesson in community history" (p. 63). Whether this reflection on the past has any value is the cause of an interesting dispute between Beka's mother and grandmother: while the latter identifies with "the old ways" symbolized by the wake, the former is adamant in her belief that "the old ways will poison the new" (p. 66). Where, then, is the foundation of the future, of the "progress" desired if the national community is to be realized?

Like Hodge before her, Edgell adopts a narrative stance that complicates the question of value and identity after colonialism by abrogating the binary divisions (past/present, Carib/creole, etc.) that might make the colonial subjects' choices easy. In the process, both the self and its community are shown to be constructed around artificial ideals; they exist in the reality of the unreal, of fantasy and dream, of what the

---

49. Gilles Deleuze and Félix Guattari, *Anti-Oedipus: Capitalism and Schizophrenia*, trans. Robert Hurley et al. (Minneapolis: University of Minnesota Press, 1983), pp. 62–63.

anthropologist Michael Taussig has brilliantly shown to be the space of "unconscious cultural formations of meaning."[50] In a telling example of this "unconscious" cultural formation, the children in the Catholic school gossip about the mixed racial origins of the local priest, Father Nuñez, and his mimicry of his European counterparts, but their discourse is predicated on a false notion of what is conventional and real:

> These comments, overheard, perhaps misunderstood, no doubt misconstrued, formed the basis of the young people's attitudes toward Father Nuñez. The majority of students in St. Cecilia's could not be expected, at their age, to perceive the underlying conflicts in Father Nuñez's personality. They had a romantic notion of how Belizeans ought to behave, and to them Father Nuñez was hypocritical adopting the mannerisms, language, and style of living of his foreign counterparts—faults they, of course, would seldom be guilty of as adults. [P. 89]

The ironic twist at the end of the quote is right on the mark—the students have already been shown, as we have seen in the case of Beka, to be caught up in the same kind of cultural crisis and mimicry as Father Nuñez. Nevertheless, there is something remarkable about their dissociation from his "hypocritical adoption" of foreign mannerisms; for although the students are being assimilated into the colonial system in ways that closely parallel the priest's "lonely journey from Xaicotz to Rome" (p. 89), their discourse has initiated a theoretical subversion of the doctrine of assimilation. For them, adoption of foreign cultures is not an ideal but a problem. As Taussig would put it, this is a first step in the demythologization of history and reified representations; unlike Father Nuñez, who still believes in the efficacy of the imperial system of meanings, the students have developed a "hermeneutics of suspicion."[51]

The Question of Closure

From Lamming's early novels to the two novels discussed in this chapter, the central texts of Caribbean modernism are dominated by a certain anxiety about endings which is also an anxiety about new cultural beginnings. At the end of *In the Castle of My Skin*, as he

50. Michael Taussig, *Shamanism, Colonialism, and the Wild Man: A Study in Terror and Healing* (Chicago: University of Chicago Press, 1986), p. 9.
51. Taussig, p. 10.

prepares to leave Barbados for the journey that will inevitably lead him to Europe, the boy G observes that "the earth where I walked was a marvel of blackness and I knew in a sense more deep than simple departure I had said farewell, farewell to the land."[52] The sense of melancholy and loss which characterizes this passage also suggests a form of identity with the landscape being left behind, so that when the exiled colonials return, as they do in Césaire's *Cahier* or Lamming's *Of Age and Innocence*, their desire for the reclaimed space of the nation is defined by their previous sense of loss. Moreover, the problem of endings in narratives of national identity is of utmost significance because, as Jean Franco has asserted in relation to Mexican literature, "it is precisely the closure of the novel that is the place of ideological ambiguity."[53] This ambiguity is, of course, triggered by the incomplete nature of modernity, the limits of modernization, and the unfulfilled dreams of nationalism in the neocolonial period. For even after the achievement of national independence, complete autonomy evades many Caribbean countries; modernization entails still greater dependence on the "world economic system," while modernity (and postmodernity) are determined by the new mass media systems from the West.[54]

Clearly independence has not resolved the problems of identity and national culture discussed in this book. Furthermore, by appropriating the infrastructure of colonial modernity, independence has complicated the process of narrative and social closure in the Caribbean text. For if the colonization of the Caribbean ushers in European modernity, then it is possible to argue that the Caribbean text seeks its autonomy by denigrating the colonial modernist project. But since official discourse in the neocolonial period still holds that the meaning and value of independence lie in the ability of the ex-colonial elite to sustain modernity, then a conflict of intentions between the politicians and writers seems inevitable. In other words, independence, by failing to resolve the question of identity and consciousness raised in the nationalist period, has complicated cultural formation in the islands; it

---

52. George Lamming, *In the Castle of My Skin* (New York: Schocken, 1983), pp. 297–98.
53. Franco, p. 132.
54. In an earlier period of Caribbean history, according to Lamming, the United States "existed for us as a dream, a kingdom of material possibilities accessible to all"; but America was also "the extreme example of Europe, stripped naked of all pretense about having a civilizing mission in the dark corners of the earth." See *The Castle*, pp. xiv–xv. In Hodge's view, the dominance of the American face of modernity is apparent in television. See Balutansky, p. 659.

seems to have legitimized economic arrangements that are weighted in favor of the metropolitan centers, but it has failed to rationalize national consciousness, which has instead been reduced to what Fanon calls "an empty shell, a crude and fragile travesty of what it might have been."[55]

In the circumstances, as Hodge has argued eloquently, the destiny of the new Caribbean nation is no longer clear or manifest: "It's much harder to point at the indicators of our domination, very difficult. When you tell people about the dangers of TV, they laugh. You can't tell people that TV or these new-style religions—the new fundamentalists—all are infiltrating us. It's hard to put that to people. So it is much more difficult to fight now."[56] In considering closure in both *Crick Crack* and *Beka Lamb*, it is important to keep in mind that although Hodge and Edgell are writing primarily about the transition from the colonial situation to national independence, they write with the privilege of at least ten years of the experiment in independence in the Caribbean region. It is not hence enough to read these novels in the traditional mode of the Caribbean *bildungsroman*; although they promise many of the formal and ideological features of this genre, and resemble other Caribbean novels of childhood in many respects, their endings are more troublesome.

In his introduction to *Crick Crack*, Narinesingh argues that Tee's departure from Trinidad is not a resolution to her crisis of identity because her inner dissonance will continue to plague her in England. He finds no comfort in her emigration: "Withdrawal from the situation by her emigration to England is not a morally affirmative position, for reconciliation can only be achieved by a mature revaluation of her condition. For Tee, personal synthesis and coherence are still to be achieved" (p. xiv). The reader's sense of ambivalence is exacerbated by the fact that Hodge has not presented us with a simple choice of ideological positions but with a series of equally tenable possibilities, placed in what Thorpe calls the "perplexing cultural situation" presented by Tee's departure for England at the end of the novel. Exile may seem to offer the girl a way out of the contradictory claims of the creole and colonial worlds, but it is not, Thorpe says, a "positive solution":

> While the possibility exists that, in a foreign country, away from the pressures of her own society, Tee might in time be able to reconcile the

55. Fanon, p. 148.
56. Balutansky, p. 659.

two cultural traditions which she has inherited, there is still the other possibility that, like the school-master Mr Hinds, her sojourn in the metropolis will merely aggravate her contempt for the local black creole culture, thus removing her permanently to the ranks of the culturally displaced.[57]

Although I find Thorpe's incisive reading of closure in Hodge's novel admirable, I don't share her belief that the narrator ever places her character, or the reader for that matter, in a situation where choices have to be made in terms of what is positive or negative. It is certainly true that the narrator has represented the creole world as more organic and hence sustaining of her character, but she has also expressed the inevitable distance that separates this subject and her previous world. As we saw earlier, the creole world may be culturally satisfying, but it is economically marginalized; the colonial world is culturally alienating yet it comes with important economic privileges.

My argument, then, is that by sustaining the tensions between the creole and colonial worlds instead of forcing the young Tee to choose one over the other, the author has evoked another form of ambiguity which allows history to enter her text. In other words, Tee's unstable position in Trinidad signifies the origins of displacement in a contingent historical condition that cannot, as I argued earlier, be willed out of existence. We can see this point more clearly if we recall that although Tee's adoption of Beatrice's middle class perspective accentuates her crisis of identity, it is a necessary form of self-alienation because it is the only guarantee of social mobility in a colonial situation. The world of Ma and Tantie contains traditions that are meaningful to those who live in the creole realm, but when they are transposed into the world of colonial modernity, such traditions become ossified and quite remote from the daily existence of the colonial subject. In one of the most illuminating moments in the novel, Tee returns home to bid her old friends good-bye before her departure for England only to discover that Ma, her only link to an ancestral African past, has died: "In the last days Ma had suddenly remembered her grandmother's name and wanted it to be added to my names. Tantie hadn't even bothered to remember it" (p. 110).

The truth is, Tantie does not have the same reverence for ancestral names as Ma did. Meanwhile, Tee's more pressing problem is to deal with a rapidly changing historical situation: "Everything was chang-

57. Thorpe, p. 32.

ing, unrecognizable, pushing me out. This was as it should be, since I had moved up and no longer had any place here. But it was painful, and I longed all the more to be on my way" (p. 110). Change and movement push Tee out; the moment of loss is painful, but it is shown as inevitable, "as it should be"—the logical outcome of her education. My conclusion, then, is that as a character, Tee does not make a choice to identify with the colonial English culture at the expense of her creole origins; rather, she emigrates to alienate herself from both, to find a third position from which she can now reinvent herself out of the various confluences that have socially determined her. Writing about alienation helps Tee (the narrator) understand her double consciousness.

Furthermore, if writing after colonialism is posited as a means of mastering the linguistic codes of colonial modernism, it is because the alternative to writing, as Edgell suggests in *Beka Lamb*, is madness or social death. Indeed, in this novel, both Beka and her friend Toycie provide contrasting forms of dealing with displacement: Toycie engages life at its most fundamental and spontaneous level—that of eros and sexuality—and thus triggers the process that leads to the mental institution and her eventual death; Beka strives to master writing, leading to the award that restores her self-esteem. But mastery of writing is not, of course, presented as a simple and singular process of liberation; on the contrary, it is cast as the result of a painful reflection on how the self (and its cultural community) are constituted in, and constitute, language. For even where the facts have been collected, there is still the problem of organizing them into a coherent narrative; it is only when all the disparate parts of the essay have been organized that the self has mastered the appropriated forms of representation. Thus the essay Beka writes is an allegory of her own struggle to rewrite herself in a world dominated by often hostile signifiers. Ironically, once she has won the essay contest she has moved closer to the colonial orb, and hence aggravated her self-alienation in the process that was supposed to pull her out of the prisonhouse of colonialism. To understand this prisonhouse more lucidly, we need to turn to the politics of representation and interpretation as they are manifested in the paradoxical relationship between history—as a project of European (and hence colonial) modernity—and the Caribbean cultural text. Michelle Cliff's *Abeng* provides a climactic confrontation between history and textuality.

7

Narration at the Postcolonial Moment: History and Representation in *Abeng*

> Being woman and Antillean is a destiny difficult to un-
> tangle. . . . The Antilles is my natural mother and it is with
> her that I have accounts to settle, like any daughter with her
> mother, before becoming completely an adult.
>
> —Maryse Condé

> With modernization everything has to be recoded, for now
> people are on the move away from home territories and
> genealogies.
>
> —Jean Franco, *Plotting Women*

By the time Caribbean literature became a major player in the cultural politics of postcolonialism and postmodernism in the 1980s, the
claim that modernity and modernization could lead to a unity of
experience, a synthesis of culture, and a unified language of the nation
in the formerly colonized spaces was being rigorously questioned.
Indeed, after two decades of political independence and economic and
cultural dependence, and the increasing influence of modern Euro-
American discursive practices such as television and film, few people
were certain that decolonization constituted a radical disconnection
from the European modernist narrative initiated by Columbus and
sustained by colonialism. Moreover, if Caribbean discourse during the
period of decolonization appropriated the narrative strategies of high
modernism to resist an ecumenical European notion of history which
imprisoned the Caribbean subject in the realm of the "other" and its

economy of representation, in the period after independence it was becoming clear that attempts to appropriate and revise the European language and its topoi were already a mixed blessing. Modernist forms could allow the Caribbean writer to "derealize" and decenter colonial systems of meaning, and even deconstruct the totalizing claims of European history, but the resulting narratives were still imprisoned in the colonial language and its phallocentric privilege.[1]

In an attempt to break out of the ideologies that had continued to sustain systems of domination even after independence, a new generation of Caribbean women writers, such as Michelle Cliff and Erna Brodber, has emerged to reopen the debate on history, representation, and identity initiated by their precursors. This generation of writers also seeks to revise the terms by which we read the West Indian experience and to interrogate the idealized narrative of the nation which values synthesis over hybridity in cultural formation and totality over diversity in history. These writers are not merely calling modernist notions of history and representation into question; they are also insisting on the need for what Stephen Slemon calls "an identity granted not in terms of the colonial power, but in terms of themselves."[2] And as Rhonda Cobham has noted in a review of recent novels by Caribbean women writers, instead of affirming a history of connections and linear genealogies, these writers use "the techniques of postmodern writing to reconstruct rather than deconstruct a postcolonial history."[3]

At the heart of Cobham's comment is an oxymoron that is the key to understanding recent Caribbean writing and the status of the modernist project in the region: on one hand, the well-known techniques of postmodernism—temporal fragmentation, parody, intertextuality, and repetition—are being used by these writers to subvert institutionalized history; but, on the other hand, these writers are striving to establish an authoritative Caribbean narrative of history. Whereas contemporary Western novelists have acquiesced to Jean-François Lyotard's definition of the postmodern "as incredulity toward metanarratives," and have even succumbed to the premise that the great

1. I use "phallocentric privilege" in the way it has been articulated by Lemuel A. Johnson in "A-beng: (Re)calling the Body In(To) Question," in *Out of the Kumbla: Caribbean Women and Literature*, ed. Carole Boyce Davies and Elaine Savory Fido (Trenton: Africa World Press, 1990), p. 131.
2. Stephen Slemon, "Waiting for the Post: Modernity, Colonization, and Writing," *Ariel: A Review of International English Literature* 20 (October 1989), p. 6.
3. Rhonda Cobham, "Women of the Islands," *The Women's Review of Books* 7 (July 1990), 31.

narrative function is "losing its functors, its great hero, its great dangers, its great voyages, its great goal," many Caribbean writers seem to use postmodern narrative techniques to affirm the continuing urgency of an oppositional history and discourse that strive for the status of a grand narrative.[4] Indeed, for writers such as Cliff the narrative of history in the Caribbean is legitimized by the writer's appeal to a repressed Afro-Caribbean historical consciousness, an erased hermeneutics of meaning, and a decentered subjectivity:

> To write as a complete Caribbean woman, or man for that matter, demands of us retracing the African part of ourselves, reclaiming as our own, and as our subject, a history sunk under the sea, or scattered as potash in the canefields, or gone to bush, or trapped in a class system notable for its rigidity and absolute color stratification. It means finding the artforms of these of our ancestors and speaking in the *patois* forbidden us.[5]

As we will see in the close reading of *Abeng* which follows, Cliff's first novel is concerned with the deconstruction of the Eurocentric phenomenon in Jamaica as a prelude to unearthing the repressed Afro-Caribbean experience in the island. Thus the reconstruction of elided black identities and African fragments long lost in the colonial archive is as urgent as the deconstruction of modernism and modernity. For Marlene Nourbese Philip, a new writer from Tobago, it is imperative that the narratives of her generation of Caribbean writers "begin to recreate our histories and our myths, as well as integrate the most painful of experiences—loss of our history and word."[6] Thus history, conceived doubly as what Lemuel Johnson considers a threat and a condition of possibility, revolving around dominant presences as much as forgotten or negated absences, "summons up a relevant genealogy of disconnections and connections."[7] The central question now is this: what form and language does this history of connections and disconnections take as it strives to represent loss and to affirm an Afro-Caribbean presence? In what ways is Davies and Fido's "reality of absence, of voicelessness, of marginalization" in the lives of Carib-

4. Jean-François Lyotard, *The Postmodern Condition: A Report on Knowledge,* trans. Geoff Bennington and Brian Massumi (Minneapolis: University of Minnesota Press, 1984), p. xxiv.
5. Michelle Cliff, "A Journey into Speech," in *The Land of Look Behind: Prose and Poetry* (Ithaca, N.Y.: Firebrand Books, 1985), pp. 14–15.
6. Marlene Nourbese Philip, "The Absence of Writing or How I Almost Became a Spy," in Davies and Fido, *Out of the Kumbla,* p. 278.
7. Johnson, p. 112.

bean women linked "to the necessity to find a form, a mode of expression" that deconstructs both the ideological machine of imperialism and phallocentricism?[8]

The uniqueness of Cliff's aesthetics lies in her realization that the fragmentation, silence, and repression that mark the life of the Caribbean subject under colonialism must be confronted not only as a problem to be overcome but also as a condition of possibility—as a license to dissimulate and to affirm difference—in which an identity is created out of the chaotic colonial and postcolonial history. In writing about the ways in which Caribbean subjects strive to subjectify themselves within the commodified space and time of colonial modernity, Cliff finds discursive value in the very fragmentation that other commentators have seen as the curse of West Indian history. According to Cliff, fragmentation can indeed function as a strategy of identity since the colonized writer struggles "to get wholeness from fragmentation while working within fragmentation, producing work which may find its strength in its depiction of fragmentation, through form as well as content."[9] Although the goal of narrative is to overcome it, fragmentation also enables writing in three main respects: First, it allows the writer to recover the colonial repressed without resorting to what François Lionnet aptly calls "the ancient symmetry and dichotomies that have governed the ground and the very condition of possibility of thought, of 'clarity,' in all Western philosophy."[10] Second, it enables the writer to inscribe herself in the previously disdained vernacular and to use it to challenge the norms of the "Queen's" English. And finally, it helps her undermine the authority of given discourse through intertextual references and parodic forms that question the historical totalities that sustain ethnocentrism.

In the first instance, an archeological quest for Caribbean beginnings outside the framework of official history is imperative. Writing squarely within the tradition of the *nouveau roman*, Cliff posits narrative as a process in which history has value not because of its teleological claims, but because of its discontinuity, its concern with blanks, ruptures, and interruptions. Moreover, the manifest discourse of colonialism is important only in its contrastive relationship to the un-

8. Carole Boyce Davies and Elaine Savory Fido, "Introduction: Women and Literature in the Caribbean: An Overview," in *Out of the Kumbla*, p. 4.

9. Cliff, "A Journey into Speech," pp. 14–15.

10. Françoise Lionnet, *Autobiographical Voices: Race, Gender, Self-Portraiture* (Ithaca: Cornell University Press, 1989), p. 6.

spoken history of the African subaltern in the Caribbean. Second, the recovery of a patois and the recentering of the oral tradition in cultures in which written forms have been hegemonic is a precondition for what Johnson calls the speaking of the New World female presence.[11]

In relation to colonial discourse, the kind of historical knowledge yielded by the narrative of decolonization appears incomplete because of its failure to develop forms that give voice and presence to the unspoken and unwritten discourse of the dominated. The question that arises from this incompleteness is common in women's narratives in other cultures and has been raised succinctly by Françoise Gaillard in another context: "How to write History when historical reality seems to come apart and can no longer be experienced except as a collection of non-totalizable anecdotes."[12] Instead of seeking to establish a unique Caribbean narrative of history, as some of the writers discussed in previous chapters try very hard to do, Cliff seeks to write what amounts to a schizophrenic text, one in which subjects realize their knowledge through their "split consciousness" and their suspension in a void between official language and the patois. Her narrative impetus here is the belief that "it would be as dishonest to write the novel entirely in *patois* as to write entirely in the King's English. Neither is the novel a linear construction; its subject is the political upheavals of the past twenty years. Therefore I have mixed time and incident and space and character and also form to try to mirror the historical turbulence."[13]

Through deliberate strategies of intertextuality, Cliff reifies the linguistic and ideological conflicts that arise when colonialist discourse is challenged by the vernacular, when official versions of history are questioned by the silent history of the poor and powerless. By establishing the antagonistic relationship between linguistic forms (especially the oral and the written), and through the interpolation of time frames and the spatialization of historical events, she represents both the value and limits of fragmentation as a condition of history and as a strategy of representation. Furthermore, as a narrative of turbulence and crisis, *Abeng* is not intended simply to evoke the value of otherness, but also to provide a genealogy of the loss of value and speech in the colonial subject. By dispersing the historical narratives of colonial-

---

11. Johnson, p. 119.
12. Francoise Gaillard, "An Unspeakable (Hi)story," *Yale French Studies* 59 (1980), 137.
13. Cliff, "A Journey into Speech," p. 14.

ism, Cliff recenters, and gives value, to margins and edges.[14] My intention in this chapter is to show that as a narrative whose goal is to disorient the reader from entrenched forms of modernism, *Abeng* finds its power in its parasitic and subversive relationship to previous texts, which it appropriates and then spits out, clearing a space for alternative systems of representation.

Intertextuality and the Journey into Speech

First, the question of intertextuality. In a powerful conceptual study of intertextuality in narrative, Lauren Jenny has asserted that "without intertextuality, a literary work would simply be unintelligible, like speech in a language one has not yet learned. We grasp the meaning and structure of a literary work only through its relation to archetypes which are themselves abstracted from long series of texts of which they are, so to speak, invariants."[15] As we have already seen, Cliff's works arise from the author's consciousness of her troubled relationship with her colonial heritage and its language, and from her dissatisfaction with Caribbean male discourses on national identity. The centering of strategies of intertextuality in *Abeng* is the clearest evidence of Cliff's determination to establish a narrative that, by evoking the disjointed forms of experience which define the colonial and postcolonial subject, posits new ways of reading West Indian identity and experience.

In this regard, the relation of Cliff's text to other texts is not only a way of decentering the Western narrative and the colonial library from its dominant position in the Caribbean mind, but also a means of deconstructing or reconstituting modernist themes and categories first raised in the works of her precursors. Indeed, intertextuality is Cliff's way of positioning her narrative within an archive defined by the opposed claims of Africa and Europe in the Caribbean episteme; intertextual reference becomes a method of interrogating the foundational status of African and European cultures. This kind of intertextuality, as Linda Hutcheon has observed in her study of form in contemporary fiction, "simultaneously works to affirm—textually and hermeneuti-

14. See Linda Hutcheon in *A Poetics of Postmodernism: History, Theory, Fiction* (New York: Routledge, 1988), p. 130.
15. Lauren Jenny, "The Strategy of Form," in *French Literary Theory Today*, ed. Tzvetan Todorov, trans. R. Carter (Cambridge: Cambridge University Press, 1982), p. 34.

cally—the connection with the past" and to situate a text in the world "of discourse, the 'world' of texts and intertexts."[16] However, Cliff's (textual) psychoanalysis of the past is modernist in one major respect—its orientation toward a future in which the Caribbean crisis of identity will be resolved.

In any case, intertextuality in *Abeng* allows the narrator to present the reader with a dual mediation of the Caribbean experience; the text echoes, revises, and sometimes amplifies both colonial discourse and its more immediate anticolonial precursors. Our reading of Cliff's novel is thus conditioned and predetermined by our awareness of its relationship to other Caribbean texts; the text constantly reminds us that we have no access to the history of the islands except through the diverse forms of discursive practices which have previously represented it. To borrow Michel Foucault's phraseology, the frontiers of the text are never clear-cut: "Beyond the title, the first lines, and the last full-stop, beyond its internal configuration and its autonomous form, it is caught up in a system of references to other books, other texts, other sentences: it is a node within a network."[17]

As we shall see later in this chapter, Cliff's priority is not the "objective" status of Caribbean history, although this is by no means an unimportant point in her concerns, but how this history is mediated by other texts and the discursive form this history takes. In all cases, her textual reflection on Caribbean historiography is highly paradoxical and informed by various kinds of doubleness. Indeed, the title of the novel foregrounds the doubleness of the Caribbean experience and the ways it is represented: we are informed that *abeng* is an African word for "conch shell," but the word has been adjusted and transformed by its function in the New World beyond its original meaning and intention. While a conch shell in Africa may be an agent of sound, speech, and the inner experiences of self, in the Caribbean it has become a mark of both displacement (calling the slaves to the canefields) and resistance (passing the messages of Maroon armies). For this reason, the conch shell is a sign of both the narrator's connection to her previously repressed African past and her functional distance from it; it is a symbolic representation of the process of historical remembering and dismembering.[18]

Even before we start reading the text itself, Cliff suggests several

16. Hutcheon, p. 125.
17. Quoted in Hutcheon, p. 127.
18. Johnson, p. 113.

ways in which the desire for an alternative history of the Caribbean is predicated on the narrating self's awareness of its placement in a state of cultural limbo and doubleness. This point is underscored in the author's acknowledgment of her literary influences, in her dedication, and in the opening epigraphs. Her indebtedness is to folklorists and scholars involved in the archeological quest for the repressed African tradition in the Caribbean, and to feminist writers involved in the establishment of a women's literary tradition.[19] Although *Abeng* is a work of fiction, it is already implicated in other, social and historical discourses which it seeks to elaborate or contextualize. In this process of elaboration and contextualization, as Johnson has noted, the author asserts her "recognition of resistance and of the self-dissolving threat that history can be."[20] In addition, Cliff dedicates the book to two authors whose texts are generated by a loss of place and genealogy: both Jean Toomer and Bessie Head wrote about a mulatto angst that represented their suspension between the white and black traditions that had socially determined them, but that they could not wholly embrace. This sentiment of loss and displacement is further enhanced by Cliff's epigraphic use of a poem by Basil McFarlane in which birth and death are encased in the same emotional and temporal frame. Both are evoked through a self-conscious elegiac tone that calls attention to the state of poetic abandonment which many colonial and postcolonial writers, especially those in exile, share.[21]

But if McFarlane's poem—and the slave lament that follows it—stress the moment of loss and displacement, a second form of intertextuality connects Cliff to a reconstructive and intransitive tradition of Caribbean writing. Indeed, we cannot read *Abeng* without hearing the echoes of other Caribbean texts. For example, the first paragraph of the novel ("The island rose and sank. Twice. During periods in which history was recorded by indentations on rock and shell" [p. 3]) provides the reader with a geological evocation of Caribbean beginnings which also echoes a famous line from Edward Brathwaite's "Islands

19. The "network" of references in which Cliff "operates" is suggested in the acknowledgments on the copyright page of *Abeng* (Trumansburg, N.Y.: Crossing Press, 1984): for "some of the details" of her book, Cliff says she is indebted to other books and works (those of Zora Neale Hurston, Jervis Anderson, and Orlando Patterson), folksingers (Olive Lewin and her group), and leading feminists such as Audre Lorde and Adrienne Rich. Further references are in the text.

20. Johnson, p. 125.

21. For the poetics of loss and exile in postcolonial literature, see Edward Said, "Reflections on Exile," *Granta* 13 (Autumn 1984), 157–72.

and Exiles"—"The stone had skidded arc'd and bloomed into islands."[22] Similarly, the line that opens the second paragraph—"This is a book about the time which followed on that time"(p. 3)—echoes notions of "before time" first raised in Zee Edgell's *Beka Lamb*.

An even more direct and dramatic example of intertextual reference is the episode surrounding the slaughter of a pig at the middle of the novel: the eating of the pig's "privates" signifies Clare's exclusion from patriarchal rituals (p. 57), but it is also important because of the way it calls to mind the famous killing of a pig in Marshall's *The Chosen Place, the Timeless People*, an incident that signalizes Saul's alienation from the world of the Caribbean peasantry. Marshall's influence on Cliff is also apparent in the latter's representation of the tension between Afro-Americans and Caribbean blacks (p. 86), which brings to mind the struggle of the Bajans in *Brown Girl, Brownstones* to distinguish themselves from native American blacks. Another important intertextual reference is Mr. Powell's experiences in New York during the Harlem Renaissance and his acquaintance with Zora Neale Hurston (pp. 86–87). In this example, a fictional character connects us to writers and texts in the African diaspora.

No doubt many other examples can be found, but they all serve a clearly defined theoretical function: they constitute what Jenny calls a "super-parole" and show how "intertextuality speaks a language whose vocabulary is the sum of all existing texts."[23] Within the context of Caribbean modernism and its discourse, Cliff's evocation of other black texts is a radical means of expanding the Caribbean social and semantic space while decentering the colonial tradition; her referents are no longer determined solely by the colonial library, and her primary references are no longer Eurocentric. Intertextual echoes are also important because of their powers of negation. This feature is particularly pronounced in Cliff's use of parody, a textual strategy that—in modern fiction as a whole—allows the author to "enshrine the past and to question it."[24] The past is enshrined because it is an inescapable part of the Caribbean experience which cannot be wished away or written out of existence; but it is questioned because it is an instrument of European power and domination. In effect, Cliff's mode of narration, as I show in greater detail below, is shaped by the doubleness of

22. See Edward Brathwaite, *The Arrivants: A New World Trilogy* (London: Oxford University Press, 1973), p. 48.
23. Jenny, p. 45.
24. Hutcheon, p. 126.

Caribbean history itself—the need to simultaneously represent dominant discourse, its referent, figures, and spectacles, and to question its
privileges; the desire to psychoanalyze the trauma of history but also
to transcend it.

Consider, for example, the following description of the queen as the
emblem of imperial power in colonial Jamaica:

> The portrait of the white queen hung in banks, department stores,
> grocery stores, schools, government buildings, and homes—from coun-
> tryside shanties to the split-levels on the hills above Kingston Harbor. A
> rather plain little whitewoman decked in medals and other regalia—
> wearing, of course, a crown. Our-lady-of-the-colonies. The whitest
> woman in the world. [P. 5]

Disjunction is an important strategy of narration here: the queen,
the symbol of imperial power and the supplement for a white mythology whose authority is derived from the relationship between sign
and signifier, is displaced within the very portrait that signifies her
power.[25] The description proceeds to foreground the obviously metonymic displacement of the picture and the plain woman it represents
and to raise troublesome questions about the value of this signifier:
Does the plain white woman have a presence outside her medals and
the crown? Without these symbols of power, isn't she just another
white woman? Of course, you cannot have one without the other: the
queen is the whitest woman in the world not because of anything
inherent in her character, but because of her symbolic presence in the
relations of power and domination which define Jamaica as a British
colony. Indeed, the narrator's description of the queen as "our-lady-of-
the-colonies" emphasizes the ecumenical nature of her power. However, the narrative counters this power through a parodic tone that
reduces the whitest woman in the world to the object of *la bêtise*.

Here Cliff's primary narrative strategy is to call attention to the
symbolic representation of white mythology and, at the same time, to
open a space in which this mythology can be reversed or subverted by
a counter-discourse built on narrative algebraization and understate-
ment. In official discourse, as in the case of the Jamaican currency, a
binary relationship—rather than an opposition—between the native
and the colonizer has been instituted to stabilize the existing system of

25. See Jacques Derrida, *Margins of Philosophy*, trans. Alan Bass (Chicago: University of
Chicago Press, 1982), p. 213.

domination. Apart from being a form of exchange, the currency is a symbolon in which the extinct Arawak is supposed to have equal value with the "sovereign crest." In Cliff's (re)presentation of this symbolon, however, the opposite effect is underscored as the narrative scrutinizes the absent Arawak and his or her relationship to the dominant: "Jamaican money bore the word JAMAICA, and the sovereign crest of the island—an Arawak and a white conqueror: only one of these existed in 1958" (p. 5). Thus the colonizer's cultural text (the currency) is represented and dispersed at the same time; it is shown to have achieved coherence or totality at the expense of the other, who now exists only as a sign with no referent.

My contention here is that Cliff's narrative derives its power from its capacity to expose the contradictions within the colonizer's economy of representation. Because the dominant social text derives its authority from its monotheist ideology, Cliff's text uses a devastating plurality to expose what the monological text represses; official or dominant enunciation is shown to have a double or uncanny element that contests its claim to ideological absoluteness or control. Also, the value of *Abeng*, as a self-consciously revisionist text, does not lie solely in what it exhibits, but also in the absent or unspoken aspects of the Caribbean experience which it uncovers from under official rhetoric. Cliff foregrounds the ways in which interrogating, or even digging up, the past resurrects meanings that both mock and haunt the dominant culture in her portrait of the Parish Church, the very embodiment of white power in Jamaica, and the deep historical secret it represses:

> The Parish Church was High Anglican—it was the church of attendance of the white governor, and members of the royal family stopped there when the queen's yacht, H.M.S. Britannica, docked in Kingston harbor. . . . In 1958, while digging near the churchyard during some renovations to the building, workers uncovered a coffin of heavy metal—a coffin of huge proportions. . . . A brass plate which had been affixed to the coffin and etched with an inscription informed the vicar that the coffin contained the remains of a hundred plague victims, part of a shipload of slaves from the Gold Coast, who contracted the plague from the rats on the vessel which brought them to Jamaica. [P. 7]

Witness the contrast between the church's self-representation as a continuation of European high culture and the abysmal slave history on which colonial society is founded. Although the narrator does not make this connection explicitly, the text suggests that the history of

Jamaica will remain half-known unless one fragment is viewed in relation to the other; the meaning of Caribbean history arises from the tense conjunction between manifest and celebrated Eurocentric meanings and a repressed Afro-Caribbean hermeneutics.

But it is when we turn to Cliff's engagement with historiography that we begin to realize that her concern with the representation of history is also part of a theoretical enterprise to rescue "Caribbean facts" from their subordination to the European sense of history as a totality with a privileged telos. Because historiography is such an important and contentious issue in Cliff's text, we can in fact read *Abeng* as a metafictional text. This is the kind of text which, according to Hutcheon, goes beyond a preoccupation with the nightmare of history and

> puts into question, at the same time as it exploits, the grounding of historical knowledge in the past real. . . . It can often enact the problematic nature of the relation of writing history to narrativization and, thus, to fictionalization, thereby raising . . . questions about the cognitive status of historical knowledge. . . . What is the ontological nature of historical documents? Are they the stand-in for the past? What is meant—in ideological terms—by our "natural" understanding of historical explanation?[26]

Let us suspend the question of the relationship between historiography and narrativity for the time being and concentrate on Cliff's examination of the nature of historical knowledge and the representation of history. At the beginning of the book, the whole question of the writing and recording of history is shown to be contested and determined by power relations and opposed desires in Jamaica. The narrator begins her quest for historical forms by tracing her "record" of history to geological formations, to periods when history was "recorded by indentations on rock and shell" (p. 3). This geological genesis of the Caribbean is important because it negates traditional histories, which posit the "discovery" as the ground zero of the Caribbean experience; at the same time, the archeologizing gesture raises the possibility that there are modes of historical knowledge which are accessible to us outside previously privileged European documents. Thus Cliff adopts what we may call an *annales* approach to history in which rocks, eye-witness accounts, coffins, and oral forms have as

26. Hutcheon, pp. 92–93.

much authority as documents: the coffin buried under the Parish Church (p. 7), the trilobite fossil Clare discovers on the beach (p. 8), her grandmother's cut-glass pitcher (p. 13), the elm trees on the family's lost plantation (p. 23), and the "CASTRO SI, BATISTA NO" sign on the wall of the church (p. 22) are all important marks of history. They represent different (if not alternative) means of making sense of the past; they are part of the museum from which the desire of history rises.[27]

It is one thing, however, to represent the fragments of the museum and record the dispersed facts of history; it is quite another to get into this history and recover its cognitive value through the creation of narrative. Clare faces this problem often in the novel. In her visit to Paradise Plantation, for example, she can clearly see the various elements that illustrate her family history, but how can she relate these fragments to each other when things seem to float and "the background could slide so easily into the foreground" (p. 25)? Indeed, what is the foreground and what is its background? How is historical value established? The truth is, "signs of a former life" do not naturally give that life meaning or significance; Clare will clearly see the traces of the slaves' cabins on the earth every time she visits the old family plantation, but this is no guarantee that she will know and understand "the former life they represented" (p. 25; also pp. 26 and 27). The signs of history cannot be mastered because the subject lacks a context and theory for establishing connections between what appear to be the dispersed and contradictory signs of West Indian history and the totalized (and sanitized) colonial version taught in school. An easy way out, it often appears to Clare, is to let desire and the imaginary become substitutes for historical signs: "She sometimes imagined that the walls of certain places were the records of those places—the events which happened there" (p. 32). Rather than seeing historical markers as signals of something else, Clare wants to invest value in these signs themselves; and when she is disappointed by historical artifacts that don't cohere with her desires, she prefers escaping from history altogether (pp. 36–37).

Why does Clare have such difficulties understanding history even when its signs are easily available to her? The simplest answer to this question is that the context in which she tries to master historical discourse, and her training and experience about the value of the

27. See Gaillard, pp. 147–48.

historical artifact, already negate the significance of forgotten or repressed histories. Boy Savage has created in his daughter a sense that history has no cognitive status unless it is informed by a vision of myth and natural disaster: "Nothing, to him, was ever what it seemed to be. Nothing was an achievement of human labor" (p. 9). The father's dystopian view of history disables Clare's archeological quest as do her mother's romantic vision of Jamaica (p. 50) and the textbook histories of Jamaica which have repressed the experiences of those who resisted the official order. But there is another, more significant, reason why Clare is inevitably disabled in her attempts to recover her history—she does not know how to master historical discourse because she has no narrative authority that might enable her to capture a fragmented history in writing. In other words, she cannot combine her meanings to reconstruct the whole.

Gaillard has made an important theoretical proposition regarding selfhood and the writing of fragmented histories which coheres with Cliff's conceptualization of writing "whole" within the fragmentary. According to Gaillard, if the identity of the subject of a narrative cannot be established, then character "is no longer the appropriate place for the performance of that totalization of meanings which goes beyond apparent contradictions. . . . Since character, now that it is itself divided, cannot synthesize an experience fragmented anyway in other respects, its intervention provides no hope of carrying out the syntactical integration of discursive odds and ends which is known as historical narrative."[28] How then does one write a historical novel predicated on a schizophrenic and divided subject? For Cliff, discourse and narrative must take the place normally reserved for character in fiction, and the tension between language and speech must also be valorized to expose the conditions that have erased the identity of the colonized subject.

The Collapse of the "Given"

As we have seen in previous chapters, the struggle between language and speech in the Caribbean text is symptomatic of two radically opposed systems of representation—the oral discourses of the peasantry and the written texts promoted by the colonial school. Clare

28. Gaillard, pp. 147–49.

Savage strives to develop her identity between the two, but because she cannot establish a fundamental relationship with either (she does not share her mother's deep passion for the folk, and her belief in official versions of history is steadily undermined in the course of the narrative), the text raises the possibility of a third discourse that is irreducible to either language or speech. In many instances, this third discourse is posited in the gap between the folk and official versions of history. Thus although Nanny—"the sorceress, the *obeah* woman" (p. 14)—and her slave revolt are absent from the colonial textbook, we are never made to believe that it is enough for the narrative to recover this repressed history and to affirm it in writing. Indeed, what strikes us about the woman warrior is not the reality of her existence, which cannot be doubted—"There is absolutely no doubt that she actually existed" (p. 14)—but the fact that in spite of historical signs that testify to her existence (ruins, for example), Nanny has not been admitted into Jamaican official history. The narrator's priority is not to prove that Nanny actually existed, but to show how her presence is negated in official versions of history because she threatens Jamaica's foundational narrative, which would prefer to trace its sources to Europe rather than Africa.

Furthermore, the narrator's almost casual reproduction of Nanny and her legends allows Cliff to emphasize one of her most consistent themes in the novel: our familiarity with the surface language of history does not allow us to escape its ruse; history evades, or is foreclosed from, even those who make it. Thus although the people in the Tabernacle church "could trace their bloodlines back to a past of slavery . . . this was not something they talked about much, or knew much about" (p. 18). The narrator's theme, then, is not the power and majesty of history, or even its eroticism, but how it eludes our knowledge or cognition. In many cases the narrative emphasizes how history is scattered around its subjects and how they relive their past without grasping its significance: "They did not know that their name for papaya—*pawpaw*—was the name of one of the languages of Dahomey" (p. 20); "Some of them were called Nanny, because they cared for the children of other women, but they did not know who Nanny had been" (p. 21). Again, we can see how the narrator makes historical discourse problematic by exposing her subjects' inabilities to confer ideological value on the signs embedded in their speech.

In the same vein, Cliff indicts official discourse for contributing to the interpretative failure of the colonial subject as it seeks to historicize its experiences: although the school and the government circulate "information" and "facts" intended to further the natives' knowledge of Jamaica's history, ordinary people find their significant experiences buried in discursive acts that alienate them. For example, color and caste are key codes in explaining social relationships in colonial Jamaica, but in Clare's school, "as in the rest of society, it was concealed behind euphemisms of talent, looks, aptitude" (p. 100). If official discourse conceals through evasion, then the author seeks a counter-discourse that penetrates the illusions sustained by such evasions to effect a postcolonial discursive practice.

But if modernity—as a project of the Enlightenment—derives its authority from its absolutist character, as Ernesto Laclau has argued in an essay on contemporary social theory, it can only be weakened from "an analytic terrain from whose standpoint this weakening is thinkable and definable." This terrain is "neither arbitrary nor freely accessible to the imagination, but on the contrary it is the historical sedimentation of a set of traditions whose common denominator is the collapse of the immediacy of the *given*."[29] In seeking the imaginary collapse of the given, Cliff resorts to wide-ranging discursive strategies: these include constant authorial intrusions into the narrative, commentary on the significance of certain words or expressions, and even the "unmediated" reproduction of discourses from other sources, such as an editorial from the *Daily Gleaner* (p. 4). In all these cases, the narrative calls attention to the possibilities of alternative meanings by enhancing its own plurality.

For example, at the beginning of the novel the *Daily Gleaner*, the official organ of the Jamaican ruling class, declares the 1958 mango season to have produced the "biggest crop in recent memory"; but almost immediately this "given" is shown to be determined by the paper's need to promote a certain image of Jamaica: "The paper ran an editorial which spoke of God's Gift to Jamaica, and concluded by telling all inhabitants to be hospitable to tourists" (p. 4). The editorial necessity to assert the "given" fact points to the Achilles' heel of official discourse—what it assumes to be collective or absolutist meanings are indeed disputed by other sectors of the society. Thus while the newspaper editorial portrays the mango as Jamaica's gift to the world and a tourist attraction, for most island people living in the United States

29. Ernesto Laclau, "Politics and the Limits of Modernity," in *Universal Abandon? The Politics of Postmodernism*, ed. Andrew Ross (Minneapolis: University of Minnesota Press, 1989), p. 67.

and England, "the mango was to be kept an island secret," not to be displayed in foreign stores and markets (p. 4). These contrasting images of a national symbol are excellent examples of Cliff's determination to devalorize the given by exposing its plural meanings. Her narrative constantly reminds us that if we read history from an absolute perspective, as the Enlightenment modernists would like us to, then we will not understand the contradictory motives behind historical acts. For example, the colonial textbook represents the abolition of slavery as a benign act by the British government, but Cliff's narrative unearths and brings into play all the unacknowledged facts and interests involved in this historical event; in placing slavery in its proper context, "it is important to take it all in, the disconnections and the connections, in order to understand the limits of the abolition of slavery" (p. 28).

Moreover, to weaken the given field of discourse, a decolonized narrative of the kind Cliff proposes in *Abeng* begins with the premise that the facts and forms of history are not easily accessible to the imagination; we have to struggle even to distinguish the historical fact from figures of eroticism and colonial desire. This kind of struggle is prefigured in Clare's attempts to come to terms with the annihilation of Anne Frank: "Why did they kill her? That was a question whose answer was always out of reach. It was hard for Clare to imagine someone, another girl, who was of her age or near to her age, dying—to imagine her dying as Anne Frank died, in a place called Bergen-Belsen, the year before Clare was born, was impossible" (p. 68). Because Clare cannot transfer Anne Frank's experiences into her immediate universe, the Jewish girl's realities remain paradoxically knowable and inaccessible: although Anne had "left behind evidence of her life" (p. 69) in the form of her diary, this is no guarantee that we can have complete knowledge of her past, what she felt in her moment of annihilation, or the real motives of those who destroyed her.

Similarly, the life of Christopher Columbus is relived in countless documents and monuments, but what intrigues the narrator is the possibility that we may not know who the real Columbus was or what the motives were for his "discovery." Was he a Marano, a Sephardic Jew hiding his identity behind Christian worship? Was he a Jew in search of a homeland for his people in a New World diaspora (p. 67)? In *Abeng*, a historical event that is one of the foundations of modern Western history is almost casually called into question: "This man, whose journeys had such a profound effect on the history and imagination of the western world, is a relatively mysterious figure in the records of western civilization" (p. 67). In the circumstances, all historical knowledge must be tentative and incomplete; historiographical fiction must be aware of its limitations—there are "so many veils to be lifted," "so many intertwinings to be unraveled" (p. 67).

Despite her awareness of the limitations of her project, Cliff strives to evoke an alternative history or different means of gaining access to repressed experiences. The narration of this history does not follow a linear, progressive scale, however. Indeed the meaning of the marginalized and erased Caribbean experience is not sought in an area of logic and consciousness; rather it asserts or commemorates itself in an arena of madness and fantasy. If European conquerors created "fantastic images to render the actual inhabitants harmless" (p. 78), writing from the margins involves inventing spectacles that alienate the colonizers in their own language and history. In this regard, to use Edward Said's words, discursive language "is like a repertory theatre that stages numerous spectacles."[30] In Cliff's text, Nanny, the Maroon heroine, enacts her history as a spectacle—catching the bullets of the oppressor between her buttocks, she renders them harmless (p. 14). As spectacle, the history of the repressed creates its own illusion of immediacy. As a form of maroonage, this history is "unruly, runaway"; beyond its "exact meaning," this history functions before our eyes, "fierce, wild, unbroken" (p. 20), testimony to an order of things outside the Western logos. To borrow Jean Pierre Vernant's theoretical formulation, the historical spectacle—as a form of commemoration— recovers memory and reconquers the past; history as celebrated by memory becomes "a deciphering of the invisible, a geography of the supernatural."[31]

Here is the narrative recall of Nanny reconquering Jamaican space and genealogy:

> Now her head is tied. Now braided. Strung with beads and cowrie shells. Now she is disguised as a *chasseur*. Now wrapped in a cloth shot through with gold. Now she stalks the Red Coats as they march toward her cave, where she spins her Akan chants into spells which stun her enemies. Calls on the goddess of the Ashanti forests. Remembers the battle formations of the Dahomey Amazons. [P. 19]

30. Edward Said, "An Ethics of Language," *Diacritics* (Summer 1974), p. 33.
31. Jean Pierre Vernant, *Myth and Thought among the Greeks* (London: Routledge, 1983), p. 80.

Now, if we recall that Cliff has carefully described Nanny as "the sorceress," then this dramatization of history suggests that for the woman warrior to empower herself, she had to transgress temporal limitations; her spectacle generates the discourse of the possessed woman who has defied the white mythology; the excessive world of magic counters the sanitized version of history in the textbook, history "lost in romance" (p. 30).

But what is the lesson to be learned from Nanny's example? For subjects like Clare who find it difficult, if not impossible, to gain access to their history and to empower themselves within it, characters such as Nanny and Mad Hannah suggest the power of "magical" practice— a semiotic site, free and indeterminate, which privileges the excluded through transgression. Clare seeks such powers of transgression, especially in her attempts to understand the extermination of the European Jews, but at every stage of her reading and rereading, she finds it difficult to figure out how such acts happened. Since her father has been the primary mediator of her historical experiences, he is posited as the barrier to understanding "because to understand would be to judge her father as capable of the acts which had formed and sustained the holocaust" (p. 75). Unable to draw parallels between the events in Europe and her more immediate colonial experiences, Clare is entrapped in the very modes of knowledge which have privileged her: "She was a colonized child, and she lived within certain parameters— which clouded her judgment" (p. 77). Clare's inability to understand amid the connections and disconnections of her childhood is related to the multiplicity of historical and social factors which hamper all her attempts to establish her identity: race, class, color, sexual identity, and gender. But a key element in Cliff's narrative method is her portrayal of Clare as a schizophrenic who has failed to accede fully to the realm of speech and language.

Let me elaborate this assertion by turning to Fredric Jameson's discussion of the relationship between language and schizophrenia in psychoanalysis. In his reading of Lacan's theory of the breakdown of the relationship of signifiers in the schizophrenic experience, Jameson observes that any breakdown in temporal relationships is also an effect of language:

> It is because language has a past and a future, because the sentence moves in time, that we can have what seems to us a concrete or lived

experience of time. But since the schizophrenic does not know language articulation in that way, he or she does not have our experience of temporal continuity either, but is condemned to live a perpetual present with which the various moments of his or her past have little connection and for which there is no conceivable future on the horizon. In other words, schizophrenic experience is an experience of isolated, disconnected, discontinuous material signifiers which fail to link up into a coherent sequence.[32]

Cliff's use of a fragmented narrative is the most obvious example of the breakup of temporal relationships in Clare's world: the Savage family lives in a world of dispersed spaces and discontinuity. If Clare seems unable to connect her past to her present, as we have already seen, it is because her social spaces are indeed schizophrenic. For instance, the family church could ideally be read as a sign of a continuous religious and cultural tradition, but Clare worships in her mother's Pentecostal church, her father's Calvinist church, and her grandmother's "private" church. Each of these symbolic spaces makes certain demands on her; they also represent certain ideological systems in contestation and underscore the set of differences which marks her life. When Clare tries to overcome the differences and divisions that define her world, she finds that the only avenue for this form of transcendence is the imaginary; but the imaginary also distances her from the historical contexts she has tried so hard to master.

In her friendship with Zoe, the material signifiers of difference "become more and more of a background, which only rarely they stumbled across and had to confront" (p. 95), but this imaginary overcoming of differences is both tenuous and dangerous. It is described as a "make-believe": "They had a landscape which was wild and real and filled with places in which their imaginations could move" (p. 95). Outside this imaginary landscape, Clare is overwhelmed by her displacement, which is inscribed by realities she cannot control; her sense of disconnection is exacerbated by her failure to establish any transparent relationship between signifiers. In her school in Kingston, we are told, Clare is on scholarship because her father cannot keep up with the payments; yet she is treated differently from the darker-skinned scholarship girls. Her privileging is certainly due to color and class (p. 96), but because the power of these codes depends on their

---

32. Fredric Jameson, "Postmodernism and Consumer Society," in *The Anti-Aesthetic: Essays on Postmodern Culture*, ed. Hal Foster (Port Townsend, Wash.: Bay Press, 1983), p. 119.

invisibility, they create confusion in the girl and deepen "part of the split within herself" (p. 96).

In the end, Clare's sojourn in the colonial landscape proves Jameson's observation that the schizophrenic "does not know personal identity in our sense, since our feeling of identity depends on our sense of the persistence of the "I" and the "Me" over time."[33] In Clare's struggle for identity, Cliff takes us to the limits of colonial alienation: we are no longer dealing with colonial subjects who are defined solely in relation to the other, for the dialectic of master and slave has become ineffective. Moreover, although the colonial subjects discussed in the previous chapters were often defined in relation to the colonial other, they still had some recognition of themselves as colonial subjects, be it in a positive or negative sense. In contrast, Clare's sense of self is defined by absolute repression: she does not even have the capacity to analyze or explain to Zoe "what she felt about their given identities in this society, where they met and where they diverged" (p. 121).

When she "drops" the patois in her final conversation with Zoe, Clare seems to have judged "the distance between them as now unbridgeable" (p. 134). Unsure about the meaning of her "I," which is not even sustained by an illusion of its uniqueness, Clare has been reduced to a dead silence about her own dreams: "She was not ready to understand her dream. She had no idea that everyone we dream about we are" (p. 166). And so we have seen Caribbean fiction shift from a dramatization of the power of the self and the uniqueness of its utterance (in *Beyond a Boundary*, for example) to a moment of closure marked by silence and emptiness. But in the quest for a postcolonial discourse the silence and emptiness at the end of Cliff's novel are portentous for two reasons. First, the existence of a gap in language affirms the continuing need for a narrative form that will take into account the contradictory impulses of Caribbean culture which Clare discovers the moment she raises questions of identity and gender. Second, it is in the gaps, the silences, and the absences exposed by contending discourses that the underprivileged Caribbean subject will find and affirm its voice.

33. Jameson, p. 119.

Conclusion

> No, we have not yet reached that decolonization of thought which would be . . . the affirmation of a difference, and a free and absolute subversion of the spirit. There is there something like a void, a silent interval between the fact of colonization and that of decolonization.
> —Abdelkebir Khatibi, *Maghreb Pluriel*

In the face of a large number of conflicting ideological and aesthetic claims for and against modernism and its influence on cultural production in the so-called Third World, the initial premise of my study was Paul Gilroy's claim that the relationship of blacks to modernity raised central issues about the validity of colonized cultures and repressed histories, subjectivity, and identity.[1] I was surprised to discover that although leading Caribbean writers such as Aimé Césaire and Wilson Harris had openly adopted modernist linguistic and formal strategies as part of an "ongoing and unceasing re-visionary and innovative strategy," and though they traced the modernist trend in the Caribbean to "the roots in the deepest layers of the past that still address us," there was strong critical resistance to modernism and modernity in the study of Caribbean literature.[2] In its simplest form, this resistance was based on a narrow identification or definition of modern-

1. Paul Gilroy, *There Ain't No Black in the Union Jack: The Cultural Politics of Race and Nation* (London: Hutchinson, 1987), p. 219.
2. Stephen Slemon, "Interview with Wilson Harris," *Ariel: A Review of International English Literature* 19 (July 1988), 48.

ism in terms of European "high" modernism, which was suspected of celebrating pure aestheticism and thus of negating the value and power of cultural tradition and history. But modernity and modernism were also resisted because the questions they raised, in relation to Caribbean literature and its symbiotic relationship to colonialism, were possibly too paradoxical to fit neatly into a nationalist discourse that was trying to effect a clean break with its antecedents.

My intention in this book has been to reflect upon two of these paradoxes and their narrative implications: First of all, there is the paradox of history and its metaphysical claims: for Columbus and the European conquerers, the "discovery" of the Caribbean initiated modernity; but as we saw in my Introduction, the implication of this modernity for the natives of the islands and African slaves was nothing less than the loss of cultures, physical annihilation, and historical displacement. Thus modernity and its art forms must of necessity have different meanings for Europe and for the African diaspora. For the former it generates or justifies the rationalist and absolutist claims that anchor the foundational narrative of modern Western culture. Indeed, as contemporary advocates of modernity as a project of the Enlightenment have reminded us, by the eighteenth century the period of the "discovery" had become conceptualized in European thought and historiography as the New Age.[3] In the sense that the Caribbean is fully implicated in the historical events that initiate Western modernist discourse, it cannot escape from the ideologies of modernity nor its consequences; it can only confront the possibilities and limitations of modernism. What Caribbean writers have done, then, is to weaken the foundational status of the Western narrative, expose what Laclau calls "the metaphysical and rationalist pretensions" of Western modernity and its absolutist theory of history.[4]

This weakening takes different discursive and narrative forms, which I have taken up in the previous chapters. In the first chapter, for example, I examined the challenge to the imperial idea proposed by Lamming in his celebration of Caliban's reversion of the master's language, and James's appropriation of bourgeois ideas of play for the cause of West Indian nationalism in *Beyond a Boundary*. Similarly, my focus in Chapter 4 was on the Caribbean's figural deconstruction of the

---

3. Jürgen Habermas, *The Philosophical Discourse of Modernity: Twelve Lectures*, trans. Frederick G. Lawrence (Cambridge: MIT Press, 1990), p. 5.
4. Ernesto Laclau, "Politics and the Limits of Modernity," in *Universal Abandon? The Politics of Postmodernism*, ed. Andrew Ross (Minneapolis: University of Minnesota Press, 1989), p. 63.

Enlightenment's theory of history which privileges the European subject. My contention that Carpentier's *El siglo de las luces* recenters the slaves' version of events and their modes of representation was elaborated further in Chapter 5, where I argued that Marshall resorts to carnivalesque strategies to undermine the teleology of modernist history and postcolonial doctrines of modernization even as she tries to listen to African voices. In both chapters, I argued that we have no access to these voices until we penetrate the modernist idea, especially its totalizing claims.

The second paradox of modernism has to do with definitions and conceptualizations. My basic contention here is that a consideration of modernity and modernism from the margins of the modern world system inevitably forces us to question previous definitions of the term itself and to recognize its variegated genealogies and contradictory categories. Clearly, the kind of modernism I have evoked in the previous chapters is radically different from "high" modernism in two respects: it is highly overdetermined by history, which it seeks to confront rather than escape; it is also closely implicated in political and economic theories of modernization. But as we saw in our examination of tradition and modernity—both as conceptual categories and figures of desire—in Selvon's Trinidad novels (Chapter 3), there is no clear transition from one term to the other; rather, they exist in a chiasmic relationship in which spaces of liberation and identity can easily be reversed.

Moreover, once they have been displaced from what I call their Eurocentric zones of origin, modernism, modernity, and modernization proffer contradictory meanings that are, nevertheless, the conditions that make Caribbean literature possible. For example, we have seen that one cannot discuss modernism, at least in the context of Caribbean literature, without engaging colonialism, its discourses, and its economy of representation. Consider the premise that Caribbean modernity is initiated by the imposition of the plantation system and the institution of colonial power—the imposition of an imperial system that leads to the loss or repression of native, African, and East Indian selves, the colonizing of cultures and spaces, and the repression of histories. If we accept this premise, it is indeed paradoxical that this genealogy of loss gives birth to Caribbean expressionism by triggering a counter-discourse of nationalism and national identity. But as I tried to show in my discussion of novels by Hodge and Edgell in Chapter 6, even when colonial modernism has given way to the new

Caribbean nation, issues of identity and heritage still remain unresolved as questions of gender and marginalized forms of expression, such as women's histories and the patois, are foregrounded. Where such national identities are found to be exclusionary or still imprisoned in colonialism, its regime of meaning, and its perverse anxieties regarding race, class, gender, and sexuality, Michelle Cliff's *Abeng* (Chapter 8) posits discursive strategies through which cultural practices can, as Gilroy says, step "outside the confines of modernity's most impressive achievement—the nation state."[5]

Whether this "stepping out" gesture suggests a postmodern or postcolonial vision, as numerous critics have suggested, has not been my concern in this book.[6] My basic assumption is that before we deal with the "post" we have to interrogate its antecedent from all possible theoretical and cultural positions. And while it is not my intention to salvage the battered reputation of modernism in this book, I share Houston Baker's conviction that for black people confined by racism and colonialism in the Americas, the articulation of a "modernized" black or African national space represented through the arts has provided "a domain of hope and an arena of possible progress."[7] It could well be that many of the claims being made for the postmodern are sustained by a previous theory of the modern which is blind to the discourses on identity and history which I have recentered in this book. Moroever, there is a certain paradox to the universalist claim that the postmodern derives its authority and strategies from its self-conscious challenge to the validity of those metanarratives which, Laclau says, "unified the totality of the historical experience of modernity . . . within the project of global, human emancipation."[8] The irony here is double: first, as the texts I have analyzed attest, modernity was closely associated with colonial domination and exploitation, not "global, human emancipation"; second, rather than invalidating metanarratives, Caribbean novels seek, in different ways, to deconstruct the Eurocentric metanarrative and to validate a decolonized narrative that will write the West Indian subject into history.

5. Gilroy, p. 219.
6. On the relationship between postcolonialism and postmodernity see the essays in *Ariel: A Review of International English Literature* 20 (October 1989). My point of view is closer to Laclau's assertion that "postmodernity cannot be a simple *rejection* of modernity; rather it involves a different modulation of its themes and categories, a greater proliferation of its language games" (p. 65).
7. Houston A. Baker, Jr., *Modernism and the Harlem Renaissance* (Chicago: University of Chicago Press, 1987), p. 11.
8. Laclau, p. 63.

Césaire once said that he became a poet by renouncing poetry: "Poetry was for me the only way to break the stranglehold the accepted French form held on me."[9] It was in the language of modernism, the historical paradoxes of modernity, and the hopes and betrayals embedded in the doctrine of modernization that Caribbean writers sought a way of renouncing colonial modernism so that they could effect a narrative of liberation. Only by subverting colonial modernism could these writers become modernists. For in the end, as George Lamming notes in *The Pleasures of Exile*, Caliban's appropriated language came with "an unstated history of consequences, an unknown history of future intentions."[10] The primary intention of my book is to confront these consequences and intentions as they are manifested on the narrative and discursive level.

9. Aimé Césaire, *Discourse on Colonialism*, trans. Joan Pinkham (New York: Monthly Review Press, 1972), p. 66.
10. George Lamming, *The Pleasures of Exile* (London: Allison and Busby, 1984), p. 109.

Index

Adorno, Theodor, 19
Alexis, Jacques Stephen, 140, 141
Althusser, Louis, 101
Anderson, Benedict, 217
Anderson, Perry, 15n
Anthony, Michael, 208
Antonio Maravall, José, 162n
Arnold, A. James, 21

Baker, Houston, Jr., 5, 12, 21, 168, 174, 255
Bakhtin, Mikhail, 188, 189, 205, 207, 208n, 217
Barnet, Miguel, 142
Barratt, Harold, 108
Barthes, Roland, 85, 86n, 87
Bellegarde-Smith, Patrick, 11
Benjamin, Walter, 154, 162, 165, 182
Bennett, Louise, 33, 58
Benston, Kimberly, 180n
Benveniste, Emile, 211
Berman, Marshall, 15
Bettelheim, Judith, 66, 67n, 188n
Bhabha, Homi, 116
Birbalsingh, Frank, 108n, 125n
Bloom, Harold, 51

Brenkman, John, 221, 222
Brereton, Bridget, 69n, 110
Brodber, Erna, 32
Brathwaite, Edward Kamau, 1, 3, 10, 14, 15, 17, 18, 169, 170n, 191, 204n, 238, 239
Bruch, Peter, 180n

calypso, 60, 61, 96, 116
Campbell, Marvis, 20n
Carby, Hazel, 52
Carew, Jan, 39, 40
Caribbean modernism: and colonial history, 9, 10; and cultural politics, 4–12; definition of, 24–32; origins of, 1–4; and postcolonialism, 231–33; and postmodernism, 231
carnival, 187–90
Carpentier, Alejo: and allegory, 145, 161; and allegory of history, 159–67; and architecture, 148, 149; and commodified spaces, 154, 155; and the discourse of history, 29, 142–44, 152, 153, 165; and the Enlightenment, 141, 150, 156, 164; on the French Revolution, 157, 158; *El siglo de las luces*, 139–67; and symbolism, 145, 146

Césaire, Aimé, 11, 16, 19, 21, 22, 23, 33, 35, 252, 256
Chevigny, Bell Gale, 143, 148
Christian, Barbara, 18
Clarke, Vévé, 214
Cliff, Michelle: *Abeng*, 232–51; the deconstruction of modernism, 236, 237; the uses of disjuncture, 240, 241; and historiography, 242–44; and intertextuality, 236–44; on language and speech, 244–47; and narrative fragmentation, 234; and postcolonialism, 231–36; the representation of history, 234, 235, 248
closure, 226, 227–30
Cobham, Rhonda, 69n, 232
Condé, Maryse, 231
Collier, Eugenia, 83n
colonialism: and culture, 5, 11, 12, 25, 27, 28, 36–38, 57; and history, 5, 7, 8, 9. *See also* colonial subject; representation and identity
colonial subject, 46, 47, 49, 77, 78, 115, 119–23, 203
Conley, Tom, 61, 64
Cowan, Bainard, 161, 165, 166
creolization, 12, 13, 14, 16, 17; and linguistic conflict, 19; as a figure of modernism, 17, 18; and modernization, 112, 113, 131, 132; and repression, 115
Cudjoe, Selwyn, 20n, 25, 26n, 35n, 72n
Culler, Jonathan, 88n, 91n, 95

Dabydeen, David, 110, 112n, 113, 202n
Dash, J. Michael, 7, 13, 25
Davies, Carole Boyce, 199, 200n, 233, 234n
Dayan, Joan, 22n, 23
D'Costa, Jean, 26
de Certeau, Michel, 4, 59, 66, 67
Deleuze, Gilles, 90, 126, 128n, 225
de Man, Paul, 63, 125, 126, 146, 151, 214
de Onis, Frederico, 144
Depestre, René, 16, 20
Derrida, Jacques, 23, 131n, 160
Donato, Eugenio, 130n
Drake, Sandra, 24
Duerden, Dennis, 175n
During, Simon, 2

Edgell, Zee: *Beka Lamb*, 217–26, 230; and closure, 229–30; and the imaginary,

233; and national culture, 217–22; and representation and identity, 225–26; and selfhood, 218–20; and subject and community, 221–23
Ellis, Pat, 202
empire, 70, 89, 91, 96, 97, 98
Enlightenment, 141, 150, 156, 164
exile, 25–27, 33–35, 36–42

Fabre, Michel, 108n
Fanon, Frantz, 30, 33, 37, 38n, 40, 43, 54, 103, 104, 107, 228
Fido, Elaine Savory, 199, 200n, 233, 234n
Ford Smith, Honor, 201n, 202
Foucault, Michel, 21, 22n, 139, 152, 155, 156
Franco, Jean, 30, 31, 99, 100, 185n, 197, 198, 218, 227, 231
Froude, Anthony, 71

Gadamer, Hans-Georg, 163
Gaillard, Françoise, 235, 244
Gates, Henry Louis, Jr., 19n, 174, 224
Gavronsky, Serge, 22n
gender: and modernism, 136, 137, 197–99; in Caribbean literature, 31, 199–203
Giddens, Anthony, 154
Gilroy, Paul, 4, 252, 255
Ginsburg, Michal, 211
Glissant, Edouard, 4, 5, 7, 8–12, 29, 33, 109, 112, 113, 140, 186, 187n, 191, 218, 219n
Goldmann, Lucien, 156
Gomes, Albert, 28, 37, 38, 116
Gonzalez Echevarria, Roberto, 11n, 29, 141–44, 147, 150, 151, 158, 160–63, 167
Guattari, Félix, 90, 126, 128n, 225

Habermas, Jürgen, 2, 121n, 144n, 150, 223, 253
Harris, Wilson, 4, 13, 14, 24, 252
Hartz, Louis, 185
Hearne, John, 5
history: crisis of interpreting, 193–96; as a dialogical process, 182; and historiography, 42, 50, 51, 60, 242–44; and narration, 139, 140, 142–44, 152, 153, 170, 178, 179, 234, 235; and nature, 165; redefinition of, 168; as repetition and reversal, 184, 185; and voice, 191–93
Hodge, Merle: and alienation, 214, 215, 217; and closure, 227–29; on the colo-

Hodge, Merle (*cont.*)
  nial subject, 203–17; *Crick Crack,
  Monkey,* 203–17, 227–30; deconstruction of modernism, 200–202; and language and subjectivity, 211; orality,
  204, 213
Hulme, Peter, 18
Hutcheon, Linda, 9, 236, 237n, 239n, 242

James, C. L. R.: *Beyond a Boundary,* 37,
  42–56; on boundaries and borders, 48;
  on colonial culture, 25–27, 36–38, 42,
  43; and cricket, 43–46, 52–56; displacement and alienation, 51, 52; and the
  heroic, 47, 48, 54; and history, 42, 50,
  51; repetition, 49; selfhood, 46, 47
Jameson, Fredric, 38, 104, 107, 128, 168,
  170, 178, 180n, 249, 250n, 251
Jenny, Lauren, 236
Jha, J. C., 110n
Johnson, Lemuel, 232n, 233, 235, 237n
Jonas, Joyce, 57, 58

Kapai, Leela, 187n
Karrer, Wolfgang, 180n
Kent, George, 8n, 27, 61, 89, 90, 95n, 99n
Khatibi, Abdelkebir, 252
Kilmer-Tchalekian, Mary A., 144n, 157
Kolb, David, 176n, 177n, 178
Kom, Ambroise, 83n
Knight, Franklin, 20n, 50n, 70n, 71n
Kristeva, Julia, 75, 78, 219
Krupnick, Mark, 42

Labanyi, J., 143, 144n, 157, 165
Lacan, Jacques, 131, 215
Laclau, Ernesto, 246, 253, 255
Laforest, Edmond, 19
Laleau, Léon, 18, 19
Lalla, Barbara, 26
Lamming, George: on Caribbean na-
  tionalism, 69; and colonialism and the
  colonial situation, 27, 28, 57–59; and
  the colonial language, 41, 80–85; *The
  Emigrants,* 89–98; exile, 25–27; on the
  Haitian Revolution, 64–65; and high
  modernism, 27; and history and histo-
  riography, 59, 60, 104–6; *In the Castle of
  My Skin,* 74–89; and mythology of em-
  pire, 70, 89, 91, 96–98; narrative authority, 86–89; nationalism, 68, 99; and
  the novel, 67; *Of Age and Innocence,* 98–

106; orality, 80; *The Pleasures of Exile,*
  35, 57–65; representation and identity,
  83–85, 91–95, 101–3; self and commu-
  nity, 74–78
Laplanche, J., 97
Laroche, Maximilien, 9
Las Casas, Bartolomé de, 2
Lawrence, Leota S., 209n
Lionnet, Françoise, 210n, 234
Lommel, Andreas, 175n
Lovelace, Earl, 30, 198
Lyotard, Jean-François, 176, 183n, 232

MacDonald, Bruce, 108n
Macherey, Pierre, 118
maroonage, 12, 20, 21
Marquez, Roberto, 7, 17, 50, 71n
Marshall, Paule: on African cultures, 169,
  170; *Brown Girl, Brownstones,* 173, 193–
  96; carnival and carnivalesque, 187–90;
  The Chosen Place, the Timeless People,
  174, 175–91; history and historiography, 29, 170, 177, 178, 179, 181, 182,
  186, 187; popular culture, 171;
  Praisesong for the Widow, 174, 193–96;
  repetition and reversal, 184, 185; representation and identity, 184, 185
masks, 174, 175, 224
Mittelholzer, Edgar, 25
Monti, Franco, 175n
Moreno-Fraginals, Manuel, 141
Munro, Ian, 83n, 99n

Naipaul, V. S., 25, 33, 34, 114
Narinesingh, 209, 228
nationalism: in the Caribbean, 43, 55, 56,
  68, 69, 99; and consciousness, 39, 43,
  55, 56; and cultural discourse, 30–32,
  217–22; and selfhood, 217, 218; and
  women, 198–201, 218
Nazareth, Peter, 111, 187n
Nettleford, Rex, 188n
Ngugi wa Thiong'o, 72n
Nixon, Rob, 34

Patterson, Orlando, 6, 60, 61n
Paz, Octavio, 136, 158
Philip, Marlene Nourbese, 233
Pontalis, J. B., 97
popular culture, 169, 171
Pouchet Paquet, Sandra, 31, 72n, 73n,
  74n, 85, 91, 95n, 101, 102n, 132

Price, Richard, 20, 21
Price Mars, Jean, 11

Ramchand, Kenneth, 69n
Reid, Victor, 107
representation and identity, 83–85, 91–
    95, 101–3, 108, 109, 136–38, 171–74,
    175, 221–25, 226
Rohlehr, Gordon, 28n, 108, 116n
Rowell, Charles, 11, 26n, 32n, 199n

Said, Edward, 17n, 28, 33, 34, 35, 36, 42,
    50, 51, 71, 72, 238n, 248
St Omer, Garth, 73n, 90
Samaroo, Brinsley, 110n, 112n
Sander, Reinhard, 99n
Saussure, Ferdinand de, 116
Scharfman, Ronnie, 22n
Schneider, Deborah, 180n
Selvon, Samuel: *A Brighter Sun*, 116–23;
    and calypso aesthetic, 11–18; and colo-
    nial subject, 115, 119–21; on creoliza-
    tion, 112, 131, 132; drama of indepen-
    dence, 131–33; East Indian culture,
    110–14; education, 120–25, 130, 131;
    and minor characters, 128, 129; and
    modernization, 127–29, 134; national
    community, 28; *The Plains of Caroni*,
    133–38; representation and identity,
    136–38; *Turn Again Tiger*, 115, 123–33
Senior, Olive, 31, 199, 200
Shaw, Donald, 157
Silverman, Kaja, 115, 215, 216n
Singh, Kevin, 110n, 113n, 114

Sistren, 197, 202
slavery: and Africa, 10; and history, 79;
    and slave community, 13; and slave
    trade, 2; and social death, 6
Slemon, Stephen, 232
Smith, Paul, 123
Sorell, Walter, 175n
Souza, Raymond D., 157
Spillers, Hortense J., 187, 190
Stoelting, Winifred L., 187n
Stuckey, Sterling, 193, 194n

Tafari, Manfredo, 144n
Taussig, Michael, 226
Taylor, Patrick, 12, 22, 43n, 49, 50n, 60,
    68, 72n, 110, 111
Terdiman, Richard, 45, 88
Thass-Thienemann, Theodore, 174n
Thelwell, Michael, 3, 5n, 30, 32, 198
Thomas, John Jacob, 71
Thorpe, Marjorie, 209, 212, 213, 215, 228
Todorov, Tzvetan, 1, 2
Turner, Victor, 41, 42n

Underwood, Leon, 175n

Vernant, Jean Pierre, 248

Walcott, Derek, 8, 9, 13, 26
Washington, Mary Helen, 191
Wilde, Alan, 19n, 23, 82, 90, 94
Wynter, Sylvia, 26, 47, 48, 171, 199

Yarde, Gloria, 72n

Lightning Source UK Ltd.
Milton Keynes UK
UKHW010004251121
394567UK00001B/62